DODGING MACHETES

*How I Survived Forbidden Love, Bad Behavior,
And The Peace Corps In Fiji*

WILL LUTWICK

A PEACE CORPS WRITERS BOOK

A Peace Corps Writers Book
An imprint of Peace Corps Worldwide

First Peace Corps Writers Edition, June 2012

DODGING MACHETES: HOW I SURVIVED FORBIDDEN LOVE,
BAD BEHAVIOR, AND THE PEACE CORPS IN FIJI

Library of Congress Control Number: 2012933423
Peace Corps Writers, Oakland, CA
ISBN: 1-935925-11-3
ISBN 13: 978-1-935925-11-8

"But he that dares not grasp the thorn should never crave the rose."

— *Anne Brontë*

"Like Alice, I chased the object of my desire into the rabbit hole, then tumbled down, landing in an utterly unpredictable world. In a situation like that, you take it moment to moment and try to keep your head intact— physically first and psychologically second. Enjoying the wild ride comes in a distant third."

— *From* Dodging Machetes

CHAPTER ONE

Coconut palms swayed in the trade winds like tipsy hula dancers. Turquoise waves nibbled the virginal seashore. A flock of multi-hued parrots landed in unison on a nearby baka tree. They opened their beaks as if chirping their songs for me and me alone. How fortunate I felt to be working in that pristine, primitive paradise, untouched by television and fast-food joints. Then again, island life was hard. People lived in rat-infested thatched huts with no indoor plumbing, or electricity. But that was what my Peace Corps adventure in Fiji was supposed to be about—escaping the decadence, materialism, and soul-killing careers of the developed world. Discovering my true identity in a more innocent, peaceful land where the shiny-faced natives couldn't help themselves from being charming. Getting back to basics. Being one with nature. Living large with the locals. This indigenous life, fragile and endangered—I was so blessed to be experiencing it before it completely vanished from planet Earth.

"Hey, Will, call maintenance and have them turn up the air conditioning. I'm meeting with some big shots from the trade commission, and I don't want to be sweating like a pig."

"Call 'em, yourself, Milton. I'm busy," I said, yanking my consciousness from the idyllic scene I'd been surveying through a wall-sized window of tempered plate glass.

1

OK, so I wasn't one of *those* Peace Corps Volunteers (PCVs), the ones who had been assigned to *the bush*. But that wasn't my fault. I didn't get to choose my station when I had arrived in Fiji a year earlier, in November 1968. I lived in Suva, Fiji's bustling capital (by island standards), and worked in the tallest structure in that region of the South Pacific. The Fiji Government Offices building was a glass-and-steel skyscraper that towered out at six stories and would look at home in any American suburban office center. I shared a concrete flat with Emmett Buck, a good ol' boy from a dinky west-Texas town, and we did have an electric oven, screens on the windows, and indoor plumbing. So I guess you could say we not only had Fiji water flowing from the spigot, we flushed with it too. And I didn't have to sleep under a mosquito net like most of my fellow Volunteers and be at high risk for getting amoebic dysentery, dengue fever, or elephantiasis, a disease that supersized the affected body parts. But we urban Volunteers had to risk diseases that our friends in the villages rarely caught, at least while *in* the villages. Such as the venereal ones, because Suva was where casual sex was most likely to happen. Luckily, penicillin was available. It was gratifying to have some accoutrements of Western civilization available, just in case you needed to bail out of a Third-World jam.

The dynamics of our work situation made it difficult for me to like Milton. Our local higher-ups thought he must be brilliant because he got his MBA at Harvard. They had never heard of Duke or Michigan, the universities where I got my degrees. So they fawned over Milton as if he were a business wizard. The truth was that he was almost as green and clueless as I was, but he was adept at self-promotion, a behavior for which I had neither skill nor interest. Our boss, Sitiveni Naitini, who was the government's director of commerce, considered me lower wattage than Milton's luminescence. That lesser support hurt my work, because I had more trouble getting cooperation from others in the Fiji government and private industry for my projects. Word would spread quickly over the coconut wireless of who was in and who was out.

But there was one advantage to playing second banana to the Harvard boy. Nobody much cared what I worked on, so I mostly worked on what I wanted. My biggest project was pushing passion fruit to the American market. I figured with a name like that, it would be an ad agency's dream product. Who cared that it tasted like sour pickles in its natural state? It could always be sweetened to excess and chemically flavored like all the other processed fruit products that Americans thought were part of a healthful diet.

I juggled two other on-going assignments in my not-terribly-busy schedule. I founded and managed a venture where oranges were shipped from Rotuma, Fiji's outermost island, to Viti Levu, its biggest, where I and 60 percent of the country's population were living. The Rotuman oranges had thick green peels and were bigger, juicier, and sweeter than the ones from our island, so it was an easy sell. Somebody just had to get the trade going. Nobody actually cultivated oranges in Fiji—they grew wild like a lot of Fijian fruits. One of the perks of paradise.

I also was doing export marketing research for Fijian handicrafts, working closely with local cooperatives to see if Americans would buy their wares. If I were to be successful, there would come a day when Fijian cannibal forks, war clubs, and whale's tooth pendants would grace wood-paneled den walls in Chattanooga and Chicago. Their owners would know nothing about their cultural significance but would buy them because they would look cool in some catalog.

თ

Milton was one of the Volunteers from the third wave of PCVs that landed in Fiji. We were invited there to spread American know-how and perform free labor in that then-British colony of 333 islands, which was in preparation to become an independent Commonwealth nation within a year. Our first contingent arrived in January 1968, and my group, Fiji-2, followed them a year later. Two more groups had arrived during the year after we landed, and several new ones were in the planning stage.

Our PCV population in Fiji had zoomed from zero to about two hundred fifty in only two years. As compared with some five hundred thousand locals, we were becoming almost a measurable minority group.

I sometimes wondered why the Peace Corps powers-that-were put so many of us in that small country, instead of in other poorer and far more populous nations in Asia, Africa, and South America, where starvation, war, and disease kept life expectancy to about thirty years. Whereas in Fiji, no one was starving, war was nonexistent, disease was minor, and the life expectancy of seventy years was about the same as in the United States. In Fiji, the locals were poor in material terms, but nobody needed riches in a naturally favored tropical paradise. And then I realized my question contained its answer. The much higher concentration of Volunteers in Fiji, instead of hellholes like Haiti or Bangladesh, was precisely because those places were hellholes. The Peace Corps bureaucrats in Washington surely didn't want too many of their young adults from affluent enclaves (average age: twenty-four, the great majority of us fresh out of college) sending letters back to their parents describing scenes of utter destitution, rampant infectious diseases, and crime run amok. That would not sit well with Mom and Dad, who might complain to their local congressperson. Nor would it impress the Peace Corps' recruiting target: other well-educated, under-experienced young adults. We wanted to live like the locals and improve the lot of poor people—just make it a pleasant place to hang out for two years. And that, indeed, was Fiji.

None of us were looking for the bullet-dodging experiences of our less-favored cousins who were serving their country and getting their cultural diversity lessons in an entirely different way in a place called Vietnam.

ᕀᕉ

One morning Sitiveni called Milton and me to his office, a room illuminated by rays of sunshine bouncing off the surface of the Pacific.

A diploma from a New Zealand college graced one wall, while the opposite one featured pictures of Sitiveni's tall, dignified wife and their two little girls. A gold-framed photograph on a circular inlaid-wood table pictured Sitiveni standing with Ratu Sir Kamasese Mara, Fiji's George Washington, both of them wearing long-sleeved, white dress shirts, thin black ties, and *sulus* (traditional gray gabardine sarongs). I marveled how those pants-alternatives never fell when Fijians wore them. Whereas, whenever I wrapped a sarong around me, I could barely make it from the shower to the bedroom without the curtain dropping.

Sitiveni swiveled around and smiled at us with rows of teeth wider and brighter than the Cheshire cat's. His enormous brown bowling ball of a head was mounted on powerful shoulders. He spoke in soothing sentences, a modest man despite a regal native lineage and a linebacker's physique. "Milton, Will, we're getting a new employee here on our floor. She'll be Mr. Docker's personal assistant, but if you gentlemen have some typing needs and she has the time, she can do that for you. But no other work for her unless you go through me first. Remember, she's *Mr. Docker's* personal assistant." He said, "Mr. Docker's," as if the man were the British prime minister.

Gunther Docker was Fiji's chief of protocol, dispatched there by the Royal Family and so garnered a lot of respect and maybe a little deference from Sitiveni. Docker was a lean, pipe-smoking blue-blood in his fifties who hailed from the Knightsbridge section of London. I didn't know what a chief of protocol did. But of course he could use a personal assistant. Couldn't we all?

Sitiveni walked Milton and me over to the other side of our floor where Gunther Docker's office loomed much larger than Sitiveni's. British and Fijian flags were mounted, one on each side of the hardwood-paneled double doors, as if saluting the entrance. But my attention was drawn to a large mahogany desk beside the doors. Because sitting at and dwarfed by the desk was a slim, enchanting Indian girl with haunting panther eyes and split cherry lips set on butterscotch skin. And surprisingly, she was not only *not* wearing a sari, but her clover-green minidress rose halfway up her alluring thighs. I craned my neck for a better glimpse, then recoiled when Sitiveni began talking.

"Milton, Will, this is Rani Gupta. Rani is Mr. Docker's new assistant. She'll be doing some typing for you from time to time."

Milton greeted her first, *damn it*, and I echoed him. Rani looked up and checked us out, the panther eyes scanning left to right. Then, with a reticent smile reflecting apparent disappointment, she brushed aside from her face an almost hip-length mane of sleek black hair and muttered a halfhearted "G'day." She turned to the pile of papers neatly stacked on her desk, a sight apparently easier on those beguiling eyes than the drooling dorks in front of her.

Sitiveni walked away, and when he was out of the picture Milton sat oh-so-casually on the corner of her desk and said, "So Rani, tell me about yourself. What were you doing before you got this job?"

Rani looked up from her work, directly into Milton's eyes, crinkled her little button nose, and said in lilting Queen's English, "Will, is it? I've loads to get done right now for Mr. Docker and don't have time for a chat." Then, looking at Milton's butt, she added, "If you wouldn't mind, this isn't a car park," and with two flicks of her left hand, she backed Milton off her desk. He crumpled to the floor as if struck by a truck.

I took a cautious step forward. "Um . . . he's Milton and I'm Will. Nice to meet ya, Rani."

She shrugged and looked away.

That brief introduction had certainly flopped. Ordinarily at such times, I would have moved on without a second thought. Yet a faint patter in my primitive brain signaled to me that there was more to this encounter than met the eye and ear. I sensed Rani Gupta and I would have other things to discuss in the future besides typing.

CHAPTER TWO

How did these three different races—Indians, Fiji natives, and Europeans—find their way to populating a group of isolated islands in the South Pacific?

According to one school of thought, Polynesians were the first to arrive in Fiji some thirty-five hundred years ago, and Melanesians arrived about a thousand years later, both groups sailing in from islands west of Fiji. They represent two of the three principal ethnicities that first settled the scattered islands of the South Pacific (the third group, Micronesians). The native Fijians today are predominantly Melanesian with some Polynesian blood in their ancestry. Individual Fijians look very similar to sub-Sahara Africans. So when I was in Fiji, it was generally assumed that the natives were not that long removed from Africa. But now prevailing thought is that their link goes back about fifty thousand years, and that Melanesians are more genetically removed from modern Africans than they are from any other major racial group in the world. Appearances apparently do deceive.

The Fiji natives were already into royalty, ceremony, sports, and revelry when shipwrecked British sailors and convicts from Australia—groups who had similar predilections—became the first European descendants to visit Fiji in the eighteenth century. There were things to trade—tools, tobacco, and guns for sandalwood and seafood—so everyone got along well, at least at first. But soon came the missionaries who did not approve of, among other things, the barbecued man-flesh that occasionally graced the menu after a good battle. Cannibalism persisted into the early twentieth century, and Fiji became widely known by an alternate moniker, *The Cannibal Islands*.[1]

Although slow to pick up on the missionaries' man-eating disapproval, the natives generally welcomed Jesus as their savior, but blended Christianity with their magical native beliefs and extrasensory powers. Even today some native Fijians reportedly lure giant turtles from sea to beach with their singing, walk on hot coals, or use voodoo to cause festering wounds to appear on their enemies or disappear from their friends.

In the nineteenth century, Swedish, German, British, and American adventurers arrived intent on milking the islands' natural wealth of cheap labor, fertile land, and sea slugs.[2] Three times in the 1850s and 1860s, American gunboats were in Fijian waters, poised to attack over monetary disputes between individual Americans, including the American consul to Fiji, and the Fijian chiefs. In 1874, after previous offers had been turned down, the Fijians got the British to adopt them as a Crown Colony. They hoped this would squash any further bickering with devious Westerners. Also their own local government, established three years earlier by British advisers, had collapsed because of run-amok spending, so they needed a bailout. As part of the agreement, the Fijian chiefs maintained control of 87 percent of the land in the islands. This Native Land, as it was officially titled, could

---

1   One late-nineteenth century aficionado, Ratu (Chief) Udre Udre, was reported to have literally devoured 872 of his acquaintances. I say *literally*, because he ate every part of his prey. Whatever he couldn't finish at one meal was preserved for the next, until every bite of the leftovers had been consumed. Apparently way ahead of his time as a food conservationist and eating champion, one day the ravenous Ratu would be honored posthumously by the Guinness Book of Records as the "world's most prolific cannibal", an achievement that one might hope will never be challenged or surpassed.

2   Sea slugs were traded to the Chinese to be used in cooking. These slimy mollusks are also noted for inspiring thousands of Japanese haiku.

not be sold, though the more commercial pieces were usually leased. That structure has persisted to this day.

Once in charge, the Brits wanted to make a pound or two on the booming international sugar market. They assumed the locals would be happy to toil in the blazing tropical sun, swinging machetes to cut the bamboo-like cane in order to make their new overlords rich. But the Fijians had no particular craving for material things and no desire to do such backbreaking work. So from 1879 to 1916, the English plantation owners brought in tens of thousands of British colonial subjects from India as indentured servants to hack away on the sugar-cane plantations. After their five-year tour of duty was up, the Indians were given the choice of staying or going back to India—but only on their own dime.

Let's see, shall we stay in this tropical paradise with no real competition as the merchant class, or shall we take a long, very expensive ride in the hull of a ship where many of us won't even survive to see the dim lights and utter destitution that is India, a land so delightful we chose a half decade of slavery over it in the first place?

So most Indians stayed, were fruitful, and multiplied. And they were joined by numerous Indian free agents who began immigrating to Fiji in the early 1900s. When I arrived in 1968, Indians had just become the majority race of Fiji with 51 percent of the population, whereas only 40 percent were native Fijians, and 4 percent Europeans. The remaining people were mixed race, Chinese, or other Pacific Islanders

૭∾

The week after meeting Rani, I had dinner with my PCV friend Troy at the Nanking, Fiji's premiere Chinese bistro. Beneath naked tubes of white neon abuzz with flying bugs on kamikaze missions, we sat on wood benches at a faux-fiberglass table and forked down chunks of sweet-and-sour pork and chicken chow mein while knocking back glasses of Fiji Bitter. Between mouthfuls, we discussed the delicate nuances of the local societal dynamic.

"Look, Will, these babes don't expect *anything*. Just tell them to meet you back at your flat, and they'll screw your brains out, then thank you for it when done. If they're really good, I might give them some munchies and brew, but why waste even that on them? It's not the money—it's the time. I need them to clear out for my next . . . ahem . . . appointment."

Troy, the unofficial stud of Fiji-2, grinned at me. One of the female Volunteers had told me that she and all the other single women met not long after we started Peace Corps training on the Hawaiian island of Molokai. They compared notes about the single guys. When it came to Troy, the consensus was *muscular, ruggedly handsome, nothing but trouble, avoid at all cost.* She wouldn't tell me how I had measured up. I was six foot three, thin, dark of follicle, and perhaps attractive in a geeky way, but in no way was I in Troy's league. You'd rarely see him with a sweet young thing in public, so you might think he was not the ladies' man he claimed to be. But whenever I dropped by his flat there was always an attractive girl going or coming. And his Peace Corps roommate Kent had confirmed both the nature and success of Troy's MO. So Troy seemed reasonably honest about his claims, though he was probably embellishing the truth just a tad when he described his take-a-number system to me.

"I'm not shitting you, Will. All those girls giggling and yelling, 'Hey Pee-see Corpse, Pee-see Corpse, Nice *bola* (body),' at us as we walk down the street, that's just the tip of the iceberg. These girls think we're the cat's ass."

"Aw, I don't know. I'm not looking for a stable of women. Dating two or three at a time is about all I can handle," I said, doing a little embellishing of my own while chewing the last bite of a fried won ton. "But there is one girl I've been thinking of trying to get to know better." I turned my head and looked directly at him. "Say, Troy, have you ever made it with an Indian chick?" I knew the possibility was remote. One of the first things we learned after landing in Fiji was that the Indian gals were totally off-limits—they weren't even allowed to date Indian guys, much less guys of other races. But if anyone could have broken down that wall, it would have been Troy.

"No way. That's like playing Russian roulette, only there are no empty chambers. Can you dig it? But I know what you mean. We all want what we can't have. It's a shame they're denying themselves the pleasure of me. But I stay away from that stuff, although there was one close call." Troy slugged back his beer and stared into my eyes. "Come on, Will, don't tell me that with all the babes in the sea, you're tracking the great white shark?"

I blushed. "OK, so there's this Indian girl who just started working at my office. Now I know they're forbidden fruit. But it's almost the seventies and the times they are a-changing, right? Well, she wears miniskirts, she's adorable, and maybe if I take it slowly and . . ."

Troy suddenly leaped out of his seat and pointed his forefinger in my face. "Will, you're shitting me, right? This girl wouldn't be named Rani, would she? Now that you mention it, I think she said she works in the same building you do. Please tell me you're shitting me."

And I jumped out of my seat too. "Oh fuck, don't tell me you've screwed her too."

Troy, the consummate bullshitter, grinned contentedly for several seconds to let me squirm, then reluctantly admitted, "Well, not really. But I wanted to, and I came *this* close." A sliver of white neon light was perceptible between his thumb and forefinger. We both sat back down. "OK, here's how it went down. I saw this cute Indian chick shopping for clothes at Morris Hedstrom's, did my usual snow job, told her she was beautiful and should come by my flat to listen to my collection of Ravi Shankar tapes."

"You have Ravi Shankar tapes?"

"No, of course not. The point is to get them there. After that, the ruse doesn't matter. Besides, she didn't know who Ravi Shankar was, but she came anyway, so that tells me she's really asking for it. Anyway, she's standing there in my living room, and I say, 'Let's go in the bedroom. It's cooler in there 'cause I have a fan going.' And she says, 'No, I'm fine here.' So I pull her toward me and kiss her, and she just stands there kind of limp. Then I slide my hand over her ass, and she pushes me away, shakes her head, and says, 'No, Troy, not with me, you don't. I must be going.' And before I can say anything else, she's out the front door. Can you fucking believe it?"

"No Troy, I can't," I said, but I was chuckling and on the verge of full-out laughter.

"Yeah, right. The bitch turned me down. Never happened before . . . well, not in Fiji anyway. Here I am risking my ass to be with an Indian babe, and she gives me blue balls. Fucking unbelievable. This girl, Rani, she's nothing but bad news. If Troy can't get in her pants, nobody can."

I breathed a sigh of relief. "That's good to hear. I mean, too bad you didn't get another notch on your headboard, but clearly this is one girl only a fool would want to mess with."

❧

Yes, Indian girls were off-limits. As Troy mentioned, groups of native Fijian girls often giggled and flirted with just about any male PCV who walked by. The Indian gals, dressed in their lovely luminescent saris, would never say a thing to us or any other males, and nothing was to be said to them. It just wasn't done. They might as well have been wearing *burqas* considering how approachable they were.

The culture of Fiji's Indians was relatively unchanged from its Old-World origins. Although the formal caste system did not survive the trip intact, their society was a place where the marriages were almost always arranged by parents who picked carefully from the proper Hindu or Muslim social strata.

There were several thousand offspring from Fijian-European coupling. Their highest concentration was in the area around Suva. There was even a Fijian word, *kailoma*, for these children of mixed race. But if there were any Indo-Fijians or Euro-Indians, I had never come across or even heard of one. They were as rare in Fiji as snowflakes.

Whenever there was an outed sex scandal in Fiji Indian society, there was a tendency for it to be rectifiable only by the suicides of all participants, male and female. If the participants resisted that form of demise, they sometimes were hacked to death with machetes by male relatives. The *Fiji Times*, the daily English-language newspaper, reported this kind of violence surprisingly often for such a small country.

Indian society in Fiji was certainly nothing like the popular *Kama-Sutra*-at-the-ashram image of Indian life that was becoming in vogue back in the States. That image had been made popular by the Beatles' visit to the Maharishi Mahesh Yogi in India the previous year. This, instead, was a survival culture of a grassroots people, those whose parents and grandparents had chosen five years of slavery as the better alternative to staying in India. They were not about to give up their fundamental convictions just because some of us in the Western world had recently decided it was time to lighten up about such beliefs.

I had already experienced an example of the power of those mores. Before I moved to Suva in June, 1969, I lived in Fiji's second-largest town, Lautoka, on the other side of Viti Levu. Initially the Peace Corps staff, in their boundless wisdom, assigned me to live with an Indian family—mom, dad, and two boys—a veritable Hindu *Ozzie and Harriet.* They were pleasant people and lived in a comfortable house. But at twenty-three, the last thing I wanted to do was to reside with a family—my own or anyone else's. I was all for cultural immersion, but a young man needed some refuge for privacy. To my understanding, though it was wrong, no other Fiji PCV was being asked to reside inside a local family's home. So I protested to my superiors and was thrilled when, after three weeks of my having unpleasant childhood flashbacks, they allowed me to swap *Chez Chopra* for a rickety government-run dormitory, aptly called the Bachelors Mess.

Twenty of us messy bachelors were living there. Two were other PCVs, and most of the rest were unmarried young Indian men who worked in various government positions. We each had a miniscule bedroom, but shared bathroom facilities and ate together in a common dining area. Our meals were prepared by an Indian woman who also did the cleaning. She and I developed a cordial relationship, but

I knew the unwritten rules and kept quiet when others were around. Amrisha was about thirty, but looked a decade older, probably owing to a harsh life. She had never married. Her impoverished family could not come up with enough of a dowry—something that considerably reduced her standing in the local Indian community. Still, she was upbeat and seemed to appreciate our conversations, limited though they were by my awful Hindi and her better, but stilted, English. The Indian men living at the Mess mostly treated her with disdain.

Not long after I moved in, our wood frame building required extensive repairs, and a construction crew of five Indian men started coming daily. They stayed for almost a month. One morning, not long after they left, I noticed that a new woman was making breakfast.

I turned to one of the Indian residents and asked, "Do you know where Amrisha is today? Do you think she could be sick?"

He replied, "It seems you have not yet heard. Amrisha and one of the men on the construction team were caught having sex. The bloke was married and his wife *somehow* found out about it." A smirk spread over his face.

"Well, is she going to be OK?" I asked.

"Not where she is going." He laughed. "They hung themselves and were found in her room." From beside his neck, he raised a clenched fist, crossed his eyes, and stuck his tongue out.

My stomach caved in. Tears welled up in my eyes. "Oh no. Oh God. That's horrible. I'm so sorry."

"Don't be. The whore was lucky they let her go out the easy way."

CHAPTER THREE

The day after my dinner with Troy, I concocted an excuse to talk with Rani. My work time had recently been consumed with crunching numbers and going back and forth to the wharf to oversee some Rotuman orange deliveries, so I didn't have anything legitimate for her to type. But that day I came up with something anyway. I wrote up the Orange Marketing Scheme's monthly board meeting minutes. The truth was there was no Orange Marketing Scheme board. I was it—the whole Orange Marketing Scheme, a name I picked for buying and selling oranges because legally, as a foreigner, I wasn't allowed to use my own name to conduct trade. When working in government, you have to cut through the bureaucracy or you'll never get anything done, and that truism also applied to starting office relationships with unapproachable women. I figured Rani wouldn't know my organization consisted of just me and a checkbook. The "minutes" were only a single page, so it wasn't as if I were going to waste a large chunk of the very valuable time of the Personal Assistant to the Chief of Protocol. But it was enough so I'd have a business reason to talk with her.

But before I could move forward, my mind stepped in front of me and threw some logic in my face. *Why are you doing this? Pursuing this woman can't lead to anything but trouble.*

And I threw convenient rationalizations back at my mind: *I just want to get to know her. What's the big deal? I can't let potential threats stop me from doing something so perfectly natural and innocent. Anyway, if it gets too dangerous, I can always stop.*

I went into the bathroom, blew my nose, tucked in my shirt, and tamed my short, cross-combed Jewfro as much as it would let me. I grabbed my page of bullshit and scurried over to Rani's desk. She sat there in her purple and white minidress, reading a well-worn copy of *Great Expectations* while sipping tea from an oversized orange Melmac cup. She looked like an auburn Alice at the Mad Hatter's tea party. I stood over her with feigned authority, waiting several seconds for her to look up.

She didn't.

"Hi . . . um, Rani, wasn't it?"

She grimaced as she put down her book and tilted her head to look at the skittish schemer towering over her. "Yes, it *was* Rani. And it still is."

"I'm Will. You know . . . the Peace Corps Volunteer at the other end of the office." I pointed toward my desk. "We met last week."

"Oh, right, the chap who sat on my desk. If you're here to see Mr. Docker, he's not here."

"No, I'm not here to see Mr. Docker, and I didn't sit on your desk. That was the other Peace Corps guy, Milton."

"Very well, then." And with that she opened her book and moved her gaze toward it.

She'd totally thrown me. But I took a breath and tried to appear composed. "Well, Sitiveni Naitini said you were supposed to do typing for me sometimes, and I have something here for you to type." I held out my page of lies as if it were burning my fingers.

But she didn't take it. She gave me the once-over again. Judging from her expression, my looks had not improved since we first met. So she turned away and pointed to her left. "Put it in the box. I'll get on it sometime after lunch."

"Thanks," I said, doing as I'd been told. She picked up her book and shut me out again. Tongue-tied, trying to come up with something, anything, to keep the conversation going, I stood there a few painful seconds, then gave up and turned to go back to my desk. I thought, *this is never going to work.*

"What is it?" I heard her voice call from behind me.

I turned again. Now I was the one getting peeved. "What is what?"

"What do you want me to type?"

"Oh, that. Just some minutes from a board meeting. The Orange Marketing Scheme."

"'The Orange Marketing Scheme?'" She rolled the words in her mouth like a wad of taffy. "That's a curious name for an organization. I mean, who names something a *scheme*. That sounds quite daft." At last she was smiling, but it was at my expense.

"Yeah, I guess it is. Maybe I'll suggest to the board that they change the name."

"Maybe you should."

❧

After disappointing incidents such as that encounter, I would contemplate quitting the Peace Corps and forgetting Fiji. Sure, it was a no-brainer that it beat being in Vietnam, but avoiding the military was not the primary reason why I had wanted to get into the Peace Corps. Staying out of the war was just a fortuitous afterthought. I had joined to make a contribution to people who needed one. My motivation was simply that idealistic and naïve.

A major obstacle toward making such a contribution was that the Peace Corps expected me to be a business leader from day one. But when I started with the Peace Corps, I was only twenty-two. I had an MBA, but how could I claim to be a *master* with no *business administration* experience? Of course, I had worked the usual summer jobs, but nothing considered professional.

My first two jobs in Fiji were in Lautoka, managing cooperatives: first a credit union and then a wholesale food operation. In both cases,

I was mostly window dressing—the real people running each of those organizations were Indian men, one of whom was arrested for embezzlement just after I left. So much for my *masterful* oversight. I had no idea what had been going on. But the men on the boards of directors didn't care all that much that I was sometimes just going through the motions. They wanted me primarily for showing off. Not me personally—any PCV would do. Apparently the latest status accessory in the islands was to have a young American on your staff. Bragging rights, I supposed, and they didn't have to pay a cent for us. Who cared whether we genuinely made a difference? This was Fiji, not the Congo. People were relatively happy and content in our island paradise. The boards of directors didn't need a bunch of neurotic, just-out-of-college kids telling them how to run their co-ops—mainly because most of us didn't know how.

We did have the academic theories in our heads. But applying them was not the same as listing them on some exam, particularly when in a developing and foreign culture, isolated from peers and mentors, books and training. There was so much about business that they never taught me in grad school. Above all, about the human side—how to get things done with and through others—which you eventually realize trumps everything else. So techniques of influence had to be self-taught on the job. But the process was grindingly slow for this inexperienced, isolated introvert who was learning by trial and error on island time. There must have been a preponderance of such limited results, because a couple of years later the Peace Corps recruiting strategy moved sensibly toward finding older, more experienced, more technically-adept Volunteers.

Looming in the back of my mind, in the back of all male PCV minds, was Vietnam. We still could have ended up dying in that meat grinder of a war that would eventually take sixty thousand American and millions of Vietnamese lives. Being in the Peace Corps had enabled me to get a two-year military service deferment, but not a lifetime exemption from military conscription. And even that deferment could be revoked before my stint in Fiji ended. People I didn't know had total control over my life. It was like that for all the Peace Corps guys, even the married ones.

What I did know was that someone at Local Board #55 in Richmond, Virginia, could right then have been in the process of getting my deferment revoked for almost any reason he might want to devise. Maybe he didn't like the Peace Corps, or he had heard that we had it pretty cushy over there in Fiji. Or he didn't like the spelling of my last name. He had his quotas to fill, after all. It was mostly a voluntary position he was in. What kind of person would choose to sit on a draft board playing God with people's lives?

A PCV in Fiji-1 went there with a deferment just like the rest of us, but then his draft board took it away for reasons unknown. His deferment was gone in an instant, and so was he. After basic training, this military neophyte was shipped off to Vietnam. Before the others in his Peace Corps group could celebrate their first in-country anniversary, he shipped out for the final time—this time for home—in a body bag. It could have happened to any of us.

I was due to go back home in a year, and my draft board then would have a full year to finger me and send my butt into war. Under the current guidelines, always subject to change if the military required it, your twenty-sixth birthday was when your life as a pawn ended. On December 1, 1969, the Selective Service conducted its first-ever draft lottery; 366 capsules, each with a different month/day combination, were dropped into a deep glass jar and picked out, one at a time. I wondered how it must have felt to know you probably had tens of thousands of death warrants at stake, as you wiggled your hand inside that jar. Guys born on a September 14 were the biggest losers—their birthday was picked number one. And young men born on a June 8 won a Get-Out-of-War-Free card by having their birthdays picked number 366. My birthday came up number 149, well under the predicted draft ceiling of number 195 for 1970, so barring the sudden cessation of what had become a military quagmire, I was a goner.

I thought about moving to Canada. A lot of guys were doing that—going up on a supposed visit, while planning on never coming back to the States again. The Canadian government disapproved of the American war and accepted such people as political refugees. In 1977, President Carter would pardon those military service evaders, but when I was in the Peace Corps, nobody thought that would ever happen. Analyzing my military alternatives was an exercise in finding the least of evils. There was nothing much I could do about the situation while still in Fiji, so I did my best not to think about it.

CHAPTER FOUR

"**M**r. Naitini would like to see you in his office. Immediately!"

Sitiveni's personal assistant, Talei, awakened me from a daydream about Rani. Talei was a pleasant woman, fiercely loyal to Sitiveni. He returned that loyalty in one way by making sure she did not have to do any work for his two Peace Corps sidekicks. Like a Western woman, Talei was wearing a satin blouse, but it was surrounded by a light-blue *sulu-i-ra*, a long sarong-like dress with traditional Fijian tapa cloth designs on the sash. It looked very dignified, unlike the red miniskirt and sleeveless white blouse Rani was wearing, which just looked totally hot.

There had been urgency in her voice that I wasn't used to, so I scooted over to Sitiveni's office. "You wanted to see me, Sitiveni?"

He didn't look up. "Close the door and sit down." *Uh-oh, what have I done now?*

"What's the meaning of this?" He handed me a typed sheet of paper.

"Oh, that. Well, you said to give my typing to Rani. Looks OK to me." I started to rise from my seat.

"We're not done yet. Sit down."

"Is there a problem?" I asked. Of course there was.

"You and I both know there's no such thing as the board of the Orange Marketing Scheme." My arms dropped. *OK, time to 'fess up.*

"Um . . . would you believe me if I told you I was just wondering how fast her typing was, so that when I have a real document for her to type, I'll know how much time to allow?"

"Would you believe it if someone told you that?"

"No. I didn't think that would work."

"Was this supposed to be . . . what do you call it . . . an ice-breaker? Were you trying to break some of Miss Gupta's ice?"

"OK, Sitiveni, you got me. Sorry. It won't happen again."

"I'm sure it won't, because now that you know how long she takes on a page of bogus minutes, why would you ever need to check that again?"

I had to laugh, and Sitiveni laughed too. *Whew. I'm in the clear. Keep him laughing.*

But Sitiveni wasn't quite done. "Will, can I speak with you, one *turaga* to another?"

"Sure. My lips are sealed, if that's what you mean."

"Well, that's good, but what I mean is you didn't just get off the boat, as you Yanks are keen to say. You've been in Fiji . . . what, about a year now?"

"Yes, I just passed my first anniversary in your beautiful colony . . . um . . . islands."

"So I don't have to tell you about the delicate racial situation we have here between the Fijians and the Indians. And you know your Peace Corps administration is bleedin' touchy when it comes to any controversy." Sitiveni paused, then moved in a little on me. "Do you fancy the Fijian girls, Will?"

That was as loaded a question as I'd ever faced. "Sure. What's not to like?"

"Will, we're both men of the world. I know what it's like to be young and single. And I know Fiji. And so I say to you with naught but concern for you personally, it's OK for you to be with Fijian girls. And by all means go after the mixed race and European ones. But young man, stay away, stay as far away as you can possibly get, from the Indian girls. Now, you're an adult, and you'll do what you want about this, but why make life difficult when it doesn't need to be?"

"Thank you, sir. That makes a lot of sense, Mr. Naitini. I'll certainly take it under advisement, SIR!" *Oh God, I'm already talking like a soldier.*

༄

I thought about what Sitiveni, Troy, and my own experience were all telling me. There wasn't a chance of getting close enough to an Indian girl to even begin having a romance. They kept their discussions with males they worked with, regardless of race, to a minimum and only about business. There was no room for small talk, much less flirting. As Sitiveni had alluded, the Indian girls were walking around in blocks of ice that were impervious to Fiji's torrid sun and romantic trade winds.

And when I was really being honest about it, Rani was no different, except for her choice of dress and her exquisite beauty. She too was a block of ice. Just like with the other Indian girls, there was no room for small talk. There certainly was no room to flirt with her. Troy thought she was just a big tease. If a lothario like him couldn't melt her resistance, what chance could I possibly have?

So I decided to abandon the chase. I was not going to be any girl's fool. I told myself that I could get some women who were actually available—ones who wanted to spend time with me, and me with them. I didn't know who they were right then, but I was sure they were out there. Somewhere. I certainly didn't want a complicated relationship. I would be out of Fiji in a year. I wanted to stay unattached for a long, long time. I decided to ignore Rani as much as possible. Why would I have wanted to risk my safety and well-being for any girl? That would have been insane.

Then I thought about getting in touch with an old flame. Kula was the closest thing I'd had to a real girlfriend in Fiji. We went out maybe five times. She was a mixed-race Euro-Fijian girl who worked in one of the many electronic appliance stores on Cumming Street— all of them owned and run by Indian men. About forty of those stores were dropped on a two-block stretch in the middle of that pristine paradise. Fiji was a duty-free port, so the stores were selling all manner of electronics gear to Aussies and Kiwis. They came to Suva on cruise ships that docked for a few hours, just so the tourists could buy those items, almost all of which were Japanese-made. You could get Nikon cameras, Panasonic amplifiers, and Seiko watches, even the kind you didn't have to wind. And Sony TVs—both black-and-white and color. They sold untold thousands of TVs each year in a country that had no television broadcasting, nothing at all to see on them besides static. But none of those products came from the U.S.—no Zenith TVs, no RCA tape decks. I wondered why. Electronic equipment manufac- tured in the States was still unmistakably the norm, at least where I came from. In 1969 I couldn't know that it was the beginning of the end for American manufacturing dominance. It was unimaginable then that the *Made in America* label would soon be almost going the way of buggy whips.

I liked to go into the shops and ask an Indian shopkeeper how much for, say, a Teac tape recorder, and he would tell me, "Usually $175, but I have too many, must sell, $129, today only." Then I'd swivel my head forty-five degrees, mimicking him, and I'd say, *"Bohoht mahanga, kuch kumti kuro"* (too expensive, lower the price). And then he'd start riffing me in Hindi like I was fluent in the language. Which I wasn't. I just knew the basics and a few choice phrases. Then we'd both laugh, and he would shake his head and say, "Oh you must be one of those Peace Corpse guys," and I'd say, *"Ji-ha,"* and then there would a pregnant pause, and I'd say, "So, really, Ramdass, how much for that tape recorder?" And he'd say, "$175. Sale just ended." And we'd both laugh again, and I'd tell him, "OK, I'll come back when the price is under $100," and he'd say, "Certainly, Sahib, don't hold your breath. Now get out of here, I've got paying customers waiting."

So I wondered how Kula was doing. I supposed she was fine. She had always been fine when we were going out a few months earlier. I knew that because I'd ask her how she was, and her reply was always, "Fine." I'd ask her what she'd been up to, and she'd say, "Not much. Everything fine." "Anything going on at work?" "No." "What do you think of Fiji becoming an independent nation next year?" "That is fine." "How about those men landing on the moon?" "Landing on the moon is fine." "Kula, what do you want to do with your life." "I don't know. Just do what I do now. Why do you ask me these questions? You're a strange chap."

Kula had a phenomenal rack given that it was mounted on a thin body—this in a time and place where implants were nonexistent. She had an alluring face, and technically did *fine* in the sack, but I never could get a real conversation out of her. I hadn't a clue what she thought about me or anything else. I guess I stopped dating her, because I might as well have been going out with an inflatable doll. It was an easy breakup. I just stopped seeking her out. That may seem cruel, but I sensed it was *fine* with her.

Did I actually want to start that up again? What would be the point? What was the point with any of the girls I went out with? We never talked. We had nothing in common. All we did was eat, drink, and rut like bunnies. There was no real foreplay, much less *aftplay*. Maybe I was reaching the point where meaningless sex was just not enough. I was too young for that to be happening. I had been a virgin until less than four years earlier, so I had to make up for all that lost time. *Oh well*, I thought, *I guess I'll just hang up my rubbers and wait till I get back to the States . . . or 'Nam.*

⟳

Sex, drugs, and rock and roll was the mantra of my generation and the *objets du désir* of my Peace Corps friends and me. These three diversions were a way to cope with the homesickness of living in the somewhat westernized culture that was Suva, but like The Rolling Stones, *I couldn't get no satisfaction.*

The sex, of course, was typified by how it was with Kula—*fine*, but it left me yearning for something more.

On the rock-and-roll front, Fiji Radio was the only English-language station, and it played mostly native and Indian music. When they did play Western pop music, it was mostly the dregs. Case in point: of all the terrific Beatles music they could have chosen, it was only the mind-grating ditty "Ob-La-Di, Ob-La-Da" that they chose to play in regular rotation. There were no record stores in Fiji. We could buy superb stereo equipment in that duty free port, but there was almost nothing to play on these state-of-the-art toys. We had to settle for the occasional tape sent from back home to discover how popular music was progressing during that turbulent period. We had missed Woodstock and all the groundbreaking new music such a legendary event had brought to the forefront. We heard *about* it, but we couldn't hear it.

As for the third front, recreational drugs were generally illegal in Fiji, as everywhere else. Alcohol was considered a different category, legal and available. But other mind-altering drugs were a rarity, particularly in our isolated collection of islands. Most Fiji PCVs probably went their whole two-year service period without any and could not have cared less. But there was a small group of us who were interested in partaking, if the opportunity occasionally should arise.

We knew drugs were a no-no for us, as it was one of the top priorities of our Peace Corps administrative betters that we Volunteers avoid all controversy. And as far as they were concerned, we had successfully done that in Fiji. That is, until PCV Mitch Thurman got busted for growing pot near his rural school site. Another teacher, a local, turned him in. Mitch was whisked out of Fiji less than twenty-four hours after the Peace Corps powers found out about his impropriety, but not before it made eye-popping headlines in the *Fiji Times*. Marijuana was mostly under the radar in Fiji before that. A few local Indians grew some *ganja* for personal use—it had been in their culture for three thousand years—but nobody cared a whit until one of our crew got caught. *A damned shame*, we friends-of-Mitch thought. Now we would have nowhere to get any, unless we got lucky when cruise ships were in port. I did hook up once with a young lady from Wisconsin that way, hanging out at the King's Wharf on a lazy Sunday afternoon. But then the next day she, her ship, and her stash were gone in a puff of smoke.

After Mitch got busted, our Peace Corps klatch was forced to find innovative ways to expand our minds. Recreational drug use was considered an almost noble calling by our generation. The obvious downside of such behavior was conveniently ignored, and the long-term effects were scarcely known. We considered ourselves seekers of spiritual fulfillment in our quest to get messed up. Lacking a dependable source of pot, we were forced to turn to other substances for our pursuit of enlightenment. But what could those substances be?

Being in information-isolated Fiji, along with the secretive nature of our mission, meant we had only one another to turn to as a knowledge base. Luckily one member of our group, a usually barefoot and sunburned agricultural PCV from Nebraska whom we dubbed *Attila the Hun*, was a veritable fountain of facts on the folk art of getting fucked up. He suggested we start with nutmeg. Yes, that garden-variety spice you sprinkle on your Christmas eggnog could also blow your mind when ingested in large enough quantities, or so Attila professed.

It sounded a little fishy, so I wrote the U.S. Department of Health, Education, and Welfare to get more authoritative information before ingesting this over-the-counter spice. I indicated that I was a Peace Corps Volunteer who had come upon an isolated, primitive tribe of natives with the unusual custom of consuming large quantities of nutmeg. These Stone Age survivors told us it was how they communicated with their gods and ghosts. But because their rudimentary language was quite different from standard Fijian, nobody outside their tribe was clear on what they were saying. Or maybe their nutmeg consumption had them speaking in tongues. I was only concerned for their health, education, and welfare, of course. Did the U.S. government have any information about excessive nutmeg consumption? What was the high like? How long did it last? Was it dangerous? Could it have harmful long-term effects on these prehistoric people?

They wrote me back and said they had nothing about overindulging on nutmeg, but would be quite interested in getting the results of my study when I completed it. I realized then that my contacting a federal agency had been quite reckless. Suppose they had corroborated my story with the Peace Corps and found out that the health of obscure native tribes was not exactly part of my job description? How could I have explained to the Peace Corps that I was moonlighting as an anthropologist with a tribe that didn't exist? I decided not to send the Department of Health, Education, and Welfare the results of my study and hoped they would just forget I ever existed.

One night soon thereafter, I was at Attila's apartment. We threw caution to the winds and downed some nutmeg. It wasn't easy. Trying to ingest the powder straight was almost impossible, as it immediately absorbed all flesh moisture in its vicinity. It covered my tongue and gums like a thick pile of brown iron filings being drawn to a magnet. I mixed some nutmeg in a glass of water. It would not dissolve. It just settled to the bottom. So the trick was to swirl it around the glass of water with a spoon, then quickly gulp down the whole concoction in one swallow, holding back the inevitable barf spasms. The spasms were, of course, my body saying, "Are you bat-shit crazy? Don't do this to me!" But I would not listen. My exalted expedition would not be thwarted by common sense. An hour later nothing had happened beyond the occasional stomach cramp and nausea pang, so I said goodnight to Attila and started walking home.

I was thinking what a bust the nutmeg had been, when I started to sense that someone was following me. I turned around. Nobody was there. I kept walking, but the feeling of being followed became more and more ominous. I turned around again and saw a dark figure in the shadows and the glint of lamplight on two pulsating eyes, and below the eyes, what seemed like metal. A freaking machete? *Oh my God—someone's after me*, I thought, and ran for my life the remaining half-mile home.

But even in my flat with the doors locked, I still felt as if my knife-wielding nemesis was always right behind me. Emmett was out of town, so I had no one to check with for verification. I would turn around, look, and though I didn't see anyone directly, I was positive he was always there waiting for just the right moment to pounce and slash. I stood in front of a mirror and fleetingly glimpsed a pair of eyes in the darker areas of the room. But when I'd look closer, my would-be murderer apparently had moved elsewhere. I tried to outwit him, faked and varied my moves, but I never could quite hone in on the elusive SOB. I continued this dog-chasing-its-tail behavior, till finally, about dawn, the nutmeg wore off, and I crumpled to the floor like a discarded marionette.

Undaunted, Attila and I next tried morning glory seeds, also professed to have psychedelic qualities. It was even more nauseating than the nutmeg as a result of the insoluble fertilizer, which was sprayed on the seeds to prevent just what we were planning for them. But the New Zealand flower seed packers did not know with whom they were dealing. Attila and I would not be deterred from our righteous mission by avoiding oral intake of a substance used in making homemade bombs and consisting primarily of bovine fecal matter. In this case, the fertilizer would also not be deterred, and immediately after ingesting the seeds Attila and I projectile-vomited them along with whatever else could possibly make its way out of our digestive systems. Once again, spiritual transformation had eluded us.

My final experiment in the realm of homemade highs was catnip. Cats seemed to get off on it, and dried up it looked as if it could have been Mary Jane's twin sister, so shouldn't the effects be similar when smoked? Made perfect sense to me. I rolled a doobie from a piece of writing paper, lit it, and inhaled deeply. Unfortunately nirvana continued to elude me, but within an hour, I did get a rash that covered most of one side of my face. It looked as if someone had pulled off all the skin layers and then pounded the raw muscle with a fork. Not a particularly good look, unless you were attending a masquerade party as a mutton chop or Jekyll/Hyde. I hid from the public until it wore off after a day or so.

After that experience, our rapturous quest was abandoned. I had to settle for booze and waiting for my ship to come back in.

CHAPTER FIVE

Two days after the meeting where Sitiveni admonished me for faking the board minutes, I was sitting at my desk going over a little green booklet I had printed for marketing passion fruit to American companies. I noticed on my right periphery that Rani was rising from her desk and heading in my direction. Turning to witness an apparently furious, pint-sized Moses walking toward me, I watched the Red Sea of office flotsam parting as she stormed my way. Could she be coming to talk to me? And why did she seem so angry?

"Kaisay hal chal, Rani? *Teek hay?"* I greeted her preemptively with a Hindi "How are you? Are you well?" pretending not to notice the furious fumes fulminating from the top of her head.

She ignored my attempt at polite banter. "Why did you give me phony minutes to type and tell me all that rot about the Orange Marketing Scheme? There is no such thing."

"But there *is* an Orange Marketing Scheme. Look, here's the checkbook." Luckily it was in the upper right drawer of my desk.

"But there's no board of directors. That's just rubbish!"

She had me there. The jig was up. "Oh, that. Well, I suppose that part is true. Sorry."

She just stood there, hands on hips, glaring at me. "I'm waiting for an explanation, Mr. Lutwick." She said *Mr. Lutwick* slowly, as if it were a criminal alias rather than a term of respect.

"Please call me Will, OK? I made a mistake. It won't happen again."

"You're bloody right it won't, but you haven't told me why you did it!" Her foot was tapping like a metronome.

"Would you believe me if I said I just wanted to see how well you typed?" *Oh, Lutwick, that didn't work before.*

She rolled her eyes. "Not when you put it that way. Come on. I don't have all day for this tomfoolery."

Man, she's quite accomplished at inquisitions. "OK. OK. I just wanted to get to know you . . . a little."

"And why would *you* want to get to know *me?*"

Holy shit. She's not going to give me a break. "Oh, I don't know, Rani. You seem like a nice person."

"I seem like a nice person? Really, is that what you think?"

"Sure, why not?"

"Oh, come on. Most chaps think I'm a . . . um . . . a *bitch*, I think you call it." She spat out the b-word. "You don't want to get friendly with a *bitch*, do you?"

"You're not a bitch. Stop calling yourself that."

"I'm being a bitch right now. No?"

"Well, you do have a point there."

Her lips curled into a transitory smile, and then she went back into fighting mode. "Look, Will. I'm an Indian girl. I may not dress like most of the others, but the same rules apply. And I know what you Peace Corps blokes are after. And you're not getting it from me. You understand?"

Goddamn Troy. He's ruined her for me. "Now wait a second. We're not all alike."

But she was already walking away.

It may come as a shock, but I was somewhat romantically challenged when I arrived in Fiji. I had a late start in life and was always playing catch-up. When my friends were going on dates in high school, I mostly stayed home. I was introverted, but the primary reason for hardly any dating was that I had no access to a car. For a boy growing up in the rigidly structured and insulated social system that ruled teen life in Richmond, Virginia, in the early 1960s, access to a set of wheels was a necessity for dating. And dating was a necessity for sex, or at least to be considered eligible for sex. Even for general transportation, it was not cool to take a bus, ride a bike, or even walk anywhere besides school. To travel that way on a date? Not only was it unfashionable, it was not even imaginable.

Why no car access? My father dropped dead from a heart attack when I was seven. My mom did the same when I was ten. (More on those events later.) So at that point, I moved in with Mom's brother Jacob and his wife, Tillie. Only Jacob drove, and he never let me borrow his car, a gold-colored 1958 Chevy Impala, even after I got my driver's license at sixteen.

Of course I had the option of double dating, but the conversations would go something like this:

"Hey Jeff, can I double with you and Rita next week for the sock hop?"

"What's the matter? You mean your uncle still won't let his *widdle* nephew drive his car?" Jeff laughed, then continued turning the screw. "Aw, I don't know. I'm not even allowed in your house." Jeff, like all my friends, was *persona non grata* inside Jacob and Tillie's modest brick abode. But Jeff was the most unwelcome of all after hitting their six-year-old son Toby in the forehead with a rock, causing a dramatic spurt of blood, though no apparent lasting damage. Jeff and his younger brother Barry had been paired against Toby and myself in a rock fight. There was no animosity involved—just a stupid game to pass a Saturday afternoon. Like *nadball*, a game Jeff and I played a few times where we'd each sit (clothed) in a chair, facing the other, about ten feet between us, legs spread apart. In turn, each player would bounce a tennis ball off the wood floor, aiming for his opponent's gonads. First boy to hit the floor writhing in pain was the loser. So Toby's rock-fight injury was collateral damage as far as we boys were concerned—nothing to get upset about. Good clean fun. Naturally my aunt saw it differently.

Jeff continued. "Do you even have a date yet?"

"No, I have to get a ride lined up first. You know how it is."

"No, I don't. Why don't you ask your uncle to drive you?"

"Aw, give me a break, I'd rather date my sister than go through that humiliation again."

"OK, date your sister, and I'll double with you."

"Eat shit and die. I hope Rita bites your dick off."

❧

The stated reason my uncle ruined any chance of my having a high school social life was for my protection. No, he wasn't concerned about a broken heart, syphilis, or a paternity suit.

"Will, a car is a weapon," Jacob told me on more than several occasions.

"That's odd," I replied on some of those occasions. "I thought it was a mode of transportation."

Jacob used to drive well below the speed limit in the right lane of the highway. People cursed at us as they passed us by, "Hey asshole, you're holding up traffic, damn it!" Road rage was a rarity in that fairly calm era, but Uncle Jacob attracted it by the shitload. Every time we'd approach a car waiting at a stop sign on a side road, he'd honk his horn. Loud. Thrice. "You can never be too careful." That was his credo for everything in life—*take no risks.* "You have to let the other drivers know you're here."

"But they can *see* you're here. Why do they also have to *hear* you're here?"

"Could be a blind spot. You want to end up like your cousin Judy?"

Judy was seven months older than me. We were in the same grade and went to the same junior high and high schools, but we were like night and day. She was petite, I was tall. She was one of the most popular kids in the Jewish cliques; she used to put on dance demonstrations with her boyfriend. I was an unpopular misanthrope and didn't know the jitterbug from the cha-cha. Judy wouldn't get caught dead hanging out with the likes of me. And although I envied her popularity, I wasn't too thrilled with her either. Her parents, Eli and Hannah, who also happened to be first cousins, were the sophisticated aunt and uncle—they went to parties. My God, they even hosted parties. At Jacob and Tillie's, only close relatives and my uncle's poker buddies were allowed on the premises and then only rarely.

After our mother had died, my older sister, Marcia went to live with Eli and Hannah, whereas I was exiled to *Chez Jacob et Tillie*. I was not consulted on the decision and, being half-grown and suddenly orphaned, I didn't have much leverage. Eli and Hannah considered taking in both Marcia and me, but they already had three kids, and their space was limited. This was Jacob's chance to step forward and do the right thing by family. And that was an issue of self-respect for him. Which is why this was one of the few times he had the stamina to chalk up a win on the domestic battlefield.

I knew Tillie was not thrilled with the idea of taking on someone else's half-grown boy. Not many people would have been. Nobody ever told me directly that she had been against it, but it was easy to pick up on. For years, she would jump away whenever I got within a few feet of her. And whatever household task she would give me, she always considered it done wrong, even if I had done it the exact way she had wanted it the previous time. Later I would see this manipulation game was part of her struggle to control her home territory, but at the time I assumed she was simply being an asshole. Whatever their shortcomings, it was a generous thing for Jacob and Tillie to suddenly take on a half-grown boy they barely knew.

Eighteen days after I turned sixteen, the magic age for driving in Virginia, Judy was killed in a car crash. There were hushed rumors of drinking. She had been on a date, a Christian boy. I didn't even know she was dating *goyim*, a somewhat risqué act in Richmond's socially isolated Jewish community in 1961. My family was devastated by the loss of its princess. Any chance of borrowing Jacob's car went out the window the night Judy died.

CHAPTER SIX

The day after Rani told me to bug off, I was in the office, nursing my bruised ego. But I was coming to the conclusion that what had happened between us was all for the best. *Bitch* did seem an apt moniker to hang around her cute little neck. And trying to be with any Indian girl seemed like suicide, maybe literally.

Sitiveni came over to my desk and leaned in.

"I have a meeting coming up at four with the Chief Minister, Chief of Protocol Docker, and some people from the Governor's office." Fiji's governor was a Brit, the official representative of the Queen. And like her, socially prominent, but politically impotent. "I need you to help Rani set up the conference room. She has all the materials. Go to her and ask her what you can do. I'd ask Talei, but she's out sick today."

My stomach felt as if I'd eaten a live gecko. "Sitiveni, normally I would have no problem with it, but to be totally honest, Rani and I had a . . . uh . . . little disagreement yesterday. It was nothing really, but couldn't Milton do this?"

Sitiveni was visibly miffed. "Milton is doing something important." *Therefore, what I do isn't.* "And what did I tell you about messing with Rani? I won't have that interfering with business."

"Oh I agree, but . . . "

"No *buts*. Just get over there and do it."

My eyes gave him the finger as he walked away. I moseyed over to Rani's desk. She was wearing a tight amber minidress that flashed *caution* to me. "Sitiveni says I'm supposed to help you set up for a meeting or something in the conference room."

She glowered at me, grabbed a key from her drawer and a bag that was on her desk, and stood up. "Follow me." So I did; like a dutiful child who knew he was about to get punished. At the same time, I couldn't help being hypnotized by the soothing rhythm of her dress hiking up and down her superb posterior as she walked.

We took the elevator up two flights to the conference room on the sixth and top floor. The ride was thirty seconds of excruciating silence. We walked down a hall, she opened the door to the teak-paneled room, and we went in. I looked out at the blue-green Pacific and noticed a few cumulus clouds floating over the water. I wished I could be floating out there with them—wished I could be anywhere other than where I was.

I braced myself for another tongue-lashing.

"Um . . . Will, I'm sorry about yesterday. That wasn't very nice of me."

"What?" I stood there flabbergasted for a few seconds before continuing, "Oh that's OK. I guess I had it coming."

"No you didn't. It's just lately I feel I have to be that way with everybody—my parents, my brothers and sisters, even my friends. It's as if they expect me to act this angry role, and so I do it."

"But why?"

"I don't know. Maybe because I'm not like them. I don't think like them. I don't behave like them. They have all these ideas about the way a girl ought to be." Rani leaned against the edge of the large oblong conference table, and I sat down in a chair. Then she continued, "Have you ever felt that way?"

"What way?"

"Different. Just different from all the people around you."

"Sometimes . . . well, actually, most of the time."

"Really? Why do you think that is?"

"I have my theories. One is that I was really supposed to be born on Mars, and they messed up and accidentally put my soul in an Earthling baby."

"So you're actually a Martian trapped in a human body," Rani laughed. "I like that. I thought there was something not quite proper about you."

"Thank you . . . I think. I don't mind being different. I never wanted to be the same as everyone else. Did you?"

"I don't want to be the same or different. I just want to be me."

"And I like that."

"You like what?"

"I like you." That wasn't what I thought I was going to say. "I mean I like that you just want to be yourself and to hell with what others may think about it. I admire that. And you know something else?"

"What?"

"You don't seem like such a bitch now."

"And you don't seem so strange."

Rani's panther eyes looked directly into mine. I felt them pierce past a protective barrier that I had never noticed before. And looking deeply into her eyes, I perceived an overpowering, restless spirit. I stood up. I was close to her. It was as if I could hear her heart beating, feel the warmth rising from her body. I meditated on the entrancing rhythm of her chest rising and falling behind her dress.

Then the sound of footsteps coming down the hall broke the spell. The door was open. We instinctively moved away from each other. The spell was broken.

It was Milton.

"Hey there. I heard maybe you two needed help. What can I do you for?"

෴

Going to college was my deliverance from a melancholy childhood. When I got into Duke University, it was my entrance into a Southern, Harvard-wannabe world of renowned professors and esoteric education, gothic buildings and storied gardens, intellectual students from families of wealth and influence. I joined a fraternity, Zeta Beta Tau, and learned how to drink alcohol, a pastime I had missed out on during high school. Our annual toga party was the most sought-after ticket of any frat event. *Doug Clark and His Hot Nuts* regularly played all night, and they were the biggest party band in the Carolinas. It was said they were the inspiration many years later for the *Otis Day and the Knights* band in the *Animal House* movie, and a ZBT chapter was one of three fraternities that inspired the film's legendary fraternity. And we were the *Animal House* at Duke, where we sponsored the Ugliest Man on Campus contest, among other elegant events.

When I went to my first toga party, I binge-drank myself into oblivion and puked up all my food and even liver bile all over my safety-pinned toga sheet, not to mention my date, Carrie. Or so I was told, because I was too smashed to remember anything that happened five minutes after arriving at the party. Carrie inexplicitly declined my delectable offer of a second date. Hangovers and date rejections aside, at long last I felt as if I belonged somewhere.

Freshmen weren't allowed to have cars, but my sophomore year I finally got my first one, a used 1963 Studebaker Lark, a get-no-respect stubbly shit-pile of gray metal, wide white sidewalls, and a ripped-up red leatherette interior. The Lark got about 150 miles to the gallon. Of oil. Although that problem didn't catch my attention until just after the used car warranty expired.

The Studebaker-Packard Corporation had once been the toast of Detroit, which itself was still the toast of America. But now the company was in its death throes. I felt sorry for them, so I bought one of their cars. Although since it was used, I doubt that helped keep Studebaker afloat.[3] It was not the first or last time I would identify with the underdog, arrogantly defying peer pressure to embrace what

---

3   Packard was dropped from the corporate name in 1962.

was in vogue. As a result of my trend-bucking, I often had taken a hit by being ostracized.

Back at Thomas Jefferson HS, I had refused to wear the peer-pressured Ivy League uniform of London Fog trench coat, Gant button-down dress shirt with a cotton hook over the back pleat, diagonally striped silk rep tie, burgundy Canterbury belt with gaudy brass buckle, Dickies khaki pants, and cordovan Bass Weejuns. Even the thugs in my public high school dressed as if they were interviewing for an executive position. But not me. Oh, I didn't go the classic nerd route of white short-sleeve nylon shirt and undersized black pants with a slide rule sticking out of the pocket. Instead, I blazed my own trail with off-brand purple shirts, green cotton pants, and loafers where, shockingly, the top piece of leather didn't wrap over the stitching as they did on the Weejuns. I got a lot of scorn for that, but what difference did it make— I didn't have many friends and wasn't going out with anyone. *Fuck 'em.*

But at Duke, when at last I had my first car, it was finally time for some serious dating. I played the field for about a year, but wasn't getting many repeat performances. Perhaps it was just coincidental, but a trend was indubitably forming because all the second-date-attempt phone calls started sounding something like this:

> "Hi . . . uh . . . Debbie. This is Will. You may remember we went out for dinner on Friday."
>
> "Oh right. Yes, I do remember. Hold on." *{Muffled talking in the background, followed by laughter.}* "You were the guy in the purple shirt with bitten-down fingernails who cuts his steak in that odd way and then chews it while talking with his mouth half-open."
>
> "Ha-ha, yup. I'm working on that . . ."
>
> "And that's some car of yours. We had to stop to put oil in it."
>
> "Yeah, it's one of a kind, all right . . ."
>
> "And then when you asked if you could kiss me good night, I offered you my hand instead. Only you still had

oil on yours and you got it all over the sleeve of my expensive new cashmere sweater."

"Was that a problem? I'd be happy to pay to have it cleaned."

"So why would you call me so soon after a night like that? Don't you think a girl would want to savor that a while?"

"Sure, but I was thinking, my frat is having a party and . . ."

[*Click.*]

Yes, maybe my unconventional car was not impressing Duke's hoity-toity coeds. Or maybe I had started dating too late, and they wanted someone with a level of romantic flair that matched my chronological age instead of that of a Bar Mitzvah boy. No, I wasn't going to be able to find a girlfriend the usual way. I was going to need something extra.

So when I found out about a futuristic thing that had just arrived on the scene, I jumped at the chance. It was called Operation Match. You would fill out a questionnaire describing who your ideal mate would be, mail it to the Operation Match office in New York, and they would convert your answers to punch cards. Then they would feed those into one of those new IBM 360s that filled a large, refrigerated room and had an astounding twenty-four kilobytes of memory. The computing machine would go through the girls' answers about ideal boys and vice versa, then scientifically figure out your three best matches. This was an exciting, modern world we were living in.

At least that was how it was supposed to work.

Billie Bobbi Berkowitz turned up at the top of my list. Billie was from Bingle, South Carolina, population 1,047. She, her two siblings, and their parents were the only Jews in town. Judging from what they named her, Billie's parents had expected a hillbilly son, instead of a Jewish daughter.

The commercial strip in Bingle consisted of Retton's Groceries, an Esso gas station, and Berkowitz's Dry Goods. Apparently Melvin Berkowitz had settled there for the vast, untapped mercantile opportunity.

Billie was not at all what I had asked for. I specified no ethnic or religious preference. I had learned since starting Duke that there were all these girls out there who did not remind me of myself, not to mention the females of my sucky childhood, which I was trying to distance myself from as quickly as possible. I, like most of the Operation Match college guys in my area, had asked for a gorgeous, tall, thin but shapely, rich young lady who enjoyed basketball, oral sex, and getting drunk. Since a gal like that could have any boy she wanted, she was hardly going to waste her time on a computerized yenta. But all the Jewish college girls were unimaginatively insisting on Jewish college boys, and in the limited universe that was the first ever Operation Match batch in central North Carolina, it was inevitable I would end up with the Berkowitz.

But these were things I figured out long after I filled the Lark's crankcase with oil and drove fifty miles west from Duke on the new I-40 to Greensboro, where Billie attended the Women's College of the University of North Carolina. I thought I was about to date a girl who had been matched to my stated fantasies, although all I had at that point was her disconcerting name and contact information. I parked the Lark and walked up the steps to her dorm, a brick building with bloated white colonnades at its entrance.

I walked into the common room and signed the book where I had to agree to get my date back to her dorm by 11:00 p.m., lest she be locked out, have to wear a scarlet *A*, and be pilloried in the main quad. One of the girls asked who I was there to see, then went back to no-man's-land. Billie soon came out.

She was five foot four with a light-brown pageboy and a bit of a beak. Her appearance was agreeable. Unlike her name, her looks would not have stood out in a crowd, but then neither would mine. She was not exactly my Operation Match fantasy, but I was no Steve McQueen either.

"So you're Will," she drawled.

"So I'm Will," I responded. "And you must be Billie."

We went out to dinner. I watched my table manners and kept the motor oil off her blouse when I got a good-night kiss. Neither of us was knocked over at first, but so began a romantic relationship that would last two years. For the first time in my life, I had a girlfriend.

CHAPTER SEVEN

The day after the conference room tête-à-tête, I approached Rani at her desk and said, "I hope you're feeling better."

"Yes, thanks." Rani kept her head down, avoiding eye contact. "I'm a little embarrassed about that. I hope you will keep our conversation private. I don't know what came over me."

"You just needed to talk. Too bad Milton interrupted us."

Rani raised her head and smiled at me. "Yes, it would have been nice to continue chatting. I'd like to have learned more about your Martian background."

I decided to take the plunge. "So how about we continue the conversation over lunch?"

Any trace of a smile vanished. She pushed at her desk, and her chair scooted backward. "I'd really like to, Will. I just . . . I just can't."

"But it would only be lunch."

"For you, it would only be lunch. For me, it would start rumors. Merely walking to a restaurant together . . . it would attract hateful stares. Too many people know me."

"So? I thought you didn't care what people think?"

"The rumors would eventually get to my family. No, I can't take that chance." She seemed to be speaking more to herself than me.

"But Rani, you can't let others dictate how you live."

"You Americans . . . so easy for you to talk like that, but you know nothing of what I have to endure, nothing of my culture. I wish I could live your way. But I can't." I could see dread in her eyes. "Don't ask me to lunch again. Please, just go."

We'd hit a brick wall. This relationship was over before it began.

∽

My roommate Emmett and I took some time off just after Christmas to visit our friend Leo on the island of Rotuma. Also, I had business going on there with some natives regarding my Orange Marketing Scheme, and I wanted to check in with the Rotuman orange traders. At four hundred miles away, it was the farthest island from Suva that was officially within Fiji. It was also the most remote; no other Fijian island was within three hundred miles of it.

Emmett and I wandered over to at Suva Wharf and looked around for our ship, the *Degei*. When we found it, we couldn't believe how small the gray and blue cutter was. Forty feet long and there were twelve of us on board, including a crew of three. Quite tiny for a forty-one-hour journey over open Pacific waters.

It was only after we'd launched that the captain, Viliame, came over to Emmett and me and said, "I hope you *turagas* brought some motion sickness medicine with you. It's going to be a rough ride."

Emmett and I looked at each other for reassurance and got none. But Viliame got a decent laugh out of it.

So I spent much of the trip with my sunburned head hanging over the railing in vomit or post-vomit mode when I wasn't sleeping fitfully on the deck. This was not your typical ocean-cruise-ship experience. You brought your own food, not that you were going to feel like eating much of it, and there was no pool, no shuffleboard, not even a casino.

But after having seen no land since soon after our departure, I had a Columbus-like moment when I spotted something on the distant horizon. It looked like the profile of a dark-green man with a bloated belly, floating on his back. But even better, it was the nine-mile-long island of Rotuma. At last our hellacious journey would be at an end.

Rotuma was distant from most of Fiji in more ways than one. Its seven thousand inhabitants were of Polynesian origin, unlike most natives of Fiji, who were primarily Melanesian. The Rotuman language and ethnicity were more similar to those of native Hawaiians, Tahitians, and Maoris than those of the much closer Fijians. The only reason the island became part of Fiji was because the British found it expedient to govern its inhabitants that way.

Leo was there to greet us at the jetty, along with several of his young Rotuman friends from his village of Upu. Rotuma had no real towns, just a necklace of village pearls dropped along the perimeter of the island. Virtually no one lived in the tangled, mountainous interior.

We stayed with Leo in his little shack. It had a tin roof that captured rain for his water supply. It was one of the more elaborate buildings on the island. I had a relaxing six days. We'd all go to unsullied beaches in the daytime with our entourage of giggling teenagers and Leo's girlfriend, Fatiaki. At night we drank beer and kava with the local men. It was a welcome respite from my semi-Western lifestyle in Suva and my frustrations over Rani. I never did get around to my intended business, meeting with the orange traders—they said they were too busy during the holidays to get together. When you're enjoying paradise, business matters can always be delayed until an undetermined tomorrow.

We celebrated the beginning of the new decade in the earliest place it arrived. Rotuma, like the rest of Fiji, was in the first time zone to the west of the International Dateline. We were on one of the remotest spots on the planet, enjoying a lovely warm beach, and the stars were flashing like cubic zirconias in a pitch-black sky. We drank abundant amounts of beer, and when the clock struck twelve we lit sparklers stuck in the sand. Leo and Fatiaki embraced and kissed passionately. Emmett and I looked at each other, simultaneously said, "Not with me, you don't," then broke out laughing. It was gratifying to put the sixties behind me, to greet something new and unknown in such a distinctive place. But my heart was still yearning for the relationship that could not be.

ઌ

Having left my life in Suva in the old decade, I returned there ten days later in the seventies. Fiji was on the verge of independence from British colonialism, to be followed by its participation as a nation in the British Commonwealth. In March 1970, six months before the official change from colony to country, Queen Elizabeth and Prince Phillip would be paraded down Victoria Parade, Suva's main drag, limply waving from inside a silver Rolls-Royce convertible shipped across the Pacific for the occasion of that three-mile drive. They would be welcomed by cheering throngs brandishing their own little Union Jacks. No revolution against the imperialists had been needed to effect Fiji's transition to independence. Neither a single sign of protest, nor a single protest sign. Everyone was just trying to get a glimpse of their beloved queen. This was, after all, a people who adored royalty at home and abroad. At least the indigenous Fijians did. But the times had been a-changing, and the Brits had seen the handwriting on the coconut shell. Moreover, the return on investment from their colonies was no longer the lucrative payoff it had once been. The royals and their associates had made their wealth and were pulling out while they still had their dignity. The sun was setting on the British Empire in that same place where it first rose every day.

In my home country, as the decade turned, much change was happening, but little of it was peaceful. America's university campuses were filled with administration building takeovers and antiwar demonstrations. Its ghettos had been burning. And the Nixon administration was at war in Vietnam and Cambodia and at home against the "nattering nabobs of negativism," which was how Vice President Agnew described the activists of my generation. We Peace Corps Volunteers in Fiji would read about such polarizing events in *Time*

Magazine, which arrived weekly—a message in a bottle sent from some far-off land, one which was becoming increasingly difficult to comprehend. Our friends back home were turning on, tuning in, and dropping out. It was as if we were watching a brutal clash of a football game through the wrong end of binoculars from the furthest seats in an empty stadium. We couldn't discern what we were seeing, but nobody would have heard our cheers and boos anyway.

My campaign to be with Rani had been annulled in the old decade. Forces larger than our interests decided that we could not be teammates, and we seemed not ready to play Jackie Robinson to the situation. That would require a lot more courage on her part than mine. We were on her turf, and it was her family, her people that we were up against. But I didn't know whether I was even up to my part of it, or ultimately where I wanted it to lead.

So I was particularly surprised when I sat at my desk at work late one January afternoon and, noticing the scent of lilacs, I swiveled around and there she stood, having quietly snuck up on me from behind. My eyes followed the line of her lean brown forearm to the end of her hand where her thumb and forefinger converged over a golden key. I gazed curiously at it while she smiled a contented feline grin, flashing a collection of translucent teeth. I hadn't noticed their symmetrical beauty before, perhaps because I had seen her smile so rarely.

"OK, Rani, what's with the key?"

"You have to guess."

I hadn't a clue what she was up to. "Is it the key to your heart?"

She laughed. "No, don't be absurd. You'll never get this close to that."

"The key to your home?"

"Oh sure. That would be a brilliant move, indeed."

"I give up."

"It's the key to the conference room, you silly bloke."

"And . . . ?"

"And I'm in charge of it and the schedule for the room. Most days it's free at lunchtime."

"Oh, wow!"

"Yeah, 'oh, wow', I like that American talk. You want to have lunch up there tomorrow?"

My heart was spinning like a yo-yo doing a loop-the-loop.

"You know I do."

"OK. Here's how we'll do it. You bring the lunch. I'll go first. Wait a couple of minutes. Take the lift and go to the room. Make sure nobody is around. Scratch on the door a little so I'll know it's you. Scratch, don't knock. Then I'll let you in."

"You certainly have this figured out, don't you?"

"Yes, I do." Her smile was radiant. "I have this *all* figured out."

೪

And so it came to pass, just as she planned it. The next day at noon she got up from her desk, our gazes met knowingly, and she left the office. I counted 120 seconds and went to the conference room, looked up and down the hall, and seeing no one, scratched the door like a cat. Even did a little meow. The door creaked open like the entrance to a haunted house. I closed it behind me as I walked in.

There she stood, cute as a panda cub. She was wearing a pink top and a red miniskirt, a seductive mixture of innocence and sensuality. I felt a jumble of extremes—awkwardness, fear, and desire. If she felt similarly, I couldn't tell. She looked happy, peaceful. But neither of us seemed able to come up with anything to say at first. A few seconds of silence passed as we alternated looking at each other and looking away.

"What did you bring for lunch?" Rani broke the tongue-tied silence.

"Roti and vegetable curry." *Oh shit. I'm shaking. Hope she doesn't notice.*

"You cook Indian food?"

"Nah, I got it from that curry place across the street."

"Smells good. Yes, I like that shop."

"Yeah, me too."

More awkward silence, so we sat down next to each other at the long table. I was taking roti and curry wraps out of the bag, putting them down, when I felt her hand graze mine. I turned and looked into those two bottomless eyes, with doubt on my face, as if to say, "Are you sure you're ready for this leap of faith?" And the bewitching eyes looked back and told me, "I know what I'm doing."

So I bent in and grazed my lips against hers so lightly I'm not sure they touched, even as I felt warmth radiating from them. And then we kissed lightly. And then we really kissed.

I guided Rani onto my lap, surprised that she would go there so soon, amazed by the feel of such a tight electric body, as her compact butt settled on top of my thighs. I was unsure what to do with my hands, but then she wrapped her arms around my neck and went in for longer deeper kisses, and my hands knew exactly where to go. Between us, we were an octopus—eight tentacles going everywhere. I stopped thinking and just lost myself in the exquisite moment.

Someone walked down the hall outside the door. Rani tensed, then darted from my lap as if it were a burning grill. The outside sounds drifted away and we both smiled, but it seemed our magical mystery tour was over, at least for the time being. Each of us silently adjusted our clothes, as if that would put us back in the mindset of our work world, but Rani undoubtedly noticed the tubular bulge below my belt because she suppressed a laugh while glancing in that direction.

Neither of us said much, just some polite talk, as we went into work-lunch mode and ate the food before us. It was as if we were now two strangers sitting at a table in a restaurant, each of us deep in our own thoughts, acutely conscious of the other's presence, but unable to bridge the divide and discuss the eight-hundred-pound gorilla lying across our laps.

What the hell are we getting ourselves into? Will we have the courage to see it through?

CHAPTER EIGHT

Courage.

Courage had been a haunting issue for me, ever since I was a little tyke. Probably my biggest issue. I wasn't brave—certainly not in the traditional sense. It's painful to admit, but I was a coward—in the traditional sense. The one foible no male should ever admit. Better to be a thief, a scoundrel, certainly a bully, than a bully's victim.

It's the most pervasive unwritten law among the males of our species. Bravery = manhood. Tormented victim = no manhood. The worst things you could ever call a boy when I was growing up—*sissy, chicken, coward, scaredy-cat*. Every boy knew that almost from Day One. It was hard-coded in our DNA.

Granted, being branded gay, with all the hatred that brings out in bullies, would have been even worse. But growing up in the 1950s, we children were rigorously shielded by adults from all things sexual even after our own sexuality kicked in. Of course we found out about sex on our own, but it actually took a concerted effort at that time. The love that dare not speak its name, true to its description, was particularly hidden from the children. I don't think I had any concept of its existence until the middle of my teen years.

In my early and middle childhood, I tried to talk my way out of fights with other boys. When the fight became unavoidable, I would negotiate. "How about no hitting in the face?" Usually I would have a bloody nose before I even finished that suggestion. I just didn't see much point in fighting over, say, who had the better bicycle. What did one thing have to do with the other? Nothing, of course, but I was failing to grasp the long-term issue: fight mercilessly and win or forever be picked on.

In May 1950 when I was four, Mom, Dad, my older sister Marcia, and I moved away from New Rochelle, the Westchester County suburb that would achieve pseudo-notoriety as the consummate hometown of Rob and Laura Petry on 1960s sitcom *The Dick Van Dyke Show*. We headed south to warmer climes, to Richmond, Virginia, where much of my mother's family had already migrated. It was only 356 miles, but in those days the cultures of those two locales were as different as they could be. I was the lone Jewish boy on my block, a transplanted Yankee from the North's most despised state. I landed smack-dab in the capital of the Confederacy at a time when several Civil War veterans were still breathing, and much of the white population was still psychologically fighting what was affectionately referred to as "The War of Northern Aggression." ("The war was fought over states' rights and had nothing to do with slavery," I was often told in my segregated history classes.).

The fabrication that the Jews killed Jesus would not officially be discredited by a prominent Christian leader until Pope John XXIII did so in 1963, the year I finished high school. Among the mostly WASP kids around me in the 1950s, that myth was commonly accepted as a legitimate grievance against present-day Jews. That he had been a member of our tribe didn't seem to hold much holy water.

One day in my first summer in Richmond, some older boys got hold of a ladder and hung me by the back of my jacket on a telephone pole in an alley. It was a half hour before a grownup happened to come by and helped the flailing four-year-old escape. Perhaps my tormentors thought that particular punishment was symbolic payback worth extra points in the get-into-heaven sweepstakes.

My parents were no help at all. The dream of the Southern Promised Land soon turned into a nightmare for my dad, for my whole family.

My father was rarely home, working seven days a week in his miniscule black-ghetto grocery store. On the Jewish male career ladder, mom-and-pop grocery store proprietor was the bottom rung, and it must have been humiliating for my dad, especially as he was married to a woman with a college degree, a rarity at the time. Previously Dad had run a pharmacy in a middle-class New Rochelle neighborhood. Baseball superstar Lou Gehrig stopped by often and became someone my father referred to as a friend. Dad lost that career when his partner and younger brother, Harry, who was the licensed pharmacist of the two, decided to move to Los Angeles, his wife's hometown. Exhausted and demoralized, my introverted forty-four-year-old father succumbed to sudden death from a heart attack one cold December night. It was two-and-a-half years after our exodus from New York.

I had no father to stand behind me just after my seventh birthday. A boy without a dad stood out as easy prey. That situation was rare in those days before single moms and divorces became commonplace.

I started school in the winter of 1951. Soon thereafter, the cherry blossom trees flowered and the weather turned warm, so my mother made me wear short pants to school.

"Mom, none of the other boys wear short pants. Everyone laughs and makes fun of me."

"They're just jealous because my William is keeping his little *shmekl* cool, and he's being so much smarter than they are."

"No, Mom, they're laughing because I look like a baby with skinny legs. I feel like I'm naked."

"Just listen to your mother, William. I know what's best for you."

It took weeks of constant complaining to get her to relent, but by then it was too late. Just a rookie, my school reputation was set in concrete. I was branded the mama's boy at John B. Cary Elementary School even before I started reading "Dick and Jane."

One day shortly after my father died, a couple of the neighborhood boys were over our house. Seemingly out of the blue, my mother told them, "When my William gets in a fight, you boys must fight his battles because he's not supposed to fight." I couldn't believe what I was hearing. *Gee Mom, why don't you just cut my balls off and shove them down my throat?* The boys, suppressing astonished laughter, responded with mock politeness, "Yes ma'am. We'll be happy to fight your William's battles for him." Of course they had no such intention, and the minute they got out of the house they were howling with laughter. They couldn't wait to spread the word around the neighborhood. Already the preferred target of the neighborhood bullies, now I might as well have put a bull's-eye on my forehead and a beat-up-this-kid sign on my back. And though it wasn't my *protectors* who attacked me, they were howling on the sidelines when I'd get slugged by some bullies.

Then when I'd get home, it was even more humiliating. Sometimes when our mother was out of hearing range, my sister Marcia, two-and-a-half years my senior, would slap me around. This continued until I got bigger than her, but that wasn't until I was about eight and she was ten. I don't think I ever hit her back. She was a girl, and boys were supposed to never, ever hit girls. That was considered not just unfair, but gutless.

Marcia had her reasons for slapping me. I was the male child, openly favored by our mother. In Mom's eyes I was supposed to become the family genius and a musical prodigy, and that must have been tough for Marcia to stomach after she had both parents all to herself through her toddler stage.

But there was another reason for Marcia to lash out at her most accessible target. One day when she was about three, Marcia was constipated, so Mom gave her an enema. And the enema freaked little Marcia out so much she could barely poop, so Mom gave her another enema the next day. And soon this cycle of constipation/enema/ freak-out became an almost-daily occurrence. For years.

During the 1940s, the American medical establishment encouraged habitual enemas, and they were used as a standard practice for healing in hospitals. Just as the more benign-sounding *colon cleansing* has reemerged on the scene in recent decades as a healthful practice. However, I don't think anyone now recommends that inserting a tube up your anus be done every twenty-four hours, like flossing. So Mom wasn't intentionally being cruel, she was just practicing the Ritalin-like parenting trend of her day.

Who else was poor Marcia going to take out her frustrations on for being rectally violated, but the new kid in the family? Understandable from that perspective, but no picnic for her brother.

Mom never pulled that shit on me. Hearing Marcia's whimpering cries put the fear of the enema beast in my gut. I would take one look at that steaming, throbbing, crimson hot-water bottle with its red rubber tail and twisted wire contraptions, and I'd run away screaming. To my little kid's eyes, it looked like a mini-Satan. So as soon as I could write, I started keeping count of my daily bowel movements. To up my stats I would cut short my toilet visits, come back a few minutes later, and poop the rest of my load. That counted as two poops in my book. Perhaps not by Olympic regulations, but it worked for me.

"William, are you sure you're doing enough BMs?" my mother would say. "You know an enema a day keeps the doctor away."

"I think that's an apple, Mom"

"Why would a person want to keep an apple away?"

"Never mind." I would shake my head in disbelief. "But take a look at this." And I would show her my daily stats, which averaged well over the 1.0 MDR needed to prevent her from practicing her demonic ritual on me.

"Very impressive, William. But too much. I'll get the Kaopectate."

❧

My mother's hopes that I'd become a musical prodigy started one day when I was four. Although he had never touched a musical instrument, her little William climbed up on the piano bench and started plunking out the title song from the operetta, *The Chocolate Soldier*. Mom, a classical music aficionado, almost had a convulsion thinking she had birthed the next Mozart. The way I see it, I was just having a flashback to a past life, which, after all, hadn't been that long before. Or maybe I memorized the score by hearing it on one of the crackly 78-rpm records Mom regularly played on our mahogany RCA Victrola. With great expectations, my mother immediately started her boy on piano lessons. Unfortunately I was a clumsy kid, so I wasn't too proficient at the keyboard, despite having perfect pitch. And like any American boy of that era, I wanted to be outside throwing perfect pitches and riding my bike, not inside practicing scales and plunking out Beethoven.

My piano virtuosity peaked at the advanced age of seven. My mother was horribly disappointed in my failure and let me know it often. Like most in that still spare-the-rod-spoil-the-child era, she believed in physical discipline. Her preferred weapon was a belt, her preferred target, my butt. I remember getting occasional beatings almost up to the day she died. Usually they weren't particularly severe. My mother doted on me, smothered me with affection and concern, but when I didn't meet her lofty expectations in school or at the piano she could have a nasty temper.

Once when I was nine, she whipped my ass with a belt, leaving red welts across the cheeks, tiny dots of blood springing up through the skin. I don't remember why she was angry, but the beating was humiliating, and I ran away from home. I went only a few blocks, and after a few hours it was getting dark and I had nowhere to go. So I swallowed my pride and went home. When I got there, Mom was a frantic wreck. She had been worried to death that some bogeyman had taken me away. She had already called the police. She hugged me tightly, screaming hysterically as the tears poured down her cheeks. She begged me to forgive her. So I did.

Parents rarely thought of physical punishment as abuse in those days. Many thought not beating your child was neglectful because it meant you didn't love them enough. Still, I don't remember my father ever beating me. I wish he had. Getting beaten by your father made you a man. Being whipped by your mother made you a weakling. Being slapped around by your sister made you a full-out sissy.

But all that was soon to change. Forty months after my father died, Mom departed in exactly the same manner—a heart attack and death, both on the same evening. She was forty-seven.

I moved in with her brother Jacob, his wife, Tillie, and their toddler son, Toby. Neither my aunt nor my uncle ever hit me. I remember thinking, *Well, this is odd. Why am I never getting smacked? Am I not loved?* Then I noticed they rarely spanked their son.

All the beatings, in the home, on the street, by males, by females, by adults, by kids—they took a tremendous toll on my dignity. It wasn't the bruises, the black-and-blue marks, the bellyaches, the bloody noses, or the busted lips. It was the humiliating ways in which so many of the attacks happened, the ways in which I had let them happen, rarely fighting back, accepting my fate as the designated punching bag for so many others' frustrations or cruelty.

One morning when I was in the eighth grade, I sat with thirty classmates in our homeroom, waiting for the teacher to arrive. Someone from the principal's office came by and told us she was running a bit late. And so, with nothing better to do, four punks, who knew me well, began taunting me, while the rest of the students silently watched the spectacle. At first I tried just ignoring it, but one of the junior hoodlums snuck up behind me and dumped the contents of a full pencil-sharpener's casing—wood shavings and black pencil-lead powder—down the back of my shirt. The crowd cried, "Awwww!" Apparently that move was not in the official playbook, but this was spectator sport, so no one intervened. Before I could do anything about the crud down my back, another boy, a head shorter than me though close to my weight, came up to me and tried to get me to fight him. We both knew his friends would join the pummeling party as soon as I'd take a swing. Now that I was thirteen, the potential injuries were getting more serious.

"Come on chicken-shit. You afraid to fight me?"

I looked down at his hate-filled face wondering why this was happening. "Fuck it, Doug. We both know what your buddies here will do if I fight you."

"OK then, you chicken-shit kike, get down on your knees and beg me not to hit you."

That was it. I snapped. I grabbed the pubescent punk like a sack of rice, lifted him over my head, and threw him fifteen feet across the room where his back smashed against the blackboard and his body slid down to the floor, crumpling in a groaning heap. I had no idea where the strength came from. It was like one of those stories where a little old lady lifts the back end of a Buick to free someone trapped beneath. The room went silent. Everyone stopped moving, their faces frozen into masks of total astonishment. I walked to a trash can, untucked my shirt, and shook out the pencil shavings. I was the only thing moving in a room full of statues, their mouths agape. I felt totally at peace for the first time in my life. Then the teacher came in the room. Everyone walked to their seats as if nothing had happened, except Doug, who had to limp to his.

Later some of my classmates came to me and said it was so very uplifting what I had done—although not so much that any of them had thought to intervene on my behalf—and that the punks had certainly had it coming.

I was never bullied again.

CHAPTER NINE

During the two weeks following our first romantic escapade, Rani and I would meet in our penthouse-like hideaway for lunch and shenanigans as often as we could. It was always dicey but thrilling going there—the staggered departures, the separate routes, the looking out for those who might catch us. Eating, talking, making out on the top floor of Fiji's tallest building with its enticing view of the cerulean Pacific and Viti Levu's southern coastline just beyond.

We were James Bond and his Soviet spy lover caught on the opposite sides of an unforgiving cold war. We were Romeo and Juliet, torn between dueling families. We spoke in muted tones and kept our clothes unfastened but loosely on just in case someone would suddenly show up at the door. And we kept the sex somewhere between second and third base, ostensibly to keep the noise level down. We decided that if we got caught eating, we'd be OK, but we would then have to desist. Even one lunch alone might suggest an "improper" relationship to many people. And if we got discovered doing anything that suggested intimacy, then we'd be in trouble, and though we weren't sure what that trouble would be, we had no curiosity to find out.

If we were entwined and we heard footsteps, we would quickly pry ourselves apart, zip, hook, and button up, smooth our clothing of telltale passion wrinkles, and start talking about the weather or a work project—both to throw off any potential snoops as well as to get our minds off the lust that had just ensued. I found this ritual exhilarating despite the obvious sexual frustration.

I would leave each session with a throbbing case of blue balls. Then when I'd go home that night, I'd get into my bed and masturbate to exotic visions of completing what we had started.

Contrary to my usual nature, I was nurturing the embryo of an adventurer and taking risks—although they seemed more the risks a twelve-year-old boy should have to tolerate than those of a man twice that age. I had already been addicted to Rani's exquisite beauty, but now I was blown away by her fierce determination and her independent attitude. Like any addict, I was in denial of my addiction, its escalating power, and the danger I was in if I continued acting out. I lived for my fix. Nothing else mattered.

∾

But there were other items on our conference room menu besides the fruit of passion. These were my first opportunities to learn who this captivating young woman was. What was her story? I quizzed Rani incessantly. I wanted to know everything about her. And after Kula and the other Fijian girls I had been with, it was exhilarating to have a conversation with a local girl that covered more than just pleasantries, sexual logistics, and beer.

"Tell me something about your childhood." I asked her one day while we ate our curry and roti wraps.

After thinking a bit, she said, "I had a happy childhood, but we were poor probably by your standards, because up to ten of us would be living off my dad's salary as a middle-school teacher."

"Wow! I don't think ten people could possibly survive on that in the States. Teachers there don't make much money."

"That's quite surprising. Teaching is so crucial, and I thought Americans were so educated and rich. Here, a teacher makes a good salary. At least when compared with others who lived in the villages where I grew up. You don't need much money to live in the rural places. And teaching is a position of respect. Even the adults called my father Master because he was a very dedicated teacher.

"I just assumed you grew up in Suva. You don't seem like a country girl to me."

"No, I didn't move to Suva until two years ago."

"So what was village life like for our little Rani?" I patted down her hair with my unstained-by-curry left hand.

"It was lovely actually. I spent most of my free time outdoors. Although I've never been off Viti Levu to compare, I really do think it's beautiful here. Rivers, forests, beaches, food growing everywhere. I particularly liked being around the rivers. They not only provided relief from the heat, they were also where my family did their laundry; caught crayfish, shrimp, and crab; and had religious ceremonies. There were ropes secured to the surrounding trees for splashing and swimming in the river."

"So you went swimming a lot?"

"Not swimming actually. The girls would just wade in the water. We were discouraged from learning to swim—I've never learned how—but we girls did climb trees. In the rivers, the kids used a fishing net made with a burlap rice sack and four strings tied in a loop to its four corners. Then the sticks went through these loops." Rani's delicate fingers went through the motions of building the net while describing it. "We put a little roti in this net and in minutes we'd catch all these fresh shrimp. My mum made the best curried shrimp. She cooked on a wood-burning stove. Nobody had electricity."

Rani looked out the window. She seemed to be watching a distant place. "The older sisters were the cooks, housekeepers, and babysitters, but because I was the baby of the family I missed out on the babysitting. My mum made our dresses, but she always wore a sari, even though it was hot most of the time. She and I worked together in the rice fields. The flooded fields gave some relief from the heat.

"We grew our own vegetables and also huge watermelons and cantaloupes. Fresh guavas and mangoes grew wild. Mangoes were pickled and guavas made into jam. When we lived on the dry, western side of the island, we would chew sugarcane fresh from the plantations. Breadfruit and jackfruit grew wild in the forests. There is nothing sweeter than a ripe jackfruit."

"Your family didn't raise farm animals?"

"Well, being Hindu, we didn't eat beef. But we did raise chickens."

"How about toys and games? Did you have those as a kid?"

"No toys . . . Oh wait, I did have this one really raggedy doll."

"Raggedy Ann?"

"No, I know the doll you are thinking of." Rani laughed. "I've seen pictures. Not her. No, this dolly was just raggedy. You know—torn, falling apart. It was a hand-me-down, so I was probably the sixth sister to get it. Nobody had toys or games. We would play games with stones and sticks, anything that was handy. You had to use your imagination a lot."

"There were eight brothers and sisters, right?"

"Yes. My father was thirty-one, my mother, twenty-eight when I was born. She was fifteen when they were married and had seven children in the next ten years, including one set of twins. Then my mum, she got a bit of a break for three years until I arrived, um . . . unexpectedly." Rani laughed.

"Well, I'm thankful for that accident. Did you feel unwanted?"

"Quite the contrary. As the baby of the family, I was doted on by my parents and all my sisters. Even my nieces and nephews call me Baby Auntie. I suppose I was somewhat spoiled."

"Yes, I imagine you might have been."

Rani's mouth tightened. "Oh, really? And why is that?"

"Well, you're quite adorable, you know. Pretty girls learn how to get their way."

She pulled back from me. "I don't think about things that way. I just believe *everyone* should get their own way . . . do what they want with their lives and such."

"And when people discourage you and even try to stop you from getting what you want—what then?"

Rani thought about it for a moment. "That is their problem, not mine. I don't mean I have to get every little thing I want. But choosing the big things in life, that's too important to let others decide. So far, I've always gotten what I really wanted, and I won't let others stop me from living my life that way."

∽

My journey with Rani was already so different from my few prior romantic sojourns. Before I got to Fiji, I had been driving in the freeway-of-love's breakdown lane. I was only three women removed from virginity. The one who broke me in was a prostitute. I had been twenty, way too old, I thought, to still be so inexperienced.

Joe Feldman had been my Zeta Beta Tau big brother at Duke when he was a senior and I was a freshman. After he had graduated, we kept in touch. He went to work at his father's fashion design firm in New York City. He had just married his college sweetheart, and they had moved into an apartment on East Fifteenth Street near Greenwich Village, when I visited him for a few nights in the summer of 1966. The first night we got soused, and I blurted something about my lack of sexual experience. The next day he surprised me with an announcement that he was bestowing a gift on me—an appointment with a *woman of loose morals* because, as he said, "I don't want to ever have to hear that fucking sob story again." I offered to pay, but he insisted, "Someone owes me a favor."

I didn't know whether Joe had ever used this arrangement to fix up his business associates or had partaken of it himself, but the ease with which he set it up made it seem part of his repertoire. Such details were not volunteered, and it would have been impolite to ask too many questions, particularly with his new wife, Jan, within earshot most of the time. After all, when getting just about the best gift a guy could ever receive, you don't want to pry too much about the delicate and illegal aspects of how it was procured.

Knowing that Joe worked in the rarified world of fashion design, visions of a stunning New York runway model, perhaps fresh to the biz and needing to moonlight, slithered into my brain. I would be losing my virginity with a goddess I could have barely fantasized, while enabling a hardworking young woman to send some well-earned cash back to her impoverished grandmother in Minneapolis or Minsk. No present could have ever been more appreciated or anticipated.

After a twenty-minute walk, I arrived at Wanda's room in a rundown hotel in the Village. *Oh*, I thought before knocking, *brilliant choice of environment for a deflowering—a bit of sleaze is a turn-on*. But said sleaze was not there for ambiance. My lady of the evening was probably twice my age, had overly processed, frizzy, jet-black hair, and wore enough makeup to paint a billboard. Her eyes had a glazed look, the little I could see them behind the layers of mascara. Judging from Wanda's appearance, Joe had gone shopping at the Salvation Army store rather than the Ford Modeling Agency.

But what she lacked in youthful vitality and superficial beauty, she made up for in gentleness and care. She knew she was dealing with a novice, and Wanda freely shared her veteran's knowledge of the *ins and outs* of the game. Here was someone who could convincingly convey that she loved her work. The only problem for me was that I didn't ejaculate. Maybe it was the letdown of her looks or my newbie nervousness. So after an hour and a half of being led through *shtupping* in almost every position you might find in a sex manual, I pulled out for the final time, waited for my appendage to stop saluting, wiped it down, and started putting my clothes on.

"That was fabulous," Wanda said. "I haven't come that many times since . . . oh, sorry about that. Hey, don't feel bad, baby. Most virgins have the opposite problem."

"They can't get it up?"

"No, their pistol goes off before they get it out of the holster."

"Well, it's nice to be unique. Don't worry about it. I know you gave it your best shot. It was me, not you." I was already getting a monstrous congested prostate, and I just wanted to take my overheated equipment and tender ego and get the fuck out of there.

But Wanda had other ideas. "Hey, sweetie, here's a thought. I have my morning free tomorrow. How about you drop by around ten for another round of lovemaking?"

"Lovemaking? Oh right, that stuff. Yes, but I think my friend paid for only one session."

"No, honey. This one will be on me."

DID SHE JUST SAY WHAT I THINK I HEARD?

Was it the challenge? A sex professional wanted another match-up with *me*—a nebbish who had whacked foul balls all night, striking out every at-bat in his debut game? But perhaps she saw some potential in this rookie that I didn't see in myself. After all, her orgasm count for the game, faked or otherwise, was well into double figures. From what little I knew of the game, her invitation was highly unusual. And when I went back to my host's apartment and told Joe about it, he was dumbfounded.

"Holy shit! This is unprecedented, Will. Nobody ever gets asked back for a complimentary refill."

His scowling wife, Jan, was standing right behind him. I gave him a squirmy look. He cleared his throat before continuing. "Well, I'm guessing about all that, of course."

"Say Joe, it's been a long night. Mind if I turn in early?"

"Right." Joe looked around. Jan had moved on, but Joe still whispered, "The porn magazines are in the bottom drawer of the dresser. But don't hit the walls or ceiling. We just had them painted."

By the next morning, I was getting paranoid. Whenever something seems too good to be true . . . Maybe Wanda's magnanimous invite was feigned to lead me into an encore that was just a setup. She was probably a heroin junkie. She might have her pimp/pusher hiding in the closet, and in the middle of copulation he'd jump out and kill me. If he did it too soon, I'd die without ever having had an orgasm during sex with another person. That wouldn't do.

"Joe, I'm a little concerned about this. If you don't hear from me by one o'clock, call the police. I'm going to leave my wallet behind."

"Will, I know this woman." He hesitated and looked around the living room. Jan was sitting on the couch at the other end, smoking a cigarette, seemingly engrossed in a book. He lowered his voice. "Well, I . . . uh . . . know *of* her through the business arrangement that I personally have nothing to do with. And from what my associates tell me, she's good people. Nothing bad is gonna happen."

"Yeah, but what's in it for her? You have to admit it's kind of weird."

"Yes, totally. But I'm telling you, she just must like you. So you got to show her that you care."

"Oh I do care about her. She took my virginity, after all. It still counts even though I didn't shoot off in her, right?"

"Absolutely. No way I want to hear you complaining about that again."

"Yeah, she's a nice lady. What do you think I should I do?"

"Take her a cup of coffee."

"That's it? But I don't even know how she takes it. Shouldn't I buy flowers too?"

"No flowers. Not for this one. Get cream and sugar on the side."

Despite Joe's assurances, I was still unconvinced. I left my wallet at the apartment and walked to Wanda's. I did take a twenty-dollar bill just in case, because, after all, this was New York, and people expected to be tipped for everything, and she was giving extra service. So if I didn't get rubbed out by her pimp, I might have to tip her. Also, what if I had to take her out for brunch afterward? What would Emily Post say was the correct protocol for après-sex with the prostitute who broke you in and invited you back gratis the next morning?

There was a diner next door to her hotel, so I went inside for the coffee. I handed the twenty to the proprietor, his black hair greased back under a dirty white paper hat.

"Christ on a cracker! Whadaya kiddin' me?

"Is there a problem?"

"A twenty-dollar bill for a ten-cent cup of coffee? You crazy or somethin'?"

"Sorry, sir. That's all I have."

"Fuckin' out-of-towners."

I took the coffee to Wanda.

"Ooh, baby, that's so thoughtful of you." After drinking it, she said, "God, I love sex in the morning on a hot summer day. Come to mama, baby."

So I'd like to say that I *came* in *mama, baby*, but no, it was another nine innings where she scored all the runs and I got lots of RBIs. Afterward, she was so contentedly exhausted that she quickly faded into sleep, and I took my leave. No pimp, no tip, no brunch, no invitation for another session.

Emily Post would have been aghast.

CHAPTER TEN

B y our seventh conference-room rendezvous, it was apparent we couldn't continue this way for much longer. One of us had to take charge of the situation.

"OK, Will. This is getting ridiculous."

"What's getting ridiculous?"

"Meeting like this in the conference room. It's been fun, but I can't keep doing it." She seemed very determined, but to do what, I couldn't tell.

"But why? I love it. It's so romantic. And dangerous."

"Oh, it's bloody dangerous, no doubt. But I'm the one in danger."

"But you said we can't go out."

"We can't. And this is too frustrating." She was pacing the room. I rolled my eyes. "Tell me about it."

"I just did."

"I mean . . . you mean?" I braced for getting dumped. This was going to be excruciating.

"Where did you say your flat is again?" *Whew!*

"Eighty-four McGregor Road. About a ten-to-fifteen-minute walk from here."

"Tomorrow night, you go home first." Her dark eyes darted as if she were plotting our moves on a map. "Then I'll leave ten minutes later. That is . . . unless . . . "

"Unless what?"
"Unless you have something better to do."
I didn't.

❧

With each meeting my addiction to Rani had deepened. I thought I could try her casually, both of us just having some fun. No complications. Nobody gets hurt. Then it got passionate; I upped my dose and still thought I could walk away. But Rani was no recreational drug. Ours was a hard-core relationship from the first kiss. There was no such thing as a casual liaison with her and for her. What did she want from all this? What did I want? Why did I find her so enticing? Did I have the cojones to go the distance, whatever that distance might be?

Doubts about my courage were being tested by our clandestine romance. Yet other external issues propelled my moving forward in this relationship that broke deeply entrenched rules.

I came of age in the early 1960s and had been deeply influenced by the civil rights movement.

I spent the summer of 1963, after graduating from high school, working in the kitchen at a children's summer camp, nestled in a pine forest in the West Virginia Appalachians. I was the only white worker, the other five, all young black guys. I became fast friends with one, Cecil, another new high school graduate from my hometown of Richmond, but of course from a different high school. All the schools I attended had been totally white despite a city population evenly split between black and white, albeit in segregated neighborhoods. Four blocks from where I lived with my aunt and uncle, there was an affluent neighborhood of Colonial Revival houses called Windsor Farms that not only prohibited blacks, but Jews as well. I had a good friend who lived there. I visited his house often, but I would not have been allowed to live in it.

But by the time I finished high school, the civil rights movement that was sweeping the country passed through Richmond as well. There were lunch counter sit-ins and demonstrations to integrate other public facilities. A single black freshman girl was admitted to Thomas Jefferson HS the year I graduated.

Race wasn't a concern in the secluded summer camp environment. As I got to know Cecil, I learned that we had similar ideas and aspirations and even shared a kindred warped sense of humor.

One afternoon someone bought a small black-and-white TV with a coat-hanger antenna into the kitchen, and all the black guys were captivated by its grainy picture. Something was on the news about Negroes marching in Washington, DC, not a hundred miles away. A preacher named Martin Luther King was about to speak. In a booming voice at the foot of the Lincoln Memorial, he said he dreamed of a world where people, maybe even his own children, would be judged by the content of their character, rather than by the color of their skin. The young men in the kitchen were raucously cheering, their eyes tearing. I had never seen black people act that way before. I looked back at the TV and instinctively sensed that not just their world, but my world and maybe even the whole world were all changing indelibly.

After Cecil and I returned to Richmond at the end of the summer, we made plans to go to a movie together. Some traditionally white theaters there had just begun to officially desegregate, but few African-Americans were attending them, and racially mixed groups at the theaters were almost nonexistent. When Cecil drove up in front of my aunt and uncle's house and they saw a black guy was driving, they tried to talk me out of going. Not because they personally had a problem with it, mind you, but "What if someone we know sees you with this colored guy? Who else will they tell? What will they do? This could cause big trouble for us—you're being selfish and an agitator. What about us?" After listening to their invective for a while, I thanked them for their opinions, then walked out the door and rode off to the movie with Cecil.

Lots of hating eyes were riveted on us from the moment we walked into the lobby together till the moment we exited the theater. I heard snippets of conversation around the concession stand about some "traitorous white boy" muttered by people who were shaking their heads. And we did a quick beeline to Cecil's car when we departed. But nothing worse took place. I found it exhilarating pushing everyone's buttons. My aunt complained some more when I arrived home, but that was the end of it, so I highly doubted any of my family's acquaintances had seen me with Cecil and ravaged them with scorn.

A week later I headed further south and started college at Duke, another school that was integrating in a token way, an institution with a mostly pro-segregation student body. I soon became active in the small, civil rights movement on campus and became known as the *nigger-lover* of my freshman dorm. I told myself I didn't care. I was used to being an outcast. Only now I had a cause more significant than flouting fashion conformity, which had been my one-boy high school crusade.

Besides participating in the occasional official pro-integration demonstrations, I went one night to a White Citizens Council rally to heckle the *good ol' boys* who would be attending. The Council was a Ku Klux Klan-like group with mostly the same membership. When they wore street clothes they were the Council and would congregate out in the open. Warmly welcomed to conduct their meetings in government buildings, they were considered a respectable group by the established powers in the South. But some nights they would don their white sheets and hoods, meet in secret, burn crosses, and on special occasions beat or murder "uppity blacks" and their sympathizers. So even in their sanctioned mode, they were not exactly pacifists known for entertaining divergent views. This time they would be meeting at night but leaving their Klan costumes in the trunks of their cars.

Only three of us were willing to go up against about a hundred "White Citizens." They congregated in a field on the edge of a forest just outside of Durham. We approached from the rear of their gathering and hid behind some trees. We heard their leader's pounding fist and rousing voice calling his minions "to combat the Jew and

Commie threat, which incites the niggahs to destroy our cherished heritage." During a lull in the proceedings our threesome yelled a few choice comments, expressing our opinions about where they could shove their racist ideas. And then we ran like hell, hoping to make it to our getaway car before they could catch or shoot us. We got lucky and lived to see another day.

It was a stupid, ineffective escapade, but it was invigorating too. I suppose one might even say it was courageous, despite our chicken-shit methodology. I was learning that courage wasn't just about picking and winning fistfights. Courage was also about putting your ass on the line for something you believed in.

⤫

I arrived back at my flat from work at the Commerce Department. It was 5:20 p.m., the day Rani was to be coming there for the first time.

"Come on, Emmett, I told you yesterday, you have to be out of here from five thirty to seven thirty tonight. She's gonna be here in ten minutes."

"Aw, shee-it, Will, where am I supposed to go?" Emmett drawled in his unmistakable west Texas accent.

"I really don't care. Just get out of here."

"How come you don't have to leave when I bring home some chickadee?"

"Could it be because both of you are too drunk to even notice whether I'm here or not? Besides, Rani and I, we're meeting in secret. This is a very delicate situation, and I have a feeling this may get serious."

"That last part's a crock if I ever done heard one." But Emmett was already getting up from our faded pink sofa, a piece of furniture that had earned its right to be euthanized probably twenty years earlier, what with springs busting through the frayed fabric in a couple of places. At least Rani wouldn't want to sit on that for long, giving us the perfect excuse to retire to the bedroom. I surveyed our home and wondered what she'd think of it and, by extension, me. Although it was nothing to write home about, at seventy bucks a month, it was probably the most elaborate accommodation for any PCVs in Fiji. The official monthly housing limit was thirty dollars per Volunteer and was paid directly by the Peace Corps office, so Emmett and I had to slip the landlord an extra ten under the table to keep our bureaucrats at bay.

Hmmm, better not let her see the Pleasure Dome, a converted bedroom so named because the artwork consisted of Emmett's collection of sixteen voluptuous *Playboy* centerfolds pasted on walls thoroughly papered in aluminum foil. But this was before *Playboy* was pushed by its more lurid competition into revealing the whole enchilada, so the shots could be considered tasteful images of the female form in sync with the historical topless couture of Fiji's indigenous female population. At least it had been that way till the missionaries intervened. With one bare bulb, a large straw mat, and a few beer-stained pillows, we thought it was almost the perfect make-out room. If only we had a black and/or strobe light (not readily available in Fiji), we would have been ready to grace the cover of *Town and Country*.

Other highlights of our first-floor flat: A flush toilet with a real wood seat and only the occasional splinter. Hot water. Electricity. Screens on all the windows. A late 1940s refrigerator with an undefrostable freezer. An electric oven. An off-balance, butcher-block table. Our gray concrete building still had its original finish. Emmett and I were immensely proud of the place we called home.

As Emmett left, I picked up his dirty clothes that lay scattered on our living-room floor, threw them into his bedroom, and slammed the door. Then I ran into the bathroom for one final smear-down of the three-inch Brillo pad of hair atop my skull. I was letting it grow, in keeping with the trend back in the States, though not so long as to put off the locals.

A knock at the back door sent a chill down my spine. I still had trouble believing she was actually going through with this. I walked over to the door and opened it slowly. Then, seeing Rani and looking behind her to ascertain no prying eyes, I whisked the little Indian into the safety of my flat.

"Good you have a back door, Will. We wouldn't want people on the street to see me coming in."

I was surprised how calm she seemed, because I was starting to shake with anticipation. "Do you think anyone saw you coming here?"

"No. I took a cab. Don't worry about it."

"YOU TOOK A CAB?" I was shocked. I had assumed she was going to walk there. This wouldn't do. "Was the cab driver Indian?"

"Yes. Most all of them are."

"But didn't he see you walk to this house? My God, you could have blown our cover on your first time here." I was sweating and starting to panic.

Her scrunched-up mouth signaled resentment at my accusation. "Will, I know what I'm doing."

Yeah, I know you do. You've done this with at least one other guy that just happens to be a friend of mine. What are the odds of that happening?

Rani continued talking, "Look Will, I didn't walk here because that would have meant somebody I know, somebody who knows where I live, would probably pass by and notice me . . . notice I wasn't going toward my parents' house after work and maybe even follow me here and tell my parents."

"But maybe the cab driver would do that."

"Far less likely, and I had him drop me off a few doors down. He doesn't know me. Then I waited till he was gone and came over here."

Oh, she's good at this. She's quite good.

"So you see," she continued, "nothing to be concerned about. Besides, why should you care? It's me that will get in trouble."

"Rani, I do care a lot about you, and I'd likely get in trouble too. Wouldn't I?"

Her eyes looked down as she thought it through. "You might. People will do anything when they are angry. And you and me together will certainly make them bloody angry. But what they'll do to you— it's nothing compared to what they would do to me." She looked directly at me. "You don't see the bigger picture, do you?"

"What bigger picture?"

"You don't see that you're a European, and that gives you a lot of power that Fijians and particularly Indians are afraid of. You certainly don't know much about the colonial system, do you? The Europeans rule. Their lives are worth a lot. Brown-skinned people—our lives come cheap. But maybe more important than race . . . for Indian women, it's far worse than if you're a man. Why do you think we have dowries? Why do you think in India, some widows throw themselves on the funeral pyre? If a baby is born a girl, they might even drown her. Because a girl means problems—money problems."

"But that's horrible." I wanted to hold her close, to protect her, but she was not done talking and therefore was unapproachable.

"If an Indian attacks you, he thinks something awful will happen to him just because you're European." Rani paused. "Won't it?"

"I don't know, and apparently you don't either, if you're asking me. But I assume if someone attacked me, he'd be treated the same as if he attacked an Indian or Fijian."

"What rubbish! You Americans." Rani rolled her eyes. "You think the whole world thinks like you do. They don't. Not here, anyway."

"But Rani, what we are doing—meeting here like this—there's nothing wrong with it. I realize it's a change for them, but people will just have to learn to accept it. And in the long run, it will make Fiji a better place."

"Oh my goodness, you truly are from Mars, aren't you?" She threw her hands up in the air.

"Then why did you risk coming here?"

"It's complicated. Can we talk about something else?" Rani switched gears, but her shaking head told me she was still irritated with me.

"Sure, you want some beer?"

"No. Anyway, I should leave now. My mum and dad are expecting me much earlier tonight than I had hoped. My father called me at work just after you left. He needs me to help him clean out a storage shed. I'm the only child still living there. I can't be late, or they might begin to suspect something. I came by just to let you know we'll have to reschedule."

She grabbed her purse and moved toward the back door to leave. I came up to her and opened my arms. I hugged and kissed her, but she was limp and then withdrew.

"I must be going, Will."

Just like Troy described their rendezvous at his place. Maybe this one is turning out to be as unsuccessful as that one—it just took longer for Rani to get to the point where she's losing interest. Or maybe the very real fear of how her people will react if they find out is getting to her. Losing her would be terrible. But what if we do keep this going and do get caught? And if the consequences would be as awful as she thinks, why is she risking it?

CHAPTER ELEVEN

What was it about my generation—our absolute assurance that we were always right, and others would just have to accept our vision of a brave new world? Was it only the energy and arrogance of youth? I grew up learning, and was beat up demonstrating, that *might makes right*. But once we came of age we were turning that on its head—*right makes might*. Then again, who thinks they're ever not right? "Power to the people," was one of our iconic slogans, but we really wanted power only for those people who thought exactly the way we did. And when told that most people didn't, we condescendingly considered them uneducated, misinformed, or the enemy. They would think differently after the revolution—you know, the one that never happened because we eventually got caught up in our own limitations to change ourselves, much less the world.

We did promote many positive trends that have become mainstays of Western culture–respect for the environment, inquiry into Eastern disciplines, rejection of unlimited consumption, treating people fairly—to mention just a few. But we were in-your-face idealists, in a hurry to remake the world into a web of psychedelic communes where peace, love, and understanding would flow naturally, and the selfish instincts of the individual would succumb to love for the tribe and all humanity. Everyone would be eternally blissed out with no work and no rules. Just sex, drugs, and rock-and-roll. Most of those visions turned out to be no more real than the LSD hallucinations some of us were having.

Maybe the prevailing trait of the counterculture's crusade of that period was its complete naïveté about the way societies worked and individuals behaved. Certainly I had been simplistic about how my romance with Rani would tear at the social fabric of her people. I understood the danger theoretically, but when you're young, you feel on a gut level that you're indestructible, you can convince people to change their thinking, and love should conquer all. I just assumed what we were doing was virtuous, an extension of the headier, integrationist days of the civil rights movement, and so everyone would quickly fall in line and feel liberated by our example—just like in the 1967 movie *Guess Who's Coming to Dinner* where the pretty white girl brings home her fiancé, a prominent doctor (played by Sidney Poitier), to meet her limousine-liberal parents (played by Spencer Tracy and Katherine Hepburn). After a little soul-searching among that group, Sidney's parents show up too, and they all do a group hug and everyone lives happily ever after.

That was how I was hoping it would play out for my precedent-breaking romantic liaison. At least the *Kumbaya* vibe part of it.

∾

My relationship with Rani was nothing like the only serious one I had before she came into my life.

Billie Bobbi Berkowitz was not different from me in terms of race, nationality, culture, education, or religion. It was probably a pairing even my mother would have approved of, at least on paper, had she lived to see the day. Billie was just the nicest, most unassuming girl a mother-in-law could want. And unlike with Rani, Billie and I did not have to meet in secret. We seemed perfectly matched, and of course that ultimately was the problem, for me at least. It *was* perfect. Perfectly boring.

Our affinity blossomed in the winter of my junior year, 1965–66. We went together to many of the weekend home games for the all-white Duke Blue Devils men's basketball team (there was no women's team) that made it to the NCAA finals that year. They finished the season number two in the country, the last time a college basketball team with such pale pigmentation would do that well. The team finally integrated the next season, its only black player joining my fraternity.

College student liaisons then would be unrecognizable to today's unfettered undergrads. Billie would hop on a Greyhound bus to travel the fifty miles from Greensboro to Durham. But that was only after her dorm mother had received signed approval for the trip from Billie's real mother. Once she arrived, Billie was allowed to stay overnight only at college-approved, curfew-enforcing guest houses off campus. If I got her back after curfew, regardless of the reason, the guest-house mother would report that to Billie's dorm mother, who would then tell Mrs. Berkowitz. Any future trips for Billie to see me would have been canceled for the rest of the semester, even if the real mother didn't give a damn. On Sundays, I'd drive Billie back to her dorm in Greensboro, being sure to get her in before the Sunday night ten p.m. curfew. Too many damn mothers.

My frat house was on campus, as were all the Duke fraternities and sororities, so we were particularly subject to the university's rules and scrutiny. The only females allowed on the premises, even during the daytime, were the African-American cleaning ladies. So the only available place for Billie and me to make out was in my Lark. The bucket seats would go down, but we didn't, what with the occasional flashlight-wielding, peeping cop out to protect society from moral turpitude. In such a regulated environment, it was a challenge for a guy to get laid, even if he were going steady with a nymphomaniac.

Billie was holding on to her precious virginity anyway. Just my luck to finally find a girlfriend who was saving it for marriage. We wrote each other a letter almost every day we were apart, further bolstering the relationship's authenticity. I filed all her letters chronologically in shoe boxes and saved them for years.

After school that summer, I worked as a busboy at the DeVille, a third-rate resort hotel in the Jewish Alps, a.k.a. the Catskill Mountains, about two hours north of New York City. The area was still in its prime as the incubator of Borscht Belt comedians and the summer retreat for affluent Jewish families from the Big Apple, though the ones that stayed at the DeVille were a bit down on their luck and also their tips. The food the busboys were supposed to eat was downright putrid, unlike that of the higher-ranked waiters who had free rein on leftovers. I got fired often at the DeVille when I'd get caught eating guest-discarded leftovers. But then I'd come back the next day, because the maitre d' was always drunk and didn't remember who I was, much less that he'd fired me the night before. The busboy gig was so paltry that I needed to paint billboards that summer just to break even.

But that was also the summer I bumped uglies with Wanda. I didn't see Billie till the end of the summer, so it didn't feel as if I were cheating. Besides, until that point we were not sexually committed to each other, and Billie was 730 miles away, so I felt I was well within my gentlemanly rights to screw a prostitute and cast off the stigma of virginity. Being a demure Southern girl, Billie agreed, though reluctantly, that if our relationship did become committed to the point where we would finally *do it* on our wedding night, one of us would have to know the ropes. So as the man it was incumbent on me to take the hit for the future of our relationship. Better sooner with a prostitute, than later with, say, a stripper at the bachelor party just hours before the bride and groom would exchange vows and bodily fluids.

That autumn, back at school, we participated in the time-honored ritual of getting lavaliered. Billie was obligated to wear my gaudy Duke sapphire and gold ring hanging from a chain around her neck as a sign to all that we were going steady. At least when within a hundred miles of each other, a clause I added to the agreement's fine print. Of course, being the guy, I didn't have to wear anything that told the world that I was spoken for. If away from school and each other for some extended time, say a weekend, certainly it would be OK to socialize with the other gender as long as nothing serious happened—the word *serious* in this case would be left undefined. To Billie, I knew it meant no touching more enticing than a business handshake. I preferred to think *serious* would kick in only when I got some girl knocked up. Billie said she could resist dating other boys during our times apart, though it wasn't as if she didn't have the option.

From that point on, we took most of our vacation breaks together anyway, doing the tedious obligatory practice of visiting either her family in Bingle or mine in Richmond. Under the watchful eyes of our parental and guardian figures, the segregation of our sleeping facilities would be strictly enforced, just like at college. I did succeed at slipping away from the noose of lavaliered commitment on a couple of unaccompanied off-campus trips beyond the hundred-mile limit. The results of these dates were somewhere between our differing definitions of the word *serious*. OK, probably closer to her firm-handshake definition.

Toward the end of that school year, my final one at Duke, we stepped up our affiliation to yet another level where I *pinned* Billie. No, not during wrestling or sex, but as yet another bizarre tribal rite. She was required to return my college ring and would now proudly wear my Zeta Beta Tau fraternity pin on her blouses and sweaters directly above the left nipple. This was a proclamation to all potential suitors that everything from the pin on down was taken, so they shouldn't get any ideas. A diamond-shaped piece of bargain jewelry, my frat pin sported twenty seed pearls surrounding the letters ZBT, a Star of David, and a skull and crossbones on an ebony background. I suppose this appeared to others that Billie was going with a guy who was either a member of a fraternity of Jewish pirates or some voodoo poisoning cult. The new agreement extended the hanky-panky minimum distance to five hundred miles and the time apart to at least one week. And it also gave Billie the right to pick out, but not order, the china. We were engaged to be engaged at last.

Why was I sticking all these disclaimer clauses into our commitments? Hell, I wasn't even pre-law. What was really going on was that a suffocating fog of claustrophobia was engulfing my relationship with our relationship. Unable to see the truth, I rebelled subconsciously—by playing semantic games with silly constraints, even as I continued to tell both Billie and myself that I truly did see us spending our lives together.

Unfortunately for our now somewhat-committed relationship, I spent that summer touring Europe without my pin-mate, thanks to a most generous graduation gift of the flight from my sister, Marcia. I happily accepted it and bid adieu to Billie for two months of gallivanting around the Old World, telling her that I just could not pass up such an opportunity. I promised her, she would be the first to see my slide show at the end of the summer. She was not pleased with losing me for an extended period, just when she had visions of our settling into a commitment to be seriously committed. Apparently, front seat tickets to watch *Will's Summer in Europe* was not a suitable substitute for constant companionship with the boyfriend.

At the end of the summer of 1967, I returned from Europe worldlier, but still only one prostitute removed from virginity. After a year-and-a-half courtship in which she had remained hymen-intact, Billie suddenly changed her mind and amazed mine by deciding to *not* wait for our wedding night. You would have thought I would be thrilled that my investment was finally going to pay off. You would have been wrong. I didn't realize it at the time, but I actually had no interest in *going all the way* with the young woman with whom I was supposed to be in love. And no, it wasn't that I had any prudish inclination that her fruit should be unplucked on our wedding night. Instinctively, but not yet consciously, I knew I could never go through with the anticipated marriage. To consummate my relationship with this recent save-it-for-the-wedding-night virgin whose primary goal in life was to become *Mrs. Me*—well, that would make the impending breakup so much more heinous for both of us. And if she gave up her precious virginity, what unique gift, besides her ill-suited name, would she have to present to the next love of her life? We had journeyed to the brink of the brink of matrimony, and at a gut level I knew I could never take the plunge.

But also I could not, *not* go through with the sex. Like any red-blooded American boy, I had asked her to fornicate with me since our second date. However, being a Southern gentleman and rather inexperienced myself, I did not make our bond contingent on that act. After a while I had stopped bringing it up. But the offer was always on the table, so I could hardly revoke it once she more or less said, "Ravage me, my prince. I'm yours."

So after a visit to my sister in New York, we left Manhattan and drove to a cheap motel in New Jersey. Eighteen grueling months of torrid torment were finally going to end. I was still thinking, *I've waited so terribly long for this—it's going to be so fucking fabulous, so fabulous fucking!*

Alas, my long-awaited love-making session with Billie didn't last long, and that was the best thing about it. Whereas I gave the prostitute two marathon sessions and gobs of orgasms, not to mention a cup of coffee, I gave the girl I thought I loved five minutes and exited quickly in more ways than one.

"Wow, that was, uh . . . swell," I said in the afterglow. "Particularly for a first time. It just keeps getting better, you know."

"You didn't seem to like it at all," she pouted, "But then you've done it with a hoo-wer. I can't compete with that." She turned and buried her head in her pillow.

I stroked her light-brown pageboy with reassuring affection. "Oh, pookie, you were so much better than her."

She turned to face me, tears dribbling down her cheeks, and then she glared at my crotch. "Then why are you already getting dressed?" I had unconsciously slipped on my underpants. And my socks. "You barely stuck his head inside my . . . down there. Shouldn't we try again? She's not even bleeding."

I looked at the door. "Well, this was like a trial run, and I wanted to save something special for next time. Say, aren't you hungry after all that lovemaking? I sure am. Let's go get some pizza."

Neither of us brought up sex again that night, and the next morning I dropped her off at the Newark airport from where she flew back home to South Carolina. I would not see Billie again for three months. I started in the MBA program at the University of Michigan, and she was beginning her senior year at the Women's College of the University of North Carolina, some six hundred miles away, one hundred miles past my circumference of frat pin commitment-land. I went out with a few young ladies in Ann Arbor, but I still thought I was Billie's beau.

She visited me there over a Thanksgiving vacation marked by frigid weather both inside our relationship and outside in the elements. Somehow we managed to go four days without sexual intercourse coming up on the agenda. I lived with three other guys in a two-bedroom apartment, so lack of privacy was a convenient excuse. The handwriting was on the wall, but I dared not look at it. I believed I was no more capable of killing a serious relationship than I was capable of killing a human being. It seemed contrary to the essence of who I was.

Three weeks later I found myself driving the Lark from my home in Richmond to hers in South Carolina with the intention of giving us one last chance. But by the time I drove up in front of Billie's house, my sad-sack sing-along with the brokenhearted pop songs on the radio had convinced me I could no longer deny the inevitable.

My legs buckled as I walked up to the front door and rang the bell. Her father, Melvin, answered it.

"Well, hi-dee-ho there, young fella. We're so delighted you're visiting us again." We shook hands, and he gave me a quick, manly tap on the shoulder.

"Yeah, me too, Melvin. Always a pleasure to be back here in beautiful Bingle with Billie Bobbi and the Berkowitzes."

Billie came to the door. We hugged and kissed like robots before she lifted her head and said, "Where is your suitcase?"

"Oh, I guess I left it in the car. I'll get it later."

After a mundane dinner discussion with the parents about family and school, they went in the kitchen, and I turned to Billie and said, "Let's go to that place in the woods."

"What? You want to go make out before dessert?" She chuckled, seemingly unaware of the demon that possessed me.

"Nah, just we haven't seen each other in a few weeks. Your parents will understand."

"I'll go. But no, Will, I don't think my parents will ever understand."

Is she on to me, or is she just doing a little parental put-down? I chose the latter and nervously snickered like a buffoon.

We drove deep into *that place in the woods.* I stopped the car and turned off the ignition. I took one look at Billie and then the dam burst. In the midst of a flood of tears, almost all of them mine, I confessed I no longer loved her. I couldn't explain why, it just wasn't there for me anymore, and I had to set both of us free. Billie was relatively calm while I cried my eyes out. She undoubtedly hadn't seen it coming. She asked what she had done, and I tried to assure her it was all my fault. Was there another woman? No. She said she had noticed things had cooled off between us at Thanksgiving. Although she wasn't expecting this now, because I just drove four hundred miles to stay at her parents' house, and who would be stupid enough to set up such a situation just so he could break their pride-and-joy's heart? After meekly raising my hand, I had to agree the timing was a tad awkward, but told her that maybe I should get some points for not doing it over the phone or in a Dear Billie letter. I encouraged her to call me if she wanted to discuss it later. She remained visibly calm in the eye of her storm—whereas I was bashing myself with the wind and wetness of a stage five hurricane.

After I had run out of explanations and tear-soaked paper towels, I backed the car out of the woods and we rode silently back to her house. I pulled the Studebaker up to the curb.

"Aren't you going to at least walk me to the door?" Good. At least she was showing some righteous anger. Although she directed it at my mannerly incorrectness, rather than at the ruthlessness of breaking her heart for no good reason.

"Pookie, I . . . um . . . I don't think that would be a good idea."

"But what am I going to tell my parents?"

"Tell them the truth. Tell them I'm a complete asshole and you're better off without me. That, they'll understand."

She hesitantly got out of the car and stood by it as I turned the key. I watched in the rearview mirror—her head was shaking and her lips were still moving—while my tires burned rubber as if the Mafia were after me. I knew it was cruel, but I just had to get the hell out of there as quickly as I could.

I checked in at the first motel I saw and gave myself a fierce tongue-lashing. Breaking off from Billie was one of the most difficult things I ever did in my life. Before or since.

She never phoned or wrote me. Turned out, she waited a year before she dated anyone, then married the first guy she went out with—and they raised five kids in . . . where else—my hometown of Richmond, Virginia. I was visiting family there fifteen years after the breakup when a cousin of mine told me that Billie had settled there. I thought she might want to catch up and so I called her. We met at a coffee shop. She finally got a chance to let out some anger, and did she ever! The waitresses must have wondered what I had done to this poor woman to warrant such a raking over the coals. She said it took her a long time to recover from what I did to her. But she also said she still cared a lot for me. God knows why, considering how badly I treated her. With all the best intentions.

Fast-forward another fourteen years. She died of non-Hodgkin's lymphoma at the much-too-young age of forty-nine.

RIP my college sweetheart.

CHAPTER TWELVE

Rani and I decided to give it another shot at my flat.

Emmett reluctantly agreed to make himself scarce. "But this is the last time I'm doing it. Rani will just have to get used to my darlin' face, next time. If there is a next time. Besides, I want to see what this little filly looks like."

"I appreciate this, Emmett. I owe you. Would, say, six bottles of Fiji Bitter clear the ledger?"

"Yahoooo!"

That was better than it sounded (not the *yahoo* part). Fiji Bitter came only in forty-two-ounce bottles, six to a case. It was stronger than American beer. Six bottles would be enough to keep Emmett grinning for a long while. Fiji Bitter was not only the beer of choice in Fiji, it was the *liquid* of choice for most PCVs. It was also the only alcoholic beverage commercially made on those islands and the only one readily available. And in that tropical climate we were thirsty all the time.

Rani knocked on the back door at the expected time, just as Emmett scrammed through the front door.

"That was good timing," I told her.

"Not really, I've been waiting by the back door the past five minutes."

"Oh?"

"I could hear you and Emmett speaking. I didn't want him to see me coming in."

"Yeah, I suppose that would have been awkward—him leaving on account of your coming here." I pointed toward the refrigerator. "You want some beer?"

"Sure, there's a first time for everything, Will." I poured us each a glass, sat next to her on the tattered couch, and turned on a Judy Collins song, which just happened to be queued up on my Akai reel-to-reel tape recorder.

"You've never had beer before? No alcohol at all?"

"No, but then I've never done a lot of things before." Rani grinned. Then she took a small sip of beer and quickly swallowed.

"Ewww. Tastes awful. How do you blokes drink this stuff?"

"It takes a while to get used to."

She was wearing a lime-green minidress. She looked so enticing and delicious. "You look lovely," then I added, "Yeah, nobody would notice you coming here dressed like that."

She pulled away. "I always wear short dresses and skirts. If I came here in a sari, then someone might suspect something. Besides, it's not that unusual in Suva. Some other Indian girls have started wearing them, at least some I went to school with. Would you stop worrying about that stuff?"

"I can't help it. Worrying is in my blood. I come from a long line of worriers. We hand it down from generation to generation, each one trying to top the last one."

Rani shook her head. "Why worry about things? They either work out, or they don't. Either way life will go on."

"I don't get it how you can be so cool about this stuff given you're such a target."

"I think about it. But not here. Not when I'm with you. There's a time for everything. I've never let what others think stop me from doing anything. Not yet, at least." She took another sip. This time, no reaction to the taste, but she flashed a rare grin. "If I should be afraid of anything tonight, it ought to be you."

"How do you figure that?"

"I'm this innocent little girl trapped in the home of a big bad man. And he's making me drink beer for the first time in my whole life." She took a couple of swigs and swung her glass around. I took it from her and put it on the table.

"Better slow down on the beer."

"Yeah, you're right. I'm done with that. But now I know what it's like. And you know something?" She didn't wait for me to respond. "I like the way it makes me feel. But it still tastes as bad as it looks."

I leaned over and kissed her. A warm, peaceful wave surged through my body starting at the lips, rippling down through my toes. Rani pushed her ebony hair behind her ear and kissed me intensely. She moved into my waiting lap, by now imprinted by her well-formed buttocks and thighs. She melted into my chest. She barely topped five feet and tipped the scales at ninety-five pounds, just over half my weight. Would I crush her? Would it fit? Would I relive those sexual disasters with Billie and Wanda?

She pulled back and looked at me. "Will, you're worrying again, aren't you?"

She had me. "Nothing important," I said.

"That's right. Nothing is important now. Just this moment."

I repeated her mantra. "Nothing is important now. Just this moment."

My doubts dissipated like morning fog.

We locked into a kiss, as I carried her into the bedroom. We laid down on our sides, facing each other in my narrow single bed. I turned on my dinky electric fan. It was a sweltering summer evening in January. We each undressed the other with deliberation. This was the first time we had seen each other totally naked. Her svelte, naturally bronzed body was as exquisitely designed as her perfect face. And even more seductive. Never had I felt such a primal animal craving.

We dispensed with foreplay, having had too many weeks of only that. I mounted her and slowly eased my way inside. Savoring the moment. Exploring each other's curves and coves as we accelerated the rhythm. Clenching her trembling prone body as she clung to mine.

Ratcheting up the tension till the final thrust and nearly simultaneous explosions. Our bodies collapsed, fused together.

I didn't crush her. No Billie déjà vu. We both scored, so no Wanda either.

Paradise in paradise.

CHAPTER THIRTEEN

I returned to Virginia after the breakup with Billie Bobbi Berkowitz and tried to explain it to my aunt and uncle one night in their den. Jacob sat quietly in his easy chair, taking it in. But Tillie had discovered a rare affinity with the small-town girl with the mannish name, and she didn't like what I had done to her. She wagged her finger in my face. "What do you mean you don't love her? How would you even know that? You young people think a couple should always be in this wonderful, lovey-dovey state, and that will solve all your problems. Well, let me tell you what love is, Mister Fancy Pants. Look at your Uncle Jacob and me." I looked at each of them. "Do we look like we're in love?"

"No. Not at all."

Tillie was on a roll. "You're darn tootin' we don't look like we're in love. You have to earn love. You have to stay together and work your problems out, and if you don't, then you still have to stay together and just work harder. If I walked out on him, what would your Uncle Jacob do? Go on, Jacob, tell him."

"Sorry, Tillie. Did you say something?"

❧

I drove back to my coldest winter ever, to Ann Arbor to complete my MBA at the University of Michigan. I was going to be able to get my degree in just one year, when normally the program took two. I wanted to do this because my student deferment from military conscription was valid for only one year, though the members of my draft board undoubtedly knew it normally took two years to get a master's degree. But I'd show them. I was able to do it in twelve months because I received credit for some of my undergraduate courses, Michigan was on the trimester system, and I took a heavy course load.

When an undergraduate at Duke, I had done the practical thing and majored in accounting. Practical because aptitude tests like the MMPI (Minnesota Multiphasic Personality Inventory) had pointed toward accounting as a good career for a young man with considerable math aptitude, a pathologically analytical mind, and the people skills of a spittoon. But my heart was never in it, and the more accounting courses I took, the more I disliked my chosen major. So when it was time to take the CPA exam in my senior year, I didn't even study, something decidedly uncharacteristic of me. Not unexpectedly, I passed only one of the four parts and never took the exam again, although I would end up spending most of my career in assorted accounting roles, including some chief financial officer positions. I just could never picture myself working at a stuffy, sterile CPA firm for two years to fulfill the employment requirements of the CPA certificate, so why bother with the exam?

When I moved on to Michigan, I decided to tweak my career toward a more creative direction. Marketing. Its chief appeal being that it wasn't accounting. I was still being *practical*—going for a career in the world of corporate business, even as the winds of sociopolitical change were whirling around me and whispering in my ear that I was not ready for the business world, nor would I ever be. In the spring of 1968, the season when Martin Luther King and Robert Kennedy were assassinated, I spent a weekend working in the Indiana Democratic presidential primary for Eugene McCarthy, a relatively unknown senator from Minnesota who had challenged and stunned sitting President Lyndon Johnson in the earlier primaries because of a single issue, his opposition to the war in Vietnam. Suffice it to say, there was a paltry number of Eugene McCarthy fans in the B-school, but I had few friends there myself. They just were not my kind of people.

The winter snows melted, and the corporate recruiters came to our hallowed halls. Like all my fellow MBA candidates, I talked it up with as many of them as would listen. To make sure they took notice of my innovative and well tuned marketing acumen, I wrote and printed a white paper called "Lutwick and You." In this unique document (one can only hope) my potential employers learned that "Lutwick is an enigma in the world of marketing, a unique combination of mathematical talent and creative genius, a man with the ability to understand both the scope of his job and the whole of your organization." I went on to quote myself about some ninth-grade class-clown experiences (to demonstrate my creativity), the diversity of my current roommate situation, which included "a Negro high school dropout" (this was supposed to show that I was in touch with an array of demographic markets), and how marketing "enables one to apply his creative talents within the context of realistic criteria." And just in case they were not already frothing with anticipation to hire me, I zinged them with "Lutwick is interested in a position of responsibility with the complementary authority to act."

This meaningless drivel went on for seven single-spaced pages, proving to the recruiter, if I had not already done so in the interview, that I had utterly no idea what I was talking about. There I was, twenty-two years young, already accumulating degrees from two of the more prestigious academic institutions in the country, but the most significant business experience on my resume was a summer job counting cars going through intersections. My fellow MBA candidates were getting oodles of cushy invitations to visit corporate headquarters in exciting cities where they were wined, dined, and lap-danced. (No, there weren't many female MBA students in 1968.) Whereas, the only bite on my job-fishing line came from the Firestone Tire and Rubber Company of Akron, Ohio, the birthplace of Alcoholics Anonymous.

This was before Firestone become notorious for an assortment of scandals. First came the accidents where radial tire tread flew off at high speeds. Then their tires were blamed for numerous Ford Explorer rollovers. And when it was revealed that their Liberian rubber plantations heavily polluted the local water supply while young children clocked in twenty-one-hour workdays, Firestone's public image absolutely tanked. But in 1968 Firestone was as all-American and respected as its crosstown archrival Goodyear, best known for its ubiquitous blimp.

So I filled the Lark's crankcase with oil and myself with hope and rattled on down U.S. 23 toward the Ohio border. Firestone went all out to make me feel like a prized recruit. They put me up at a Holiday Inn and even gave me three dollars toward dinner, although I had to dine alone because, strangely, nobody from the company came to welcome me to Akron. I figured they must all be working late marketing Firestone tires and rubber.

The next morning I spiffed myself up in my best business suit and drove to company headquarters, a hodgepodge of rectilinear beige buildings placed right behind the three-stories-high tire at the front gate. I met with the Director of American Rubber Marketing, a middle-aged gentleman named Todd, who told me they were looking for someone just like me, although with "maybe a little more real-world experience." With perspiration dripping down the left side of my face (stressful situations and buttoned collars always made me sweat that way), I told Todd that would not be a problem—I'd just get the experience on the job while I was proudly working at Firestone. I told him I couldn't wait to try out some of my ad jingles such as, *Firestone Rubber, it'll put some bounce in your life, Don't be a sap, buy our rubber*, and for their other division, *Tires, without them you'd have to walk*. Todd looked at me with a puzzled expression and then said that they had an ad agency for coming up with their slogans. I asked if we would be having lunch with some of our fellow marketing experts, and he said we would not even be having lunch with each other. Apparently, I had been invited there on an "unexpectedly very busy day." After about thirty minutes, Todd said that I "far and away stood out" and I'd be hearing from them soon. He told his secretary to show me the way out. I told her I wanted to look around the compound first, but she said that "unauthorized people are not allowed to walk unattended just anywhere they want" at the headquarters of the world-famous Firestone Tire and Rubber Company. I told her it was OK because I'd be working there soon, and she said, "We'll see about that."

I drove back to Ann Arbor from Akron feeling sick to my stomach, no longer able to delude myself over how badly my jittery confidence façade and banal advertising slogans had bombed on my only onsite job interview. Then and there I gave up on ever having a career in corporate America. It would have to be "Lutwick and *Someone Else*." I should have followed my heart, not my insecurities. I never should have majored in accounting or gotten an MBA. But because I did, I decided, by the time the Studebaker crossed the Michigan state line, to try to use that education to work in the nonprofit sector, where hopefully my education would be of some use to organizations that were shunned by most MBA graduates. I was disappointed with myself, but it also felt as if an immense burden was lifted off me and that a new *Lutwick* would emerge from the ashes of the corporate pretender.

The next day I called the Peace Corps and asked them to send me an application. Eight years earlier on the steps of the Michigan Student Union, a few blocks away from both the Business school and where I was living, presidential hopeful John F. Kennedy first announced in a campaign speech his vision of what would become the Peace Corps after his election.

The application had a question asking where I would like to serve. I closed my eyes, and the answer immediately came to me—*a really isolated island in the Pacific Ocean*. I wanted to get as far away as possible, both figuratively and literally, from everything I had known in my twenty-two years.

Two weeks later I got another rejection letter for my collection— from Firestone. A slight sting to my ego, but no surprise, and it brought closure to me for thinking I might ever belong in corporate America.

Two months later I got accepted by the Peace Corps and was informed that if I proved psychologically fit I would be sent to the Fiji Islands, where I would work in the Co-operatives Program. Having no other career options and knowing that being in the Peace Corps would help keep me away from Vietnam, it was a no-brainer. But I was also excited to launch this exotic adventure, working for the people of this place I knew nothing about. I was to fly to Escondido, California, in October 1968 to begin three months of training—first there, then on Molokai in Hawaii, and finally in Fiji.

And that was how I managed to find my way to become a Peace Corps Volunteer in the Fiji Islands.

CHAPTER FOURTEEN

Rani and I started a new clandestine routine—meeting at my flat two or three times a week. After work, I'd walk home. About ten minutes later, Rani would leave our office and hail a cab. She would have the driver drop her off within a block of my building varying the particular drop-off place each time. She'd sneak over to my place, check for spies, saunter up the walkway, then cut around to the back of the house and knock on the door. We'd almost immediately and wordlessly move to wild, eager sex in the fading daylight. Afterward we'd lie together on our backs in my narrow bed in the sultry Fiji air while my small plastic fan cooled down our radiating bodies. And while the clouds outside the window turned crimson, Rani would nuzzle up to me, and I would kiss her and stroke her glossy black mane.

On one such rendezvous, she lamented about how she hated all the sneaking around.

"You know I love coming here, being with you. It's the one thing I look forward to. But then I leave and get on the bus. It's awful going home—the worst feeling in the world, lying to my parents over and over again, wondering how long I can get away with this."

I rubbed her shoulders. "What do you tell them?"

"I tell them I'm with a girlfriend. I've told this one friend of mine, Sumi, to cover for me if they ever need to check. What's that word, you know, for someone who says you were with them?"

"Alibi?"

"Yes. She's my alibi. Sumi and I went to secretarial school together, and she had a boyfriend there, so she understands this type of thing. Actually, lots of the girls there had boyfriends."

I was quite surprised to hear that. "I thought Indians aren't supposed to have boyfriends and girlfriends."

"They're not. But they still have them and they keep them secret. Not all the girls do this. I have five sisters, and none of them had boyfriends, as far as I know."

"Maybe they successfully hid them."

"Yes, I suppose that's possible. But then, all of them had arranged marriages while still teenagers, and so did both my brothers. My sisters are all older than me and were happy to be traditional Indian girls, to marry young and then start having babies. I'm just not ready for that and don't know when I will be. The girls at the Derrick Technical Institute . . . that's where I went to secretarial school . . .we were learning to work in the world of business, to make our own money. So we want to work and have some fun before we settle down to a life of husbands and babies, cooking and cleaning. We're modern girls and probably the first group of Indian girls in Fiji to be like this."

"But you still have to keep relationships with the opposite sex such a big secret."

"Well, of course. If you get caught, you have to stop. And it could bring shame on the family."

"And then the parents have to arrange a marriage quickly?"

"Maybe, but arranged marriages exist more for financial reasons than how would you say . . . social ones."

"What do you mean?"

"Most Indians in Fiji are poor, and they want to get the girls out of the house at a young age because they are a money burden on them. And the older they get, the more dear they become. So, if a girl can earn money like me, then the hurry for an arranged marriage goes away. I turn over most of my paycheck to my parents, so there is no rush for me to be married."

"Doesn't giving them most of your money tie your hands in terms of doing what you want?"

"No, it's just the opposite. If I move out, they lose that paycheck. So that gives me more ability to get what I want, at least from them. Even though I'm already quite old to be unmarried at twenty, they stopped pressuring me about having an arranged marriage. They talked about it more five years ago. But then I got a full academic scholarship to the Institute, so this is all profit for them."

"Oh wow! That's quite impressive."

"Thank you. You can imagine that my father being a teacher—he is very proud of that scholarship."

"And well he should be. But tell me, don't almost all Fiji Indians still have arranged marriages?"

"That's true, but it has started changing, probably just in Suva, which is different from the rest of Fiji. A couple of my classmates, once they were caught having boyfriends, they married them. Their parents, of course, were not pleased. But if the fellow was from a good family and had good prospects, then it was an easy decision. And they'd rather see the girl married than not married at all."

"So the girls were pregnant?"

Rani laughed. "No, of course not."

"But you said they had boyfriends and got caught and then were pushed into marriage"

"Yes. That's true. But few would have had sex like we just did."

"Why not?"

"Because you have to be a virgin when you get married, of course. No respectful Indian man will marry a non-virgin." She said this as if, *doesn't everyone know this?*

So why the hell are you having sex with me "like we just did," and what will you do if this doesn't lead into a marriage? Those two obvious questions popped up in my mind, but I knew I didn't want to go there just then. "So if they don't have sex, what do these boyfriends and girlfriends do?"

"They meet in secret. Maybe they go to a beach or a river, some-place where they are unlikely to be seen and recognized. As for sex, they just go slow with it because they know the girl has to remain a virgin. So at first they kiss. And then maybe they touch, you know, the sensitive places, outside the clothes, then inside the clothes." Rani was giggling, and despite her deep tan skin, her face took on a slight rosy glow.

Hearing Rani talk of sexual brinkmanship was an aphrodisiac to me. But I was genuinely curious to learn more. "So then what happens?"

"Oh, they usually break up because they can't go any farther and so they get bored with each other. Or, like with my schoolmates, if they think they love the other person, and their parents accept them not having an arranged marriage, then they get their permission to marry. Then they get married and have real sex at last."

I was beginning to get a headache, trying to fit the Fiji-Indian methodology of sex, money, family, love, and marriage into my own conceptual framework. It was much more complicated than I had thought.

Rani put her hand on my shoulder. "I guess being an American, you wouldn't understand what it's like to have a girlfriend who won't . . . I think you say . . . go all the way with you."

I had to grimace as my prior relationships flashed across my brain's movie screen. "Yeah, right, Rani. Dating in the States is one nonstop orgy even for a shy guy like me." I moved closer to her and took her hand. "But even though my mind is somewhat boggled by all you're telling me, I now get the sense that if you and I got caught, your fam-ily would be upset, but they would also eventually come around and accept us as a couple."

Oops! Should . . . not . . . have . . . gone . . . there.

She thought about it for a moment, then replied with more than a hint of scorn, "That might be true except for two things. One, we have no plans to get married. And two, you're European. Neither of these would be OK with them, and the most unacceptable thing of all would be if we *did* plan to marry, and that's *because* you're European. That's something no Indian in Fiji is ready for."

❧

In addition to our Monday-to-Friday dalliances, sometimes Rani would come over my place on the weekends. Usually there was nonstop partying under our ceiling, because my friends who were having a *real* Peace Corps experience living out in the bush wanted a break from the *real* Fiji. Where else to go but where the city lights were the brightest, the Fiji Bitter the coldest, and having sex the easiest? Living on the equivalent of forty U.S. dollars a month (excluding housing) made staying at hotels out of the question, so the few of us who lived in Suva had our homes turned into hotels, or at least flop houses, on a regular basis. Every Friday a batch of eager American faces would show up at our front door, so we had to take them in and share the urban Fiji experience with our country cousins.

Most weekends you'd find some of the sassy locals that were attracted to our group, hanging out in our living room. They considered us a curious breath of fresh air after more than a hundred years of less approachable Europeans. If nothing else, we did know how to get down and party. And celebration was deeply ingrained in the Fijian spirit.

We adopted colorful people like Aminiasi who preferred we call him Amnesty. He was a smallish Fijian man with a long goatee, weathered chocolate skin, and gleaming ebony eyes. We knew him from his term as one of our instructors at our Peace Corps training on Molokai. Amnesty was of regal lineage but had fallen out from the aristocratic Fijian lifestyle. He would eat our food and drink our beer, and in return he would share his *talanoa*, stories orally handed down through the generations of a mystical Fiji before the white man came. That Fiji was *Bulu,* an underworld inhabited by ghosts, snakelike spirits, and a giant bully named Flaming Teeth. It was ruled by dueling shark and octopus gods who controlled the Earth's weather and food supplies. And Amnesty was also a *voo*, a witch doctor who cast good and bad spells on people. So you wanted to stay on his good side because he got quite ornery with those he disliked, particularly when drunk, which was most of the time. Fortunately he liked everyone in our crowd.

I introduced Rani to this collection of American misfits and native Fijian characters. They took to her, and she to them like a newly hatched turtle to the sea. No Indians were in this throng of partygoers, so Rani didn't have to worry about anyone snitching on us. And as she would tell me, "For the first time in my life, I can really be myself around people. It's so freeing, not to have to worry about every little thing I say or do and to just be with people so accepting and fun."

And this environment was the perfect Petri dish for our relationship to develop. In this simulation of a community, Rani and I could be a couple around others and not just when alone. We could talk about things other than just the liaison and its difficulties. By not being under the microscope, we became part of a group and closer to each other.

Our assemblage was a makeshift tribe of South Pacific quasi-hippies, and Rani was happy to join the caravan even if it actually wasn't going anywhere. My home was a haven from the regimented lifestyle of her childhood. Although it seemed at those times to be on the other side of the world from us, her birthright culture surrounded our refuge oasis, waiting to pounce on her every time she walked out the back door.

∾

Our lunches continued in the conference room, our former Lovers' Lane, and this gave us some more slack time to explore the nonphysical side of our relationship. I was still trying to locate some of the pieces of the puzzle that made up my perplexing paramour. As I attempted to understand her culture, I wondered what she knew of mine.

"When you were growing up did you know much about the United States or Americans?"

"No, why would I?"

Rani had a knack for putting me on the defensive. I wasn't used to people being so direct. "I thought maybe you'd learned about us in school or read about us in magazines."

"Not really. Of course I knew the United States was out there somewhere in the world, but we weren't exposed to Americans or American culture as kids. In the villages we saw the occasional European chap, but those were always Brits, Aussies, or Kiwis, and they usually were missionaries. With our being Hindus, they were not interested in us. They were there to convert the native Fijians."

"So how did you and your family get along with Fijians?"

"Really well. In our villages there were also some Samoans and Rotumans and some of the Indians were Muslim. Everyone got along, and we took classes together too, but as we got older the Indian girls were discouraged from socializing with the boys. A lot of my friends in the lower grades were Fijian girls. My family was friends with all the people. The political tensions between Fijians and Indians— that mostly was going on in the government and in Suva, not in our villages."

"Really? That surprises me. I realize they are usually polite to one another, but all I hear is that the Fijians and the Indians dislike each other."

"Well, I don't know about that." Rani's face perked up. "Listen. Here's an example of how it was. When I was very small, there was a powerful hurricane that flooded and destroyed most of our village. The rivers had swelled their banks and even cattle were washed away downstream. Most of the people lived in flimsy homes and thatched huts, and all of them were destroyed. As meager as my father's salary was, it enabled us to live in a concrete house that somehow survived the storm. Many people had no place to go, and my parents invited them to stay with us. I remember sitting on a bed surrounded by Fijian families huddled together, getting shelter. One corner of the room was set up for Hindu praying, and an Indian man I didn't know was chanting there. I still can picture all that, even though I was only two years old at the time."

"You're kidding. You remember something from when you were two?"

"I would not lie about that." Her vocal tone registered some indignation. "It was a life-threatening storm. People were very upset. I guess that is why I can remember it."

I wasn't about to further challenge the veracity of Rani's remarkable memory, so I went elsewhere. "It seems Hinduism was important in your family?"

"Yes. We mostly prayed in the home. Hindu temples were very rare in the villages, so most religious celebrations and holidays were celebrated in homes or on riverbanks. Rivers are considered sacred by Hindus, and we had a lot of ceremonies there at holidays, weddings, and such. Priests would read from the sacred texts, the Vedas. My family worshipped many gods, but in particular we worshipped Krishna, who is believed to be the highest of them all."

"Oh yeah, I think the Beatles are into him, and I read that some young people back in the States are starting to dig Krishna too. They shave their heads, wear orange sheets, and hang out at airports, clicking finger cymbals while chanting 'Hare Krishna' over and over. Then they ask the crowd for money."

"Hmmm." The sour look on her face told me Rani was not impressed by Westerners *digging* her religion. "The only Indians who dress anything like that are the priests, and they would never behave that way."

CHAPTER FIFTEEN

We knew it would happen eventually, though we behaved like it never would. We liked what we had between us. We wanted to freeze that moment and pretend it could go on forever.

How could we have expected to keep our romantic liaison quiet in a small city, a tight island culture? It had been eight weeks since we had first kissed in the conference room. Four since we started meeting at my place. The *coconut wireless* would allow no secret to last for long. And so word reached Rani's parents, Kiran and Mani Gupta, that their youngest daughter had been spotted more than once in the company of a young European man. Rumor had it that he was an American, one of those Peace Corps workers they had read about in the local papers.

Not only is she sneaking around with a boy, but a European, one of THEM. *They took over our mother country, then wrenched us from our homeland. They tricked our grandparents to come to Fiji as indentured servants, virtual slaves. How could she do this to her parents? Her father is a teacher, a respected man. She will forever be marked as a fallen woman. People will not say that to her parents' faces, but this is what they will think whenever they see them. It is a curse on the whole family. They must not have known or they would have put an immediate stop to it. That wicked American man has stolen their child's most precious gift, and she can never get it back. But what does he know of our culture, our ways? He is a man, unable to control his urges, and he was brought up in America, the land of sinful behavior. It is for the girl to say "No," and if she says "Yes" before her marriage, then she is undoubtedly nothing but a . . . a whore.*

She must be stopped.

∞

"How did they find out?" I asked as I held her hand. We were in the conference room. I had sensed something was wrong when I saw Rani muddle into work that morning. The light was gone from her face. She didn't look at me. She didn't smile. So I suggested we go to our usual place when she could get away. Her body was rigid, but still I was surprised how well she seemed to be taking it.

"Our neighbor told my father. Also, my brother Sunil, he found out from his friends and told our dad. So for him to hear it from two people on the same day, that's very bad."

"So what did your father do?

"He told my mum to make me stop seeing you."

I felt my stomach sink. "And is that what she told you?"

"Yes."

"So is this good-bye?" For a fraction of a second, a part of me hoped she'd say "Yes." I didn't know whether I could handle the gathering storm. But no way was I going to abandon her to the wolves. No matter where this road would lead us.

She clenched her fist. "No. Not unless you say it is. I've come too far to give up that easily."

"Then I'm in it too, sweetie. You know your family—so what do you think we should do?"

"We do what we've done, but let's wait a couple of weeks. Look, Will, I told my mum that you and I are just good friends, we like the same kinds of things—books, movies—and people are getting the wrong impression. I told her, we are not having sex, of course."

"And she believed you?"

"I don't know. Would you? She said she wants me to stop seeing you, but I could tell that her heart wasn't in it—she knows I have strong feelings, that I usually get what I want." Rani looked down for a moment and then up at me. "And she said she understands."

I was flabbergasted. "Is that for real? But why would she even say that?"

"I don't know. Maybe because she knows I'm different from everyone else in my family. She just . . . understands . . . me. She recognizes that I have to live my life the way I want to live it. Maybe she resents that she's been given the job of disciplining me. Maybe she sees a life for me that wasn't available to her."

"Your mom sounds amazing. I can see where you inherited your strength. I hope to meet her someday."

"I hope so too, but not yet, not now."

⁓

We cooled it for a couple of weeks, hoping to throw the unseen spies off our scent. I resented going through the charade and missed our alone time together, but I had no choice but to defer to Rani's judgment. Meanwhile, we decided to try something different—openly going to lunch together. But not just the two of us. I invited a couple of male friends, from the government Cooperatives Department in our building—Inoke, a Fijian with whom I had collaborated at marketing passion fruit, and a close Peace Corps friend, Tom. Rani invited two young women that she had known from secretarial school, one Indian and one Fijian. We chose our favorite restaurant, the Nanking for this experiment in interracial lunching. The idea was to show the watching eyes of Suva that Rani and I were just friends, just part of a youthful crowd that worked together, and so went to lunch together on occasion. It was something that would not garner attention elsewhere. But we all knew we were living where even something this casual was just not done. Still, change was blossoming and we were going to help fertilize it a bit.

Rani and I were about to meet the others in the building lobby when she got a call from her Indian friend, Tarita, saying she just couldn't risk tarnishing her reputation. Rani told her that she understood, but when she told me about it, she was upset and proclaimed her friend a coward. As the only Indian woman in a now mostly male group and with her reputation already tarnished, this was not going to look quite as innocuous for Rani as we had hoped. But she said she was determined to keep going.

We took the elevator to the lobby where we met our three lunchmates, then stepped out into a warm, cloudy day. Tom said, "Let's go blow some minds," but I gave him a cautionary look and shook my head. The five of us walked together the three blocks to the Nanking, chatting and laughing, searching for shade beneath the overhanging second floors that jutted over the sidewalk, held up on stilts like a movie set for old Dodge City. The noon-day crowd, mostly men and about half Indian, parted before us. Jaws dropped and eyes widened when they saw us approach. And the more astonished they looked, the more we chatted and laughed as if this were the most ordinary assortment of people to be having lunch together.

When we went inside the Nanking, we grabbed an unoccupied, rickety table and sat down. The guys sat on the side that faced the window. The gals faced the back of the restaurant.

I was glad it worked out that way because a small crowd of young Indian men starting gathering outside and I didn't want Rani to have to endure watching that through the meal. They shaded their squinting eyes, all the better to watch the freak show inside the restaurant. A Chinese waiter saw them and ran toward the front door making a shooing gesture and they dispersed. But gradually they came back after a couple of minutes like squirrels at a picnic table trying to appear innocuous, yet hungry for a peek. Tom, Inoke, and I didn't say anything about it to Rani and her Fijian friend.

The outside light darkened somewhat, and I heard thunder in the distance. It began to rain as our lunch was served. The crowd eventually dispersed, and we ate our meal in relative obscurity.

We finished our food and exited the restaurant, then gathered in front on the sidewalk. We had brought umbrellas with us. Afternoon rains were a daily occurrence in this, the wet season of a town that received 130 inches of rain per year. As planned, Rani was walking next to the Fijian girl and in back of me when I heard some terse Hindi words, snarled from under a cluster of black umbrellas going in the opposite direction.

"Bijaru. Tum bhrashta bijaru hai." (Whore. You're a filthy whore.)

I turned to see Rani stopped in her tracks, a hand held to her heart. She turned around to search for the source of the insult, but was unable to pinpoint it in the mass of moving umbrellas. She recovered and continued on her path. I walked back to her and asked, "Are you OK? What did they say?"

"Just keep walking." Her lips were pursed with anger.

Bijaru. I hadn't known what the word meant then. It would not be the last time I would hear it.

༄

We would play on the outdoor basketball court at the University of the South Pacific, maybe the only basketball court in the South Pacific. Fiji in 1970 was not a time and place where the all-American game of hoops was popular. Team sports reverence was reserved for football (soccer) and particularly rugby, at which native Fijian men were world-class players. One day the Fijian team would become world champions despite the relatively small pool from which to pick their players. But there were some locals who picked up basketball quickly from us in the Peace Corps. We managed to get an impromptu league together mixing PCVs and Fijians on four teams. Tom was on a competing team and after a particularly grueling game where my team lost by one point, we sat together on the nearby grass cooling off, gazing out at the endless blue Pacific down the hill from the campus.

"So, Lutwick, what is it with you and the Indian chick?"

"You know, Tom, I ask myself that question all day long, and I come up with a different answer each time. It's mostly all I think about. I'm definitely attracted to her and care tremendously about her, and she's the most exciting girl I've ever been with."

"Exciting? You mean like in the sack?"

I smiled. "Well, definitely there too. But I meant she's just so unusual, coming from her background where the women are so isolated and restricted, and then she decides she'll make up her own rules. It's like she's a cultural radical, but where did that come from? There's no underground movement here in Fiji for things like that. She's a revolutionary army of one. I wish I had her bravery."

"Gutsy babe, no doubt, but . . ." Tom squinted at my face as if searching for some revealing sign. "Is this the real deal, Lutwick? Is this little girl sweeping your scrawny ass off its feet? Am I going to have a wedding to go to?"

"Whoa, Tom. You're really jumping the gun there. I've been seeing her for about three months. And I tell myself, or at least I used to, that I don't want to get married till I'm at least thirty."

"Thirty? Shit, man, you don't have that kind of time. You do know, you're playing with fire, don't you?"

I released a groan. "Of course. Her parents know about us now, so it's going to be really tough for her to get away."

"Tough? I saw the look in those beady dark eyes watching us eat lunch. They want blood. You're going to have half the population of Fiji banging at your front door with pitchforks and torches, wanting to string you up. And I when I say torches, I don't mean flashlights."

Tom had a penchant for whimsical overstatement, but I wasn't in the mood for it. "I'm not worried about me. I'm worried about her. She's the one they'll blame the most."

"So why . . . why are you doing this, Lutwick?"

"We're back to the *why* questions again. But this is all about emotion, not logic. It went from curiosity to friendship to desire to need very quickly before I realized what was happening. Yes, I was naïve, but I wanted to be naïve because I wanted her so badly. And now I'm swept away in something that is bigger than me, bigger than us, and though part of me is afraid, I can't back out. She can. She might have to. But I have to see this through."

"Are you in love, Lutwick?"

"If you mean in love, like get-married-and-live-happily-ever-after love, I don't know. There's too much shit swirling around us for me to get an accurate reading on that."

∾

Rishi was my other Indian girlfriend in Suva. Well, not really. She was Indian, female, and a friend, but not a girlfriend in *that* sense. She was a Peace Corps groupie, but again, not in *that* sense. It was just that she liked to befriend PCVs and invite us to her home for food, drink, and compelling conversation. I seemed to be her favorite, so I went there about five times during my time in Suva. She was an affluent Indian in her late thirties, married to a successful merchant, and they lived in an airy clapboard house on a hill overlooking Suva Harbor. It was filled with modern teak and mahogany furniture and Indian tapestries that were kept clean by a Fijian housekeeper. Rishi was a dead ringer for Frida Kahlo, an Indian of another feather, although unlike the Mexican painter, Rishi was chubby, a status emblem of Fiji-Indian success. She talcum-powdered her face to appear fairer, and it left a layer on her cheeks and forehead that gave her skin the coloring of a chocolate doughnut dusted with powdered sugar.

She called me at my office to invite me for tea and crumpets soon after Rani's parents had found out about our "friendship." When I got there, I noticed we were alone. We sat on her veranda with our cups of chai, watching a silvery tourist ship pull into the wharf in the distance. Rishi buttered a crumpet and handed it to me.

"Where are our other Peace Corps friends? Is Arjun joining us this evening?"

Rishi ignored my questions. "Will, my friend, I understand that you have taken up with an Indian girl."

I was so startled, the scalding tea went up my nose, and I sneezed it out into my napkin.

"How could you . . . how did you find out?"

"You, young chap, are the talk of the town. The Indian part of it, anyway. The Europeans and Fijians would probably enjoy seeing the Indian community squirm, but they probably don't know about this yet."

"But this girl, she and I, we're just good friends. Nothing else is going on."

Rishi bit her lip, peered into my eyes, and tapped my forearm. "That's a very good response. Just keep saying that. Nobody will believe you, but you still must say it."

I had to avoid agreeing with Rishi about the depth of the relationship, but protesting might also make me suspect. I knew she was scrutinizing the tone of my voice, facial expressions, and even my body language. Rishi was a friend, but she was also a lie detector and a gossip. "What are people saying?"

She took a dainty sip of tea, then put the cup aside. "Among my friends, the more modern Indians, they say they don't have much of a problem with it. Not that they would ever want it taking place in their family, mind you. It just is not done. Eventually that sort of thing was bound to happen here, although we didn't think it would be quite this soon. But among the poorer classes, I hear people are quite upset. They think it is scandalous and should be stopped."

"Do you think they will do anything about it?" Although I was hanging on her every word, I tried to come off as only academically interested.

"Not much to you, if that is your concern. You're European, so there is some apprehension about confronting you. Quite frankly, most Indians don't know how to conduct themselves with someone of your race about things beyond work and pleasantries. But also you are a boy, a man, so they will blame the girl first, because she is the one who is considered most sinful and should know better. And mainly because she is one of us. Then again, if you are with her when they attack, then you are fair game too. But this is considered a family issue. It is they who are expected to handle it. They will be shamed into stopping it."

At least she thought the mobs would wait for the family to act first. Better to be in combat with only one family than Tom's picture of a swarm of angry villagers with pitchforks and torches. "And you, Rishi, what do you think of it."

She flicked a mosquito away from her ear and sighed. "I have nothing against it personally, of course. But to be honest, I would rather you had not gotten involved with this person because nothing good can come of this for either of you. Or anyone else, for that matter."

"What do you think I should do?"

She hashed it out in her mind, then replied. "You can do one of three things at this point. You can continue to see her in secret, but that will be impossible now. People will know. You can end the relationship, which would probably be the best thing, but she will always be scorned by her community unless she convinces an Indian man to marry her anyway. I understand she is quite comely, and some of the more educated Indians may be getting less strict about marrying a virgin. Or you can marry her."

"And that would solve the problems?"

"Absolutely not. For almost all Fiji Indians, it would be the worst betrayal of all. Surely you know the history of the Indian people with Europeans, and it is not pleasant. On the surface all the races in Fiji get along day-to-day, but just beneath it there is much mistrust and anger."

"Yes. But I'm an American, not a Brit or Aussie or Kiwi."

"All the same to them, young man. All the same." Her eyes honed in on mine. "But then you two are just friends anyway. Isn't that so?"

Unable to look her in the eye, I turned away. "Yes. Of course."

She picked up the bone china teapot, raised her eyebrows, and asked in an overly polite voice, "Now then, Will, how about another cup of tea?"

∾

Rishi was right. I sure had gotten myself in the middle of a riddle with no reason or rhyme. Like Alice, I chased the object of my desire into the rabbit hole, then tumbled down, landing in an utterly unpredictable world. In a situation like that, you take it moment to moment and try to keep your head intact—physically first and psychologically second. Enjoying the wild ride comes in a distant third.

We were lying low for a while, so seeing Rani every day at the office was driving me nuts because I couldn't be alone with her. Sure, we could talk—and maybe do a little more—in our secret rendezvous room, but once you're used to first class, no way can you go back to flying coach. It might have been easier just to go cold turkey and not see her at all for that period, but that was impossible because we worked together.

So I decided to get a car. That way we could at least go a few places—friends' homes or restaurants in a couple of tourist hotels on the outskirts of town, where fewer people might recognize Rani. Undoubtedly it would raise eyebrows and blood pressure, but at least it was unlikely anyone would do anything about their prejudices in a Euro-touristy environment. And a car would facilitate our clandestine meetings at my home by obscuring her identity, as she would enter and exit inside a traveling steel container. Certainly it would be no panacea, but a car might lower the anxiety level.

The problem with getting such a vehicle was that I wasn't allowed to own one. This rule had nothing to do with Fiji's laws for foreigners. It had everything to do with the Peace Corps administration. They considered it un-Peace-Corps-like for Volunteers to own a vehicle. We were, after all, supposed to live life on a par with the locals that we served, and only the richest could afford their own cars. However, if the Volunteer's host employer gave him full-time use of a company car, then it was acceptable to our higher-ups. This happened quite often in the rural areas, where an agricultural cooperative worker might have to drive around to local farms, or a fisheries PCV would visit docks and beaches along the coast. But it was rare in Suva, where such business requirements were fewer, and buses and taxis were plentiful.

I could have appealed to the Peace Corps powers-that-were to relax the rule for security reasons in my unique circumstances, but they were among the last people I wanted to discover my no-longer-quite-secret affair. In our Peace Corps training, the two commandments that were drilled into our heads were: *Stay out of Fiji politics* and *don't offend the locals.* So even though one could and should argue that my liaison with Rani was a private arrangement between two consenting adults and nobody else's goddamn business, the situation still shattered those cardinal Peace Corps rules. I had managed to offend over half the population of my host country. Not an easy trick to pull off intentionally, much less without even trying.

We PCVs looked on our Fiji Peace Corps brass as clueless drones living a haughty, affluent lifestyle, as insensitive to the local culture as tourists. In short, they were our Fiji Brits—they just wore shorter socks and spoke English with a Yankee accent. They socialized with the aristocratic set, and their contact with Indians and Fijians was primarily with top government bureaucrats, rarely with less patrician classes as equals. Although all their servants were Fijians and Indians. Our elitist characterization was perhaps unfair, inevitable because of our differing roles, but I wasn't expecting much empathy from our higher-ups on the car issue.

On top of that perceived dynamic, the Nixon presidency began the month after I arrived in Fiji, the first time Republicans had ever overseen the John F. Kennedy-initiated Peace Corps. Although they at first paid lip service to supporting our mission, Team Nixon became increasingly distrustful of us save-the-world do-gooders. They knew that the great majority of PCVs were against the Vietnam War, and the word came down that we were to keep our dissent among ourselves. By March 1970, a dozen Volunteers in other countries had been dismissed because of their open opposition to the war. Eventually Nixon would try to eradicate the Peace Corps by eliminating its budget, failing only because of political and public pressure. Apparently the president and his inner circle were more comfortable pursuing foreign policy with Second and Third World countries from behind an automatic weapon than from behind a plow or schoolbook as was our *modus operandi.*

A new Peace Corps Director had recently been appointed for Fiji by the *Nixonistas*, so we Volunteers became increasingly unlikely to engage our local Peace Corps management except when unavoidable.

It was not uncommon for PCVs to be *deselected* and then sent home before their two-year terms were up. Of the 117 of us who started our three-month training in my Fiji-2 group, merely 67 would make it to Fiji, an attrition rate of 43 percent even before we began working. A handful left of their own accord, but most departed early by the organization's volition. They were kicked out for allegedly not being an acceptable emotional match with the intended role of living in a developing country while being an always cheerful ambassador of American values. Nobody even pretended it had anything to do with whether they had the functional skills to do their proposed jobs.

The late 1960s had been a time of considerable adulation of the power of psychiatrists to predict success and failure, and the Peace Corps had subscribed to that philosophy with religious fervor. We had one such shrink from my alma mater of Duke University playing God with us throughout our training on Molokai. Dr. David Saperstein clearly was the most powerful person in our lives for those three months, though he barely got to know any of us directly. He was away from our training site most of the time, coming to Molokai only on occasion to evaluate our behavior and wield his ax. But even when he wasn't around, we lived in fear of what others might report to him about us. So we Volunteers-in-training continually played a hiding game of survival where we tried to seem as meek, malleable, inoffensive, and unemotional as possible. It was like trying to get *on* jury duty. Oddly, that was considered the best profile for being an outstanding Peace Corps Volunteer.

Although the good doctor no doubt deselected several potentially effective PCVs because their brains were *not* flatlining, someone with a severe mental illness managed to slip through our group's filtering process only to be fired and sent home when the condition blossomed in our host country. So Dr. Saperstein was hardly infallible in his diagnoses.

Six years after my group completed in Fiji, a PCV (whom I shall call "Fred" to keep potential lawyers at bay) in Fiji's neighboring island Kingdom of Tonga, killed another PCV (whom I shall call Julianne) by stabbing her twenty-two times. She had been spurning his advances for several months. The local Peace Corps administration was aware of the problem because Julianne had been trying to transfer to a different island solely for that reason. Nobody seriously tried to claim Fred was not the perpetrator. The Peace Corps administration decided its interests would best be supported by trying to minimize the crime, despite the fact that the victim was also one of their own. They, really meaning the American taxpayers, picked up all the defendant's legal costs, sparing no expense. The Peace Corps imported Tonga's most renowned lawyer, who was living in New Zealand at the time. And they also brought in a psychiatrist from Hawaii to brand Fred a paranoid schizophrenic, although earlier he had passed their rigorous psychological deselection process. Not a single psychiatrist was living in all of Tonga; therefore there was no counter-expert to challenge the schizophrenic argument. Because the defense held all the cards, Fred was predictably deemed insane rather than convicted of murder. Then the U.S. State Department intervened with the local government and had Fred extradited to the United States, assuring the Tongan prime minister that he would be institutionalized till he was no longer dangerous.

However, the hospital that the State Department planned to put Fred in took only voluntary patients. So when the culprit arrived home, he simply refused to submit to institutionalization. The Peace Corps did try to have him arrested, but the Washington police said they had no right to do that. Fred surprised everyone by agreeing to be examined by a psychiatrist at that same hospital. The psychiatrist said Fred had suffered a "situational psychosis" when he stabbed and killed Julianne, but he was no longer a threat to anyone.[4]

---

4   All of the information about the *Fred* case up to the footnote number is based on an excellent article by Phillip Weiss, "Stalking Her Killer," *New York,* May 21, 2005. The opinions about this case that follow the footnote number are those of Will Lutwick.

Thanks to the Peace Corps brass' active intervention and State Department incompetence, Fred got away with murdering a sister Peace Corps Volunteer.

Of course I did not know of this ethical capitulation by the Peace Corps higher-ups at the time. Not being one of their psychiatrists, I did not have their aforementioned capability to predict the future. But I did have enough present concerns about my Peace Corps superiors that I didn't want to ask them to bend their rules about getting a car. Luckily, they were not particularly in touch with what we Volunteers were doing in their base city, much less their whole jurisdiction. And I was happy to keep it that way.

If my adversaries in the Indian community had understood the Peace Corps dynamic, they might have simply walked into the local Peace Corps office right there in Suva, expressed how profoundly their community had been hurt and offended by my odious behavior, and I would probably have been out of the country within twenty-four hours, even before I had time to present my side of the story or say good-bye to my lovely partner in crime. As with that mentally ill Volunteer in Fiji or the murderer a few years later in Tonga, they would have apologized for my outrageous behavior and sent me back to the States to be someone else's problem.

❧

Despite our local Peace Corps staff's perceived obliviousness, I couldn't chance one of them seeing me driving around our smallish town in a car that had not been assigned to me. What to do? And then I connected the dots and had a eureka moment. I hastily convened a meeting of the board of the Orange Marketing Scheme, the front organization I had used to buy and sell oranges from Rotuma. The board members all resided in my head, so they were able to convene almost immediately. They voted unanimously to buy me a car to be used in our quest to put a Rotuman orange in every hut in Fiji. I was humbled by their business acumen and generosity.

Of course I never could have afforded a car, even a run-down one, on what the Peace Corps paid me. I had to dip into my life savings back in the USA and have my bank there wire some cash into the Scheme's checking account. Once it arrived, I perused the *Fiji Times* classifieds and found an eight-year-old Ford Anglia for sale, a diminutive vehicle just roomy enough for our needs. One Sunday, I took a bus to the seller's address just outside the Suva city limits, kicked the tires, and wrote a check, the equivalent of five hundred U.S. dollars, to an Indian gentleman who probably never would have sold me the Anglia had he known for what nefarious purposes I intended to use it.

Programming myself into driving on the *wrong* side of the street, I drove my car home and to work the following Monday. I had said nothing to Rani about it and waited till the end of the day to show her our royal coach powered by the steel equivalent of sixty-two wild stallions. She was ecstatic when she saw it and was even more thrilled when she realized what relative privacy it would afford us. She stepped into her coach, kept her head down, and I drove her away to my flat where our drought ended in deliciously raucous fashion. I then drove her home for the first time, dropping her off at a spot secluded by a grove of mangrove trees a block from the house. I watched her walk to it. As she stood at her front door, she turned and nodded in my direction. I drove home and went to sleep. The next morning the coach had happily *not* turned into a pumpkin.

We were back in business.

CHAPTER SIXTEEN

"They want to meet you."

Rani and I were sitting in my living room drinking Fiji Bitter while George Harrison's guitar gently wept on my tape recorder. I spit out my beer so hard it spray-painted the nearby wall. I ran into the kitchen to get a towel.

"Did I hear that right?" I exclaimed as I blotted up the spewed beer.

"I think you did," Rani was laughing, "Judging from your reaction."

I sat beside her on the couch. "This doesn't seem possible."

"But it's true. Now remember, officially we're just friends. There's no sex involved, right? So my parents want to meet Will, my friend from work. It's all very innocent. On the surface."

"And all four of us know what lies below that surface—anger, people going crazy, and lots of sex."

"Maybe, but until proved otherwise, they want to believe that it's only a friendship. It allows them to meet you, check you out, and if others find out about it, they can always tell them 'Rani says they are just friends and we believe our daughter.' If the other people scoff then that makes them look bad, while my parents end up looking smart."

"Even though your father told your mother to stop you from seeing me."

"Yes, even though."

Rani's voice was dropping, and I could tell she was getting annoyed by my cynicism, so I moved on. "Where should we meet and eat? Are they going to invite me over to your house? Perhaps meet at a restaurant?"

"No, that won't do. We'll have to meet here."

"Why here?"

"Because a neighbor may see you go into or out of my house, and someone will definitely see us if we go to a restaurant."

"Oh, so we're going to hide them too?"

"Yes. They don't want people to know we'll be meeting."

"But you just said they can tell them, we're just friends."

"Yes, *if* others find out. But that doesn't mean they *want* them to find out about it. Will, don't push me on this. It's complicated."

But I sensed a crack in the façade and wanted to bring the wall down. "Look Rani, here's our chance to bring the whole thing out in the open and show the Indian community that if your parents are willing to meet me then maybe our being together is not such a bad thing. We could change the public's way of thinking about this, enlighten them, and create a breakthrough. I just think . . ."

Rani pushed an open hand toward my face. "That's the problem with you, Will—you think too much, but know too little. Just because you want something doesn't make it so."

I was disappointed and she knew it, so she stood in front of me and lifted my head toward hers and kissed my pouting lips. "Look, Will, it's my family and my community. You don't need to understand everything about them. That's what you have me for."

❦

"Guess who's coming to dinner, Emmett?" We were standing in our living room.

"I *dunno*. The queen? Tricky Dick? The girls from the Golden Dragon?"

"Nope—Rani's parents."

"Does this mean I got to get lost again?"

I nodded.

"Shee-it, Will. I'm getting tired of being told to get lost like I'm your little kid. Why can't I stay?"

"Think about it, Emmett. Do you really want to be here when I meet the parents?"

Emmett grinned. "Say no more, my friend. But this really will be the last time I vacate the premises for your butt, and I expect a complete report afterward."

∾

I suggested I prepare the meal myself, but Rani insisted on being the head chef. And on reflection, I had to admit that this was too crucial a meeting for me to try my hand at cooking curried mutton for the first time. I was trying to impress people for whom the ability to tell the difference between tasty and terrible Indian cuisine had probably become part of their genetic code. Truly my inspired suggestion that I do the cooking had been an all-time worst what-was-I-thinking moment. Rani's cooler head prevailed.

I had never cooked Indian food and was only eating it when with Rani, ubiquitous as it was throughout Fiji. Even the native Fijians had somewhat adopted curried dishes into their diet, so Indian-style food was the most commonly available grub wherever you went. When I had lived in Lautoka at the Bachelors Mess Hall, curry was on the menu most nights. But exactly what was curried was often hard to tell. The curried courses were usually served with taro—think gray Hawaiian poi before it becomes liquefied—or stringy white cassava, both bland, starchy root crops with low nutritional value. Add some processed meat substances from tin cans and that was dinner most nights. But sometimes we had my favorites—squid guts and fish head soup. There's nothing that whets the appetite more than looking into your bowl and making eye contact with a face even a mother fish would push away, if only her fins were hands.

So by the time I got to Suva and was able to decide what I'd eat each night, I'd gotten curried out. There were no Western-food restaurants outside the foreign-touristy hotels so most of the local PCVs opted to cook at home or eat at the Nanking, because Chinese food was at least somewhat familiar to our American palates. This was long before haute cuisine and any ethnic fare beyond Italian and Cantonese would gain a toehold on at least some American dining habits. My taste buds, like those of most of my comrades, were decidedly redneck. Bloody, marbled steak dripping with liquid fat was our ultimate dish. None of us were aware that such a diet was a heart attack on a plate.

Rani whipped together a meal of curried mutton and side dishes made with spinach, okra, lentils, and eggplant—to make our guests feel at home. And with their daughter cooking, why wouldn't they? My flat filled up with the unmistakable, mouth-watering scents of various Indian delicacies. Maybe I had misjudged the scrumptiousness of Indian cuisine.

Mani and Kiran Gupta arrived as planned, after the sun had set. They emerged from a cab and traversed the cement walkway with a handful of hibiscus flowers. I opened the door and looked down to see a middle-aged woman in a yellow sari and a man in a white short-sleeved shirt and ivory slacks. The woman was about as tall as Rani, but fuller in form. She had twinkling dark eyes like her daughter's, although they were less bewitching. Her husband was a baldish, gray-haired man, ten inches shorter than me. Rani came to the door, inserted herself in the middle of the throng, and cheerfully introduced us all to one another as if this were an everyday acquaintance being made. I could tell she was the only one even remotely relaxed—the rest of us displayed frozen smiles and shocked eyes, our feet nailed to the ground. Rani grabbed the flowers and wisely suggested we go inside, not needing to add "before anyone spots us." That broke the spell and we proceeded into my for-once clean flat. I could hear the back door closing as Emmett vamoosed.

Kiran's English was limited, though Mani was as fluent as his daughter. His being a teacher, I had expected that. As we walked toward the kitchen, I figured this was an opportune time for me to try my Hindi on Rani's mother and I suppose for her to practice her English on me, so we had a conversation where I would say things in broken Hindi: "Today, weather is lovely?" "Where you will find beautiful yellow sari?" and "Indian food very delicious." And she would reply to me in English: "I am good very thank you," "Yes, I make," and "Rani make curry the sheep meat of New Zealand." This stimulated self-conscious laughter from all parties.

Rani told me to sit in the living room with her father while she and her mother finished preparing dinner.

"No, no, your mother is the honored guest. She should sit. I want to help." *You can't actually be serious about leaving me alone with your father. And why was I just talking in stilted English?*

"Will, my mother and I cook together all the time, and you don't know the first thing about making Indian food. Really—go talk with my dad."

"Oh, OK." *I'll get you for this later.*

Rani's dad carefully settled into my falling-apart couch, as the mother-daughter team meandered their way into the kitchen. I could hear them chatting in Hindi and laughing (*at me?*). I stood in front of Mani and mindlessly asked, "Would you like a glass of beer, Mr. Gupta?"

To which he replied, "No. Thank you very much. I don't drink alcohol, Will."

Way to go, Lutwick. You've lost him already. My lightning-quick mind calculated that asking the same question of his wife, much less his daughter would not be the best move at that moment. *Perhaps a toke of ganja, Mr. Gupta? On behalf of my people, I would like to thank yours for that contribution to civilization.* Even I was not that clueless, but the night was young.

So I sat down on a chair facing the father of my lover, a man who I knew must resent every cell in my body for the awful position my presence had put him in. And I grinned.

And he grinned. And he said, "Nice flat you have here."

And I said, "We like it."

And he suddenly seemed quite intrigued. "We?"

I gulped. "Well, I mean, I have a roommate. Another Peace Corps Volunteer. His name is Emmett, and *he's from Texas.*" I said that last phrase louder and slower, as if Mani should be impressed by my roommate's state of origin.

"Ah, Texas. That is where the cowboys come from."

"Yes, the cowboys and Indians . . ." *I DID NOT JUST SAY THAT, DID I?*

"I beg your pardon?"

"Oh I'm just joking, Mr. Gupta." *Not quite the best comeback, fool.* "I mean, we have our Indians in the United States too." *Gee, did that sound condescending enough?*

Mani stared at me and shook his head slightly. "So I have heard. But they are not really Indians, are they? Why do they call themselves Indians if they are not from India?"

"Well you might not believe this, but you actually look similar." *And I look like a complete fool.* "As I understand it, Christopher Columbus . . ."

Mr. Gupta held up his hand to stop me, frowned, and shook his head vigorously from side to side. "Never mind, I know the story. Stupid man. He thought he was in India, but he was on some little island in the Caribbean Sea as far from India as you can get. How could he mistake that place for the great subcontinent of India and a tribe of tent-dwellers for people from one of the world's oldest civilizations?"

"I think he was given a bad map." *Yup, that explains it, all right. Maybe I should just throw in the towel right now and invite Mani and the missus to check out Emmett's artful collection of chesty centerfolds we had adorning the walls of our Pleasure Dome.*

Rani must have been overhearing our conversation because she dashed into the living room, gave me the evil eye, and said, "Will, maybe you should set the table. Dinner's almost ready."

My eyes said, *thank you for rescuing me before he wants to kill me.*

And her eyes shot back, *What do you mean, "before"?*

We sat down to dinner around the off-kilter butcher block table in my kitchen, barely large enough to seat four. I faced Rani's mother, which was better than facing her father. Although Mrs. Gupta and I could barely have a conversation, I think she had figured out the gist of what had been going on in the other room, as she looked at me with sympathetic dewy eyes, like those from a Margaret Keane painting. I returned the warmth with appreciative smiles. I took an immediate liking to her and found it ironic that I could communicate more easily with her nonverbally than by speaking with her husband.

The conversation went on in English and Hindi, only Rani and her father understanding all of it, but the two of them did some translating for Kiran and me. Having already gagged on the foot in my mouth, I spent the rest of the dinner being very cautious about what I said. I tried to behave under the pretext that Rani and I were "just friends." And she pretty much ignored me the whole night, I suppose under the same pretext. Although perhaps my living-room performance with her dad had something to do with her remoteness. Touching her had become the most natural thing in the world for me to do, particularly in my home, but I was careful to keep my paws to myself.

Mani asked about my life before Fiji, and I gave him the G-rated version, which was all he wanted, if he wanted even that much. We spoke about our work. He talked about his teaching middle school. He was reassigned to new schools every few years, so the family had to regularly move around the island of Viti Levu. At one point I brought up Fiji's impending independence, but I backed off when I realized that they were nervous about how Indians would be treated under the new form of government. *Stay out of local politics.* Nothing deep or personal was discussed, and I sensed this level of formality was common for them around the dinner table. Nothing was spoken about the unspeakable *friendship*. After all, Rani and I were just friends and everyone was happy to leave it at that—at least for one evening.

I was surprised how much I liked the dinner Rani and her mom prepared. So this was how genuine Indian food tasted. Or maybe my taste buds were maturing. It was a shame that I was too uneasy to fully enjoy the cuisine.

The evening ended with tea and sweet rice pudding. I would have driven the three of them home, except I needed to keep the car a secret from the Guptas. Had they seen the Anglia and its license plate and asked their friends to be on the lookout for us, more would become known of our sinister behavior. So I had parked the car a block away instead of in my dirt driveway as I usually did.

The four of us walked out to the street, I hailed a cab for the three Guptas, and we bid adieu.

When they were safely out of sight, I ran through a damage assessment for the evening: *Batting .500 in this league—not too shabby. Although getting a lucky single with Mom may not be enough to make up for grounding into a triple play with Daddy Gupta.*

∽

Three days later, Rani came to work and told me that she had something vital to talk to me about, but it had to wait till we could be in private. Her anxious demeanor signaled that whatever-it-was would be intense. So we waited till we could get some alone time in our usual place.

Rani paced the floor. I had never seen her so visibly agitated.

"It's my brother Sunil. He's threatening to beat me and my mother up." Her voice was stressed and cracking.

"What the hell?" I threw my hands in the air. "But why?"

Her voice got louder. "Why do you think, Will? It's because of us. Me, for being with you, and my Mum, for not finding some way to stop me from being with you."

"It's none of his goddamn business."

"That doesn't matter. And my father won't stop it. He thinks it should happen."

"But why—we had such a nice dinner the other night."

Rani stared at me and rolled her eyes. *OK, so I overestimated my charm.*

"He wouldn't dare do it," I said, but then added, "Do you think he would?"

"He definitely would. He's always been cruel—a mean bully. When I was younger he used to punch me in the stomach. It knocked the wind out of me and I would cry. Then he would laugh. Or he would hit my arm. It left bruises that lasted a long time. He did that to all my sisters. He thought it was funny. I hate him."

"How could he get away with that? Why didn't your father stop him?"

"As the oldest son, he has almost father-like status in the family. And he's just a lot more aggressive than my father."

"Where does he work?"

"Burns Philp, in the stockroom. He manages it. Why are you asking?" Burns Philp was one of the two prominent department store chains in Fiji, and their flagship store was in Suva.

"Because I'm going to go see him. I can't sit on the sidelines any longer waiting for something awful to happen."

Rani had already impressed on me that I should never lash out at the people who threatened her. She knew they would always take it out on her when I wasn't around, and this was most likely to happen with her family members who could be with her whenever they wanted. I agreed with this strategy. It reminded me of the nonviolent civil disobedience techniques of the civil rights movement. Ironically, those techniques were pioneered by another Hindu, Mahatma Gandhi, to be used against the same British colonials who were about to give up their *ownership* of Fiji. Karma was going and coming around like crazy. With most of the population against us, and nobody but ourselves to back us up, we could not win by physically fighting.

But keeping one's anger in check takes a heavy toll on the psyche, particularly for someone as hung up as I was on the courage issue.

Rani said, "I don't think it would be a good idea for you to meet him." But then she cocked her head and looked at me curiously. "What would you do if you go see him?"

"I don't know." I was a bundle of rage and confusion. "I'd want to beat the crap out of him or at least threaten him, but I know that will result in his retaliating against you. I suppose I'd just try to say I'm a good guy who treats you well. And that you're old enough to make your own decisions. I'd appeal to his better side."

"He doesn't have a better side."

"I can't just stand around doing nothing and wait for him to beat you and your mom."

"Still, I don't like it."

"I have to do it. It can't make things any worse. It may help."

"OK, but be careful. Don't mention that he threatened me and remember, we're simply friends, not having sex."

"I can't say that. It's not true and nobody believes it."

"He won't bring up sex, so don't you either."

"I may be a fool, but I'm not an idiot."

Rani was pressing her hands to her face, looking not unlike the *Scream* painting. "Oh God, I hope this doesn't make it worse."

∽

I showed up at Sunil's warehouse late in the afternoon that same day. I certainly wasn't going to schedule an appointment knowing he'd probably never keep it, and if he did, what kind of entourage or weapons might he bring along? And going to his home would certainly be out of the question with his wife and children there. Surprising him at work would be the best way. Less likely he'd cause a scene there too.

"Do you know where I can find Sunil Gupta?" I asked a burly Fijian man who was unloading a large box from a truck.

"Over there." He pointed to a small wood and glass enclosure built into the side of a wall inside the warehouse.

As I walked over I mumbled my rehearsed lines, took a deep breath, exhaled, and then knocked on the door. A thin, wiry Indian man in his mid-thirties opened it and said, "Yes, what is it? Are you the auditor from Sydney?"

I said, "No, my name is Will and I'm a friend of your sister, Rani."

A weighty moment passed. He stumbled slightly, as if I'd pushed him, and then regained his composure. "I'm busy. What do you want?"

I pushed my way into his office before he could close the door on me.

"I want to talk to you about Rani. I won't be long."

Suddenly his tone changed from belligerent to business-pleasant. "Very good, sir, please have a seat." He pointed to a chair with his upturned palm.

"Sunil, I understand you disapprove of my relationship with your sister."

"Really? What gives you that idea?"

"Oh just . . . she said you didn't like the idea of our friendship."

"I don't know why she would say such a thing. I didn't even know she had a European friend."

I ignored his feigned naïveté and started spilling my prepared speech. "Look, Sunil, I really care about . . ." *Oops take it down a notch*, ". . . my friend, Rani, and I would never do anything to hurt her in any way, and I will always be fair to her."

"So?"

"So there's absolutely nothing for you to be concerned about."

"I'm not concerned. Would you like some water?" His smile was almost as wide as his face.

"No, I'm fine, thank you." His politeness was disconcerting. I continued, "Yes, well, uh . . . Sunil, there is nothing wrong with your sister and I having this uh . . . friendship."

"I agree. It is fine that you have this *friendship* with my sister."

Did he just say the word friendship *in a mocking tone?* I regained my composure. "Besides, Rani is old enough to make her own decisions. I mean, about who she will and will not associate with."

"I completely agree."

"Yes, well that's really good to hear. So do you have any questions for me, Sunil? I'm very open."

"No, sir. None that I can think of."

"Well, I'm really glad we've had this little chat, Sunil." I was beginning to relax.

"Yes, me as well."

"It's always good to talk and clarify any misunderstandings before they get out of hand. I can't tell you what a relief it is to me to know that you are OK about me having a friendship with Rani. She's such a nice girl."

"Yes, she is."

"Well, I guess I should go now. Are you sure there isn't anything you'd like to know about me?"

"Not a thing, thank you. I now know all I need to about my little sister's European friend."

CHAPTER SEVENTEEN

I watched a guy get killed at the Golden Dragon.

At the time I didn't know he was dead, but later the buzz on the coconut wireless said that a man had been killed there. I'm assuming it was the same guy. I don't think it was ever reported in the *Fiji Times*. Probably bad for tourism, the Dragon having been a magnet for travelers from all directions looking to party.

The incident happened before Rani and I met. The Golden Dragon was the PCV-preferred hangout because it was the rock-and-roll epicenter of Fiji. Well, that, and the beer flowed freely. And there were always lots of single women. There wasn't much rock music played anywhere in the islands, live or recorded, but somehow they had a very danceable house band—*The Dragon Swingers,* fronted by the son of the nightclub's owner. They played an impressive "Proud Mary." I don't know where they found their material and influences because Fiji Radio, the only English-language station, was mired in truly awful bubble-gum music when it played Western music at all. But *The Dragon Swingers* and the handful of other Dragon bands played music that was surprisingly hip, at least based on what we remembered from when we left home in 1968.

On this particular Friday night, the Dragon was way more crowded than usual. I was there with my Peace Corps pals Tom and Charlie, drinking beer, enjoying the sounds, looking for some action, our usual *modus operandi*. The usual coterie of island people were there doing the same thing. Charlie was also there on business. He lived in a Fijian village not far from Suva. One of his work projects was starting and promoting a Fiji Battle of the Bands contest that became quite the rage and helped spread the devil's music throughout the islands. He had spoken with the members of that evening's band between sets to get their support for the contest.

Workers from American Samoa staffed a freighter in port where a New Zealand Navy ship was also docked. From their respective Polynesian and European appearances, most of the males in the club that night probably came from those two vessels, swelling the size of the crowd to be much larger than usual.

Everything had been calm until I noticed some angry shouting between one of the Samoans and a Kiwi sailor on the other side of the crowded dance floor.

"Hey Charlie, Tom, look over there," I said. "I do believe a fight is about to break out between those two."

Tom turned around. "Yeah, they look shit-faced, but this place is too crowded to give them enough room to fight."

But the two testosterone-infused inebriates were not going to let logistics stop them. The Samoan threw the first punch, a hard right to his adversary's jaw that knocked the New Zealander down. He sprawled out cold, face-down on the floor. The people surrounding them backed up. This movement rippled through the tightly packed crowd as people banged into one another. In about fifteen seconds, the chain reaction had traveled through the whole room. Scores of men and more than a few of the women took their cues as if choreographed, and their fists and feet were flying. It was a barroom brawl—island style.

The sight of punches thrown by drunken Fijian men was not uncommon. Usually the next day all was forgiven and forgotten. But I had never seen a donnybrook erupt, and this one felt onerous.

Our party of three, true to our Peace Corps credo, pushed back away from the pugilists, dodging errant punches and flying chairs. I wanted to get out of there, but there was no way to move through the battling crowd toward the staircase, a mere half-room away.

And then it happened. Being tall, I could see over the combatants and noticed a Samoan standing up across the large room and beneath him, viewed through a forest of flying appendages, an apparently unconscious man lying face down on the floor. Judging from where he stood and his general appearance, the Samoan was the man who had initiated the melee.

Then he lifted one foot up to knee level and brought it down hard on the man lying defenseless beneath his shoe. I couldn't see clearly, but I sensed the Samoan was putting all his power into pulverizing the unconscious man's head. And then the Samoan repeated his blow. I felt nauseous, and the voice in my head screamed in outrage at me, *DO SOMETHING!*

I yelled, "NO! NO! STOP! SOMEBODY STOP THAT GUY!" and tried to get closer to the scene, but it was hopeless. The melee was such that I couldn't move in any direction. But that inner voice asked me, *Is that true you can't move, or is it really fear that holds you back?*

I couldn't believe what I was witnessing—mob violence and a stomping in my Pacific island paradise—violence perpetrated on dozens by dozens over apparently nothing and nobody doing anything to stop it. Why didn't the stomping victim's friends who were fighting nearby him intervene to save him? Why didn't someone?

Why didn't I?

Eventually enough people left to enable my friends and me to get out of there while the battle continued. No police had yet shown up, if they ever did. But I kept wondering what I should have . . . could have done to prevent the violence. Maybe I should have at least gone to the police to tell them what I had seen, but I hadn't clearly seen the Samoan's face. I would not have been able to identify him, but dozens of others probably could, so I felt it was their responsibility to talk to the authorities. Certainly the victim's buddies would step forward to finger the worst evildoer. I doubted anyone was prosecuted because so many were brawling. Any injuries to someone participating in a brawl were his own damn fault. Right? Apparently whatever happened at the Dragon was going to stay at the Dragon.

And so on and so forth went my justifications for inaction.

Months later, after I had confronted Rani's brother about his violent threats, I thought back to that horrid, surreal spectacle and recalled being torn by my inertia over getting involved.

Listen to me rationalizing why I didn't do more about the Dragon killing. Yes, I talked to Sunil after he made threats of violence. But what if violence does break out around Rani? Will I just stand there and make excuses, or will I protect her no matter what?

I knew what the right answer should be, but the question still lingered.

❦

Rani was wearing oversized movie-star sunglasses when she showed up at work the next day. I surmised something terrible had happened. We adjourned to our conference room privacy. She removed the glasses, revealing deep blue-black blotches surrounding her left eye. I couldn't believe anyone would do this to her, much less her own brother. She paced the floor shaking clenched fists. "He came over to our house and acted calm and friendly at the door, but when he got inside he went into a rage. 'How can you disgrace our family?' he yelled at me. 'You're just a dirty whore.' Then he punched me in the eye."

I was stunned. "That fucking asshole! I want to kill him." I moved toward her. "Oh baby, I'm so sorry."

Rani pushed away my attempts to comfort her. "Luckily I saw it coming and partially blocked his fist, so it didn't do more damage. Otherwise it could have . . . well, who knows? Then my mother came over and started yelling at him to stop, and he pushed her so hard she staggered backward across the room, hit the wall, and fell to the floor. She just sat there trying to get her breath back. She was so stunned. I could believe he'd hit me—but my mother? How could he push his own mother so violently like that?"

"Where was your father?"

"He was in the bedroom. He heard what was going on, but he didn't come out. At least not at first."

"Unbelievable. Then what happened."

"I ran to the kitchen and grabbed the first thing I found—a big fork. Sunil followed me and leaned his hand on the table to balance himself. He must have been getting winded; he's not particularly fit. And then he yelled, 'Put that down, whore!'"

"And did you?"

"Yes I did," Rani's fierce look was replaced by an impish grin. "At first I moved like I was just putting it on the table, but then I plunged it down hard on the back of the hand that he was leaning on. I could feel it going in like I was stabbing a melon and the blood gushed and he screamed and screamed."

Although I thought, *Fantastic, hope he bled to death,* the words that came out were "Oh my God. That sounds awful."

"No it wasn't. It was great." Rani's grin widened into a satisfied smile and I laughed. She continued, "I felt like I was getting him back for years of his picking on me. He grabbed me with his good hand and was about to punch me again when my father *finally* came out of the bedroom and said, 'OK, Sunil, stop. That's enough. Go home now.' And Sunil whined, 'But *pitaji*, the little bitch stabbed me.' He was crying and holding his hand up like a wounded paw for my father to see. So my father said, 'Go wrap it up in a towel and get out of here. There will be no more fighting.' So Sunil did what my father told him and left. And that was the end of it."

"The end of it?"

"Well, my dad and I both went over to my mother and helped her up. She was still dazed and maybe in shock from the whole spectacle. She accepted my help but pushed my dad away from her and yelled at him, 'How could you let your son do this?' And my father said, 'I'm sorry, but I didn't think he'd hurt *you*.' And I yelled at him, 'Oh, so it's OK if he punched your daughter in the eye? I hate you, Father.'

He said nothing back to me. My mother ignored him and came to me, patted my hair and neck, and hugged me and asked, 'Are you OK, baby?' I told her I was and she pulled away and yelled some more at my dad. Then she stormed off to her bedroom, but she was walking funny as if something was wrong with her back. My father spent the night on the couch."

"Do you think she'll be OK?"

"I hope so. She was really sore today and was lying in bed when I left."

A group of mynah birds flew across our window view as if they were black rocks skimming the Pacific's horizon. Behind them, Joske's thumb, a steep green volcanic plug, stuck up through low-hanging clouds like rings on a finger. A lull fell upon us, and Rani could tell I was contemplating what to do next.

"Don't even think about it."

"I have to. We can't let him get away with this."

"He didn't get away with it. I stabbed him in the hand. I don't think he'll try to hurt me or my mother again. That is unless you retaliate."

"But I can't just sit and let this happen."

"You can and you will. It's my life on the line, not yours. If you do anything over this, he'll come back again, but next time he'll bring some of his buddies too. No matter what we do, we'll lose by fighting this. All the Indians in Fiji hate us. You can't come over here from the other side of the world and expect to win this kind of battle."

"Then we should go to the police."

"The police?" Her mouth twisted into a sneer. "No, I don't want them in on this. Anyway, they will just consider this a family matter. They won't get involved. They won't care."

I gulped. "Should we stop seeing each other?"

Her eyes were on fire. "Don't ask me. That's your decision."

I felt as if I'd just been punched. "I'm not quitting. But you're the one who is in danger, and staying with me will keep you in danger." There was no way I could any longer pretend we shared the risks of our liaison equally.

I hugged her tense body, but there was no response, though her breathing gradually settled and her heartbeat slowed. We were both gathering thoughts, coming down from the shock of the beating, wondering what might happen, and what we should do next.

Finally I broke the silence. "After this, why would you even want to keep seeing me?"

She thought about it for a moment. "Because I really like what we have, and I don't want to give it up. Not because of other people, that's for certain. I like being with you, and I can really be myself around you and your friends. I can't do that anywhere else. I believe that there is nothing bad about what we are doing. And I'm stubborn." A trace of a smile crossed her lips and lit up her bruised face. "And why would you keep seeing me?"

"Because I love you, Rani." I blurted out the unplanned declaration. This was the first time I'd said the three magic words, and it seemed I was doing so at the worst possible moment. *So why am I saying it? Is it because she got punched, or do I honestly mean it?*

"And I love you too, Will." Her first time too. *Does she mean it or is she saying it only because I did?*

We kissed. We silently held each other for several minutes. The relationship had just been ratcheted up another notch. All was right for a moment. But then the moment passed and we walked out into a world hostile to our simply being together. And there was no solution to make that stop.

∽

A few days later, my friend Jeff came from the States to visit me. I was in junior high school when his family first moved into a house across the alley from where I lived with my aunt and uncle in Richmond. I used to hang out at his home and often ate dinner with his family. Mine never reciprocated. He was not even allowed in my house. Nothing personal. Well, there had been that incident with the rock fight, but my aunt had a no-friends-allowed policy anyway. None of my friends or her son's friends were allowed in their house, and she and my uncle had no friends of their own.

During high school, Jeff and I hung out together a lot. With Jeff at six foot five and me at six foot three, we were probably the two tallest Jews at Thomas Jefferson High School, though no official stats were kept.

Jeff was doing well after college, living in Mountain View, California, and selling medical instruments for a small manufacturer. After his arrival in Fiji, he expressed interest in an authentic indigenous experience, so we drove the Anglia out to visit my PCV friend Bill who lived in the *real* Fiji barely thirty-five miles away. On one hand Bill, like all Volunteers in the bush, had to rough it—no indoor plumbing, no electricity, no bright lights or cold beer. On the other hand, he was treated like a king in his castle—his hosts provided all his meals, and cleaned his *bure* (hut) every day. To do his laundry, the village women would take his clothes to the river and beat them with rocks to loosen the grime. Once the clothes dried, the women pressed out all the wrinkles with a benzene iron. It was sort of like camping for two years, but with servants to do all the work.

But not all of the bush Volunteers had it so cushy. A few were at sites on islands so remote, they were the first nonnative people the villagers had ever seen. In general, we urban PCVs felt guilt toward our rural brethren and sisters. But it actually was a two-way street. After all, they were having the kinds of experiences you would think a Peace Corps Volunteer should have. They would return home after their Peace Corps service with glorious stories that would someday impress their kids and grandkids. Such as "I survived dengue fever and amoebic dysentery and lived in squalor to fight poverty." Whereas, the only yarn the urban PCVs would be able to spin would be "I risked gonorrhea and worked in an air-conditioned building where I went to bullshit meetings to fight poverty." Clearly we city Volunteers would pay dearly with yawn-inducing stories for our mildly plush lifestyles. And our punishment would last for the rest of our lives, whereas the bush PCVs had to suffer for only two years.

And then there was the money issue. Excluding housing, all of us were expected to live on the equivalent of forty U.S. dollars per month no matter where we were assigned. Sure, you could do that in the villages because there was nothing to buy. You might even save a few bucks during your two-year tenure. But no way could you live on forty dollars a month in Suva, with all its temptations and halfhearted reminders of the consumer society back home. We urbanites were like junkies feeding our materialistic addictions with third-rate heroin. The PCVs in the bush had gone cold turkey and were living the blissful natural life that the hippies back home pretended they wanted. We Suva volunteers also had to provide crash pads when the rural PCVs came into the big city to party. We provided them food and drink, but they knew how guilty we felt and only occasionally contributed anything back besides a pool of vomit from the inevitable overdrinking. They were such amateurs.

So visiting Bill was payback to a bush Volunteer for all the B&B hosting I had done, although Bill had always been one of the more generous and considerate guests. Jeff and I found Bill's *bure* on a hill overlooking the school compound at the edge of Verata, a native village. A flurry of fluttering white chickens and skinny Fijian kids with arms a-waving announced our arrival. My car kicked up a billowing auburn dirt cloud that coated a couple of nearby huts. Despite that faux pas, Bill welcomed us profusely as we handed him the traditional guest gift, a kilo of *yaqona* (kava) powder to be mixed with water to produce Fiji's ubiquitous ceremonial beverage. The gift was for our Fijian hosts who would be preparing our dinner. We would all drink it later.

We entered Bill's one-room shack, where Jeff and I would crash on the floor that night. The floor was quite comfortable, with layers of straw and several mats. Traversing it was like walking on a giant sponge. Sleeping on such a surface would not be a problem, particularly after a night of kava consumption. I could smell the breeze coming off the Pacific a half mile away, filtering through clusters of banana and guava trees. The porous straw walls of Bill's home enabled the wind to go right through it. So lack of a fan would be tolerable too. Rats, bats, and mongooses regularly prowled the villages at night, but they would hide in the darkness during our visit. To discourage the ubiquitous mosquitoes we'd burn green spiraling mosquito coils that stunk like cheap incense. With its walls bedecked with banners of naturally colored tapa cloth, I had to admit Bill's home was way more inviting than mine, even without any twentieth century flourishes.

Jeff and I hadn't expected such a to-do, but the village elders decided that our presence was worthy of a feast. An unlucky pig was to be roasted in our honor—in a *lovo,* a traditional circular open-pit barbecue dug out of the ground.

We walked past thickets of pink bougainvillea and crimson hibiscus flowers to the main part of the village, where we could observe the cooking process. A fire already filled the pit. It was primed with burning coconut husks. Once those were flaming, chunks of coral and river stones were thrown in. When those were glowing hot, some Fijian men used poles to push some of the rocks and coral aside, making way for our deceased and soon-to-be delicious friend Porky. His gutted carcass had been partially stuffed with banana leaves. We watched as four men each grabbed a leg, carried the pig, and then lowered it, so it was lying evenly on top of the fire. They used the poles to push some of the hot rocks into the pig's belly. The leaves steamed as they hit the searing rocks, and the smell of roast pork exploded in the sultry air. On top of the sizzling carcass, the men put fish and vegetables wrapped in more banana leaves.

After all this food baked for a couple of hours, the sun had set and grass-skirted Fijian boys lit torches. We entered the chief's *bure* to eat dinner. Three doors opened into the dwelling, and I figured any door would do me, but I was wrong. Only one door was suitable for honored guests and high-ranking village males. Another was for other village men and a third for the women and children. They all led into the same room, but the rules were important to Fijian natives. I went through the common males' door and was laughingly admonished to leave and come back through the appropriate portal. Outsiders were expected to screw up, but were still urged to follow the rules.

We sat cross-legged on the soft, matted floor in an oval around the center of the room where the food was placed. The first course was a yellow-fin tuna soup. Jeff, being the true outsider and therefore the most honored guest, was served the silvery scaly head floating in a pink broth. In Fijian culture, the head of whatever animal was to be devoured was always considered the most desirable portion. Luckily for Jeff, he was sitting next to a village man who was getting an eyeful of Jeff's first course.

Using intuitive sign language, Jeff asked the Fijian, "You actually want this?"

It was an easy trade and they exchanged bowls.

Bill said he couldn't count the number of times he had to delicately pass the honor on to someone who might genuinely appreciate it. Meanwhile, he often craved the crab that other Fijians were eating, but shellfish were considered unsuitable for a man of Bill's lofty stature because they lived their lives traipsing on the seafloor where all the pee and poop fell from the fish swimming above. Or so the theory went.

Jeff was lucky he wasn't served the pig's head, which was thankfully devoured elsewhere. The dinner was savory, and after it, all the men settled in for a festive evening of drinking the *yaqona* (kava) we had brought. The women often drank it too, but in the villages it was more a tradition for the men hanging out socially. Kava is an unregulated substance in the United States despite its tranquilizing and intoxicating properties, and it certainly wasn't regulated in Fiji. I never got buzzed from it, though some Volunteers swore otherwise. Mostly it left my mouth feeling numb and me feeling heavy and groggy. Perhaps that's why it was often referred to as *grog*. Many men in Fiji drank enormous amounts of the substance. Doing that over many years can make one's skin take on the texture of an alligator's. The drink's taste was not something a Westerner would savor. Imagine throwing cardboard, sawdust, some rotten apricots, and water into a blender, then downing the results. Fast. But when in Fiji, even in Suva, there were times when you had to drink it, lest your host get miffed.

Yaqona was served at all Fijian ceremonies—birth, death, marriage, a new chief—with elaborate procedures. But this night we would drink it with only the daily dose of formality. The grayish-brown opaque liquid was made by grinding the roots from a pepper shrub into a powder that was put inside a narrow cloth sack. The sack was immersed in a large wooden bowl of cold water where our kava-tender would wring it out for about fifteen minutes. Next, he dipped a *bilo* (half a hollowed-out coconut shell) into the concoction and brought that to the first person in the group of thirsty drinkers. In this case, I was the fortunate recipient, an honor just in itself. Bill had told them, Jeff would not know the proper response, so he was spared the embarrassment. Just before I took the bowl, I did a traditional cupping of my hands and clapped them once, so it sounded like a *dull thud*, which was what I would soon become. I slowly took the bowl, brought it to my face, and swallowed the contents in a single gulp. Everyone in the *bure* was seemingly impressed, so they also did the cupped hand-clap. Only they did it three times. Then the kava-tender went back to the bowl and repeated the cycle until everyone had some. Only then did he drink some himself. The mix/serve/drink/clap process repeated for hours until all participants staggered to wherever they were crashing for the night.

Back at Bill's hut, I almost had a heart attack when a rhinoceros beetle flew into my face just before I fell asleep. These black finger-length mini-monsters are proportionally the strongest animals on Earth. If they were the size of an average human, they could lift a sixty-five-ton object. Fortunately they didn't bite people, but were a major pest to Fiji economically because they *single-mandibly* destroyed coconut trees, the source of copra, Fiji's second-largest export. In my circumstance, we just opened the door and the varmint flew away.

After a night of kava-enhanced slumber, I awoke to the realization that it had been so relaxing to spend some time in a Fijian village where I could get totally away from that soap opera taking place a few miles down the road. I couldn't believe how tense I had become in recent months, noticing it only when I got this respite away from the source of the stress.

But the respite would not last long. Shortly after Jeff and I set out on our return to Suva, we had an unexpected visit. As I was driving, our conversation was interrupted by the loud *thwack* of a large rock hitting the middle of the Anglia's windshield. Had Rani been with us, I would have assumed it was no accident. But she wasn't. So even my paranoia would not endorse the idea that someone who knew my car had waited by the side of the road overnight just for this moment. Though the thought did occur. The probable cause was simply a large road rock being kicked up by a vehicle coming from the other direction.

I pulled the car over to the side of the road, and we got out to inspect the damage.

Which was slight.

At first.

Just a crack in the middle of the glass.

Which spread as we watched.

A spider web rippling outward.

Over the course of sixty seconds, the web devoured the entire windshield.

As we watched.

Helplessly.

We got back in, but we could see nothing through the glass but a sun-powered light show. I wrapped a dirty T-shirt around my hand and punched the crinkled glass. But contrary to my understanding of the laws of physics, the windshield fragments fell mostly inward, collapsing into thousands of little pieces in the car's interior. It was only then that I realized we were parked facing uphill. After we had cleaned out the more lethal glass chunks, Jeff crouched over the hump on the floor adjacent the back seat for the remainder of the ride. And yours truly was happy that a menagerie of only insects went splat in my face for the duration of the bumpy ride home.

CHAPTER EIGHTEEN

To my surprise, the ensuing weeks went by with no major incidents, so Rani and I planned a day trip with Bill. The destination was a highly recommended beach on Laucala Bay about a twenty-mile drive from Suva. Bill rode a bus to town on a Friday and spent the night at my place. The next day we drove to Rani's home pickup spot, the nearby mangrove tree cluster. She was conservatively dressed for a day at the beach but still looked sensual in a blue sarong bottom and pink stretch cotton top over her bikini.

Bill switched from the front to the back seat. Rani got into the car, turned toward Bill and did a double-take. "Where's Joyce? Are we picking her up on the way to the beach?"

"She couldn't make it today. There was a parent-teacher event at her school, so she just couldn't get away. She sends her regrets." Joyce was an alluring blond Peace Corps Volunteer and a member of our weekend party cabal.

I started driving, resting my right arm on the car door as I pulled onto the street. It was a rare cloudless sky and hot already—ideal beach weather, but Rani was unusually quiet and leaning a frowning face on her fist.

So I asked her, "What's up, babe?"

"This is not going to look right. Maybe you two should go without me." She was staring ahead, avoiding eye contact.

"Why? What's the problem?"

"How can I explain this if you still don't understand it? If Joyce were here, it might look like I'm coming along as her friend to spend the day with her European male friends. Not perfect, but at least that appears somewhat respectable, and Indians may hold back making a scene in front of a white girl. Two white blokes and an Indian girl . . ." Rani shook her head. "Everyone who sees us will think I am a prostitute."

"Fuck 'em," I said, "I don't care what they think anymore. Things have been going OK lately. We went to that *Easy Rider* movie the other night, and nothing happened. I think things are really starting to change."

"That was because we arrived separately, and we were mostly in a dark theater when we were together. After the movie we were in the lobby, and the few Indians there were staring me down with hate in their eyes. A couple of them know me."

"Should I turn around?"

"No, just keep going. You think nothing will happen so we'll see about that." She turned away from me.

I shook my head, frustrated. I asked Bill, "When do I turn off the King's Road?"

The directions were to take a right on a rutted dirt road and follow it to the end, and that's where the beach would be. We had no map, so we had to totally rely on the directions that Bill had been given. Word had it that it was the best little beach on this side of Viti Levu, and it was quite secluded, so I thought it unlikely anyone would disturb us. And if they did we'd just get in the car and drive away.

I turned onto the dirt road, tickled Rani, and looked at her with my lips posed in a pout. She laughed a little. We approached our destination. But what we saw there was not reassuring.

At the end of the road, there was no beach in sight, just a bumpy outcrop dropping to a bank at the mouth of the Rewa River, Fiji's widest. A few tiny boats with outboard motors sat on the muddy bank. Each of the boats had a man standing next to it. And each of the men was Indian. What lay beyond was open sea, with land visible in the distance.

I parked the car and walked through brush to the path, which sloped down about fifty feet to the boats. Rani slumped down in the seat, by now almost a reflex when we'd stop the car. I scanned the men to see who seemed the most amiable and went up to one who was picking at his teeth with a dry blade of grass.

"*Namaste.* I was told there is supposed to be a beach at the end of this road. Do you know where it is?"

The man pointed across the bay at the distant land—a yellow strip that jutted out to the sea. It seemed to be three or four miles away.

"Oh great," I said. "So how do I drive over there?"

"No road, no car. I drive you in boat."

I didn't like this. "How much to take me and two friends across and back later today?"

He hesitated, then said, "Four dollars."

"OK, I'll give you two dollars when you drop us at the beach and two dollars when you come back for us this afternoon."

"Not a problem, sahib."

"Let me check with my friends."

I explained the situation to Bill and Rani. I was surprised Rani agreed to go, but she said, "I'm tired of hiding too and think maybe you're right that I should stop worrying about what other people think about us. And these men, at least they won't know me. Why should I care what they think?"

"You're sure you're OK with this? We don't have to do it." Now I was the one getting squeamish.

"Let's just get it over with." And with that she jumped out of the car. The decision was made.

We got our gear, walked to the white wood boat, which was only as long as a three-person canoe. We stepped in without saying anything. Our driver, whose name was Janki, seemed unfazed when he first saw Rani, though I noticed astonished looks and angry muttering among his fellow boat drivers. Rani shot me an *I-told-you-so* glare as she sat down next to me. Janki waded into the water and walked to the other side of the boat. He jumped in and pulled the cord on the engine. It putt-putted to life and off we went.

Although we were heading toward the beach in the direction the three of us were facing, Janki spent most of the fifteen-minute ride at the other end of the boat watching us instead of our destination, turning his head to face it only occasionally to get his bearings and fine-tune the boat's direction. Rani turned her head to the side, but I watched Janki most of the time. His frozen gaze kept switching between Bill, Rani, and me. His face was thoroughly drained of emotion. And that seemed stranger than the usual look of scorn that passed over their faces, when most Indian men first spotted us. Then he put on sunglasses. Perhaps he sensed my increasing concern and was deliberately hiding his eyes from us. But still I noticed the rigid line of his mouth, and his teeth seemed to be grinding, though he wasn't eating anything.

The boat rounded a cove and slid onto the yellow sand beach that covered one whole side of a mini-peninsula jutting from Viti Levu. We got out of the boat, and I paid our driver. He seemed more relaxed when he thanked me, and we agreed that he would return at three o'clock. He headed his boat back toward the riverbank.

We had almost the whole beach to ourselves. A group of Fijians was near the end closest to the main part of the island. The men were casting a fishing net into the water, and a woman went into the bay in her floral print dress. Some children were playing in the bay near the shore, laughing and splashing about. I figured their village must be nearby, and they had walked to the beach. About ten white people were already glowing pink at the far end of the beach. We picked a spot in the middle, where a small grove of coconut palms provided some minimal shade.

We spread our mats on the hot sand and stripped down to our bathing suits.

"I kind of hope he doesn't come back, although I have no idea how we can get back to the car without him." I told Rani and Bill.

"Oh, he didn't look too bad to me." Rani's voice was surprisingly light. "Better than I expected. At least better than the other boat guys looked."

"He wouldn't dare try anything." Bill chimed in. "There's three of us and one of him." Bill always did take the optimistic point of view.

We enjoyed a delectable picnic lunch of roti-wrapped curried fish and vegetables that Rani had prepared and washed it down with a local chartreuse-colored soda pop of which the only identifiable taste was sugar. We had brought some beer with us, but I wanted to be entirely sober for the return, not knowing what to expect. Rani looked spectacular in her green and purple bikini. Her lush bronze skin, long black hair billowing like a flag in the sea breezes, and petite perfectly proportioned body were ideal for the beach, for any beach anywhere. I had never seen an Indian woman wearing any kind of bathing suit, much less a bikini, and the taboo rarity of that sight made it that much more tantalizing. Rani wore hardly any makeup—how did I ever get so lucky to end up with such a natural beauty? Moments like that made the craziness we endured seem somehow worth it.

By three o'clock we were sunburned and sleepy. We donned our street clothes and waited. And waited some more—our driver showed up forty minutes late. Janki said nothing about his delay, but with his head turned down, asked for his money while avoiding looking at us even though he had his sunglasses on. I gave him the two dollars. We got in the boat and roared off toward our destination. We had been on open water for only a minute, when I noticed the tiny vessel was rocking back and forth. The sea was as calm as could be, so it made no sense. Bill leaned toward me and covering his mouth, said, "Don't look now, but our driver is shit-faced."

But I did look as Janki stood straight up and shook a small half-filled bottle of scotch-colored liquid as if it were the severed head of a vanquished opponent. He unscrewed the cap and drained the liquor down his throat, some of it trickling down his neck. Then he threw the empty bottle in the water and raised both fists in the air like he had just won a race. Next, he spread his legs and stood with both feet on either side of the boat hull, deliberately rocking it back and forth and laughing at our increasing anguish. And then he let out a primal howl for his captured audience.

"What the fuck is the matter with you?" I yelled, and he grunted back something indecipherable. Bill, Rani, and I were clinging to the boat as Janki laughed and rocked it so hard that water was sloshing into it from one side, then the other. If he rocked it any harder, it would pitch over, and we'd all be in the bay.

Rani clenched my arm and screamed above the noise of the boat's engine and the sound of splattering water, "I CAN'T SWIM!"

"You can't swim well, you mean." I clarified, as we clenched the sides of the tipsy vessel.

"No. I never learned. I told you that when we started going together."

"You can't swim *at all*? But you live on an island. As a child you went to beaches and rivers all the time."

"Just listen to me, Will. I CANNOT SWIM! What are we going to do?" Rani's large pupils looked double their usual size. There was nothing I could say to comfort her because I, too, was beginning to panic.

We were already at least a mile from the beach and getting further away every second. I could swim, but not well. I didn't think I could swim even half a mile. And Bill said he was not much better than me. The water was deep—very deep. None of us would survive being dumped into the middle of the bay.

I asked Bill, "Can you handle an outboard motor, because I don't know the first thing about boating?" And he looked at me with mouth twisted in angst, his head shaking in the wrong direction.

Oh God? This is it? This is how my life ends?

I tried to use body language to calm our tormentor. I motioned to him to sit down. I tried to seem friendly and reassuring. "The joke is over. We got it. Ha-ha." He pointed at me, laughed, and finally sat, temporarily winded, and put the outboard in neutral. A moment of calm.

OK, he's not stupid enough to kill us because he knows we'll take him down too. He's pickled, but only a few other boats are on the bay. It would not be easy to hit them even if he tried, given his condition. If we stay calm, we're going to get out of this alive. We're going to be OK. Please, God—we have to come out of this OK.

Our tormentor smiled at us, taking stock of what he had wrought—two clueless white boys and an Indian girl—all shit-their-pants scared to death.

Bill said, "He's in a good mood now. Let's keep him that way."

Janki said something directed to Rani. She crumpled down, and her eyes were tear-filled, but angry. There was only one word he said that I could decipher—*bijaru*. This wasn't just about a crazy boat driver getting blotto, trying to scare his passengers. This was yet another case where just the sight of us lit the fuse on an explosive mixture of primal hatred and jealousy in a total stranger.

Filled with my own fury, I stood and moved toward our driver. I wanted to grab him, but I'm not sure what else I would have done. We needed Janki to get us back to shore alive. But it was all moot anyway. He put the motor in gear, and we took off like a bullet. The thrust knocked me down on my back. I was lucky I hadn't swerved to the side while falling, because the boat was so small that I would certainly have ended up in the bottomless sea, reflexively grabbing the tipping vessel and taking all the others with me.

He cackled with amusement at this sight and veered the vessel left and right, zigzagging its way along the glassy surface of the bay. Our path seemed aimless at first, but soon we were passing alongside a stationary two-story boat with about twenty people visible. It appeared that all of them were Indian. Janki pulled even with the larger craft and put the motor in neutral. He stabbed the air with his forefinger pointing at Rani. Then he pointed at Bill and me. I knew enough Hindi and body language to get the gist of what he then said:

"Look everyone, look at the filthy whore. She fucks not one, but two white devils. She is surely the filthiest whore in all of Fiji, and I am going to make her pay for her sins."

Rani covered her face with a towel as our driver ranted on. I yelled in mixed Hindi and English to the people in the other boat. "No, no, this is not true. You see, he is drunk. This man is crazy and bad. She is not *bijaru*. She is my friend. We are all only friends." When I realized how ridiculous I must have sounded I stopped, but I took some solace in their knowing that because I had spoken some Hindi, they would see that Bill and I were not just tourists who picked Rani up at a bar. *Oh great. So we're local Europeans who picked her up at a bar. Who gives a damn what they think—we'll be lucky to be alive in five minutes! Concentrate on how to get us out of this mess!*

Again I lurched forward toward the drunk as he started the engine, and again he revved it. The boat roared away, I fell backward, and he chortled with glee. The zigzagging and the tipping of the boat from side to side had filled about a quarter of it with water, but Janki seemed to care not a whit that he too might go down with the ship. I was getting nauseous while Rani was already puking over the side. I tried to comfort her, but she pushed my arm away. Only Bill seemed composed, but he was probably in shock behind his aviator sunglasses.

We passed another boat—this one small like ours—an Indian family, of course. Janki repeated his antics. "Look at the slut in my boat. Look at these two white boys she fucks." The family looked more stunned by Janki's drunken performance than by Rani's presence. This pleased me, despite the desperation of the moment.

More zigzagging, more rocking. And then I realized we were almost back to the shore where we had begun several hours earlier. *Maybe we still might come out of this nightmare alive!?!*

Except that when we got closer, I saw seven of Janki's comrades, men he had probably recruited after the morning trip, because there were only two boats left on the shore. The men were jumping up and down and yelling at us. I could tell it certainly wasn't because they were happy we made it back alive. A couple of them toppled over on each other, undoubtedly smashed. A glint of sunlight off the blade of a cane knife caught my attention. The nightmare would continue.

What do these maniacs have planned for us? Dear God, please get us through this alive. I'll do whatever you want. I apologize for all my trespasses and any other bad shit I ever did. We don't deserve to die. Please . . .

Then another voice in my head interrupted. *Will you stop with all this whining? Calm down, for Christ's sake. Here's what you should do.*

And so the second voice hatched the plan.

I told Bill and Rani about it as the boat pulled toward the shore. There was no time for discussion. I handed Bill the car keys. As soon as we hit shallow water, we jumped out of the boat, surprising our host. And then we tipped the boat and Janki over and into the drink. The Indian men screamed and hooted, then chased us as we scurried toward the car. We avoided the exit path where the men were and forged one of our own up the embankment, cutting our legs on the tangled, thorny vines. Rani stayed with me while Bill veered off from us, and we yelled back at the men. They followed the two of us while Bill scooped up some large rocks in his towel.

I wanted to turn around and face them down, but I knew that they would grab Rani if I did. As they followed us, I contented myself by screaming every expletive I knew. I could feel the adrenaline pumping through my body. It felt enlivening to release all that anger after having to suppress it on the boat. It also felt as if I were floating through a delirious nightmare.

Rani and I got to the car, and Bill caught up with us. According to plan, Bill gave me two large rocks as I stood facing the angry men and Rani stood between me and the car. All movement stopped as the men reached us and contemplated our pathetic armament, given that theirs included a couple of machetes. They faced me from about seven feet away, but somewhat downhill, both sides considering their next move. One of them spat at me, and that seemed to impress his friends, as a couple of others followed suit. Because they were spitting uphill, they didn't hit their target, but I got the message and the feeling was mutual. I flashed on the movie scene that Tom had mentioned where Doctor Frankenstein faced down the angry villagers who wanted him to turn over his creation to them. This lynch mob, however, was real.

Bill scrambled around the Anglia, unlocked it, got in the driver's seat, put the keys in the ignition, and pushed open the riders' door. Rani backed off toward the car, and the mob lunged forward. But I wound up for the pitch and said, "Who wants his head split open first?" They got the idea and held steady. Rani folded the seat down and got in the back, keeping her eyes on the drunken mob as they kept theirs on her every move.

Bill turned the ignition. The angry pack moved forward again. I took a step back and got ready to throw. I slowly backed off from the crowd and jumped in the front seat, slammed the door and yelled, "Floor it!" Bill did and we screeched off down the furrowed road as we watched the mob vainly running after us, eating the cloud of dust we left behind in our wake. I heard two simultaneous hits on the back of the car—maybe machetes, maybe rocks. We weren't about to stop to investigate.

For a few minutes as we put more distance between us and our horror show, we congratulated one another on a job well done, releasing any remaining angry energy in hoots and hollers. But once that zeal dissipated, the reality of how close we had come to being killed started sinking in.

We rode the rest of the way to Suva in dead silence.

CHAPTER NINETEEN

It was an understatement to say that my relationship with Rani was not accepted by her Hindu family, but to be fair it would not get green-lighted by my Jewish one either. Luckily, in this sense, my parents were long dead, though no doubt tossing and turning in their graves. I pictured my protective, judgmental mother trying to get clearance from the powers above for at least a one-night haunting, where she could give me her two cents' worth and set me back on the road to pursuing someone more like the girl who married dear old Dad.

It had been almost two years since I had seen anyone from my family and they were eight thousand miles away. International telephone communication was so expensive then, I made only one call to the States during my two years in Fiji. A few months before Rani came into my life, I phoned my sister Marcia to warn her that I had a dream where she was killed in a car accident. This was a déjà vu of a nightmare my mother had fifteen years earlier about other family members being in a highway collision. That one prophetically came true the day after she dreamed it, when two of them were seriously injured in just such a crash. In my mother's case, she had not warned them. So I called Marcia to sound the alarm, thinking perhaps this ghastly gift of clairvoyance might be hereditary. Luckily my fortune-telling skills would not be so prescient. Or maybe I altered destiny by giving

Marcia the heads-up a day early, affecting her behavior just enough to save her life in the process.

Later I would recall that my mother's dream had foreshadowed her unpredictable heart-attack demise by only a few months. So perhaps by calling my sister and messing with the universe's cause-and-effect tapestry of pulleys and levers, a.k.a. fate, I had saved my own life a few months later. Certainly it had hung in the balance during the boating incident, along with the lives of Bill and Rani. The universe, after all, does work in mysterious ways.

With my parents deceased, I hoped no other family member would pick up that baton of parental judgment with regard to my liaison in Fiji. My guardian aunt and uncle almost never wrote, so I didn't know how they were taking the news I sent them, although I expected they and most of my family hoped I would come to my senses and end the romance before I left Fiji. Marcia, older than me by thirty-one months, had fallen into a motherly role after our real one died. So it would only be a matter of time before she began to send smoke signals in the form of little blue aerogrammes that indicated this match did not please her.

But then I had somewhat consciously provoked her predictable response. In my letters I emphasized the more controversial and dramatic aspects of the courtship. I enjoyed writing of my harrowing adventure. And I aimed for a truthful, but entertaining and dramatic read. I thought Marcia might be impressed by her mild-mannered brother finally casting aside his life of playing it safe. This was not too bright on my part because I should have known it would not play well with my sister. But then getting family approval for my unconventional romantic relationship was not high on my list in 1970, my year of rebellion.

Marcia wrote back that the tropical sun must have driven me mad, and from her vastly more mature vantage point, she feared for my safety as well as my sanity. Rani was just so different from us, not being Jewish, white, American, college-educated, a mainlander—OK, Rani and I did not share many attributes. But that was the allure. I hadn't been happy in my childhood, so why would I want to be with someone who reminded me of it? Like most people at the time, Marcia could not fit this *Hin-Jew* thing into her paradigm. I might as well have told her I was going out with an inflatable doll. A non-Jewish one.

One evening at my place, I said to Rani, "Hey, sweetie I just got an aerogramme from my sister."

"Does she know about us?"

"Oh, yes. I wrote her all about you and me." I was beaming with pride.

Rani tapped her fingers on the coffee table. "And what does she think about it."

"Well, she doesn't like it. But that's because she hasn't met you yet. And she is concerned for my safety. And she . . . never mind." As usual, my mouth was running at least a couple of seconds ahead of my brain.

"And never mind what?" Rani's fingers suddenly stopped tapping.

"Well she also thinks because we're so different from each other, it could be a problem."

"'A problem?'" Rani hashed that around in her pretty head for a moment. "Is that her way of saying because I'm not white she doesn't like me?"

"More like because you're not Jewish."

"So your people are afraid of mixed couples too. They are just like my people."

"Well, yes, but it's different with the Jews. Although many other Americans, and some Jews too, would hate seeing us together simply because they are bigots."

She tilted her head slightly. "How is it any different for the Jews?"

"The Jewish population is small, and we are historically unaccepted, so some Jews are afraid we could be assimilated into the other religions, and Judaism would eventually disappear. And the Jews in Europe were almost completely exterminated when the Nazis took over, so you can understand why Jews might be somewhat paranoid about that."

"Yes, but what is important for us is that your people . . . your family disapproves of my relationship with you." I was learning that

Rani was like a dog with a rag. Once she focused on something, there was no way of distracting her until *she* was ready to let go.

"Well, they wouldn't actually say they didn't like us being together, to your face."

Rani squinted and moved in on me. "So what? Sunil wouldn't say he disapproved of *us being together, to* your *face.* Then he punched me in *mine.*"

"See, that's the difference. Marcia would never punch me in the face." *Touche!*

"That's because you're a man and she's a woman. And I presume you're bigger than her."

I let out a sigh. "Yes, she's not much taller than you. Well, she did slap me around when she was bigger than me . . . when we were little kids." By this point, my mouth was now a full lap ahead of my brain.

Rani gritted her teeth. "So she *is* like Sunil. Just like Sunil!"

Of course, whether these two ladies might ever get a chance to wrestle *mujer contra mujer* was still up for grabs. But I didn't want Rani thinking these things about my family. If she were to meet them someday, I wanted her to feel comfortable, not combative. This conversation had been a splendid example of how I was not too savvy at understanding human behavior, much less influencing it in a fortuitous direction.

I had to admit we were challenging both families and cultures with our button-pushing romance. Although the dynamics might differ, Rani and I had become equal-opportunity offenders.

℘

The nefarious boat incident had knocked the wind out of our sails, as we realized complete strangers would go at least to the brink of murder to intimidate us. But though it made us more skittish, it also steeled our resolve to take the romance out of the closet and into the glare of Fiji's sunlight.

So armed with this contradictory attitude we went out on a few occasions to movies or a restaurant. Thankfully the stares seemed to be dying down, as if the shock value of our verboten relationship had dissipated, and people had moved on to something else to gawk at. Or maybe I was getting used to the stares, and they became part of the scenery. But Rani noticed the changes too.

"Do you think people are finally getting used to us?" she whispered one day at lunch at the Nanking.

"Could be. But I kind of miss being a celebrity," I said, and she smacked my hand playfully.

Our fellow diners went from loud to mute. All eyes turned toward us.

"So much for anonymity," I said as I pushed some chow fun around my plate. "But at least they are being a little more discrete and polite about it. As long as neither of us makes a sudden move, they don't seem to notice us—kind of like prey around their predators."

"Yeah, I guess that's some progress, but see how they like this." Rani nonchalantly flipped her long dark tresses over her shoulder as a score of eyes perked up to watch. "But some of them would still like to kill us if they thought they could get away with it."

"Speaking of such people, how's Sunil doing? Any more fallout since you stabbed his hand?"

"Not a word. I think he's afraid of me now. But my mum said something interesting." Rani covered her mouth as she started giggling.

"What is it? What did she say?"

It took her a while to stop laughing, and I loved that she felt comfortable being herself in a restaurant, despite the cold stares. Then she came in close and whispered, "She said my breasts are bigger since I started seeing you."

"Are you kidding me?" I had to laugh too. "I had no idea I had that effect on women. That's the nicest compliment anyone has ever paid me."

Rani looked somewhat baffled by my response. But she continued, "She says she likes you, but she told me not to let my dad find out."

"About your breasts or that she likes me?"

"Both."

"So I guess your mom doesn't buy the we're-just-friends story anymore. And yes, your dad—how is he taking our *friendship*."

"Not good. He goes around telling everyone our relationship is going to kill him."

I raised my head and peered into the panther eyes. "Come on. It can't be that bad."

A shadow passed across Rani's face. "Really, Will, I'm just repeating what I've heard him say. He says that to me. He says it to my mom, my uncle. I think he even tells his friends and the other teachers."

"That's terrible," I said. "He's being rather dramatic, don't you think?"

"He's reacting like most Indian fathers would react in a situation like this."

Was she defending his behavior? "So I guess he's not buying our friendship disguise, either."

Rani rested her cheek on a clenched fist, looked down, and released a sigh. Her response was clear and on target.

๑๏

Three days later, lightning struck in the form of a heart attack. Mani Gupta was dead; his prophecy, fulfilled. He was fifty-one.

It was 10:00 a.m. the following day when I found out. I was at my desk, and Rani had not yet showed up for work. I had a gut feeling she was not out with a sore throat. Her friend Sumi, the only person to whom she confided anything about the liaison, walked into our office and headed toward my desk. I watched as she approached me, the maroon skirt of her sari flowing beside her legs as if in slow motion, each step making me more apprehensive. Her head was shaking, and the whites of her eyes were pulsing in a way that signaled danger.

Then she hit the brakes in front of me and started speaking in a monotone. "Rani . . . asked . . . me . . . to . . . tell . . . you . . . her . . . father . . . has . . . died."

I felt as if I'd just been kicked in the stomach. "How did it happen?" I asked when I recovered some composure.

"They were eating dinner—Rani, her mom, and her dad. And then he suddenly got up and said he was having trouble breathing. He was walking to the couch when he grabbed his chest and fell to the floor. Rani went outside and hailed a cab, and they got him to the hospital, but it was too late. Mr. Gupta was already dead when they arrived. They said it was a heart attack."

"Oh my God! That's so awful!" I watched our conversation as if I were hovering above it, because this of all things could not actually be happening. Not here. Not now. "How is she? How is Rani taking it?"

"Very badly. Of course she is taking it very hard." Sumi threw a dismissive look my way. "And her mother is also taking it very badly."

"I must go to see her . . ."

Sumi put a finger to her lips, then looked around to see if anyone were watching us. Satisfied that no one was, she leaned in a little. "Rani said for you to leave her alone . . ."

I reeled back. "Leave her alone? She can't mean this. She's just upset. Understandably, but . . ."

"Let me finish, will you? She just wants you to leave her alone... for now. She'll contact you when she's ready. Don't go to her house. She's afraid of what they might do to her."

I sighed and shook my head. "Should I go to the funeral?" *Where did that come from?*

"I don't know. Why are you asking me?" And with that Sumi turned away and hurriedly exited the room.

∽

Days of mental anguish followed. My lover was grieving the death of her father, and I could do nothing to help her, except stay away. I felt a lump of responsibility for her father's demise, and the more I thought about it, the more the onus spread inside me. I had a part in making the woman I loved fatherless and her mother, a woman who liked me despite all reasons not to, into a widow. This was more responsibility than I could handle. I had thought I was simply getting into a romantic relationship. I had not signed up for these heavy layers of guilt and responsibility. With all good intentions, I had been complicit in destroying lives. Who was I to challenge another culture's traditions and values?

I then tried to tell myself that it wasn't our fault. *If anyone is responsible, it's those meddling bigots who told Mr. Gupta my relationship with his daughter brought shame on his family. And it was a heart attack. If Rani and I had not become a couple, he might have died at the next stressful episode in his life. Right?*

And then the guilt-ridden voice in my head countered: *But Mr. Gupta had no other significant stress in his life, and nothing could be as stressful as the position I put him in. Who am I to take an innocent man's life, and for what? Lust for a woman I may leave behind when my Peace Corps time in Fiji is up? What kind of monster have I become?*

I thought about my own parents, both of whom were felled like Mani Gupta way too young by heart attacks—my father at age forty-four and my mother when forty-seven. I remembered Mom had occasionally said, "William, you're worrying me to death," and "It's killing me that you don't practice harder at the piano." And so I blamed myself for murdering her. Ten-year-olds, after all, are still in the grip of the egocentricity of childhood. It was natural for me to think her sudden passing was all about me.

However, I was the lucky orphaned sibling when it came to guilt over Mom's demise. One of our aunts told Marcia point blank, "You killed your mother. She worried herself to death over *you*." But I didn't learn of this until many years later. And it was also much later I found out that if anything external to her had caused her early ending, it was my mom's reaction to my dad's passing. She was miserable during the forty months between their deaths but felt she had to keep going for her children. So one could reasonably argue she welcomed death and was happy when she reunited with the love of her life on the other side. At least I'd like to think that's how it played out.

Fourteen years after first flagellating myself with parenticide guilt, there I was retrieving the dead albatross from the attic in my mind and wrapping it around my neck once again. Although this time it was for my paramour's parent.

I could not be with Rani to help her grieve. I could not even be in contact with her. Unanswered questions racked my brain. Did everyone know of her father's prediction? Were they blaming Rani? Her mother? Me? Were they taking it out on those two in this their darkest hour? How was Rani holding up? Was she even safe now?

And what would become of the star-crossed lovers after this disaster? Would she even want to see me now if she could? Was she regretting our romance? Indeed, regretting ever meeting me?

It was maddening not to be able to communicate with her. I paced the floor in my flat always in the same formation—like a zoo tiger gone claustrophobic from his caged confines. I was unable to do anything in the physical world about the situation, while thought balloons exploded in my brain, telling me to do *something*. Anything. I wanted to go to her home, scoop her up in my arms, and run away with her. I pictured her family and friends screaming that we were murderers and throwing things at us as we made our getaway to some haven, any refuge where we could finally be left alone. I wanted to be there for her grieving, to hold her close and make it all better. But I knew none of this would happen.

Her father was dead. He was not coming back, though I wished I could turn the clock back a few days and use all my strength to prevent the minute hand from going forward.

I went to work in a fog. I felt I had become a zombie, dwelling in a world between life and death. I could see others, but they couldn't see me. At least I hoped they couldn't.

A few days after Rani's father died. I was sitting at my desk staring at the blank wall in front of me, hoping for some sort of saving vision, when I heard someone say my name seemingly from far away. I was pulled back into the world of the living.

"Will, I'm trying to talk to you?"

I slowly turned my head to the right. It was Sumi.

"I have a message from Rani."

I felt like a man dying of thirst in the desert, and here was a woman with a canteen suddenly appearing from nowhere.

"Oh my God. Well, what is it?" I wanted to reach out to Sumi and shake the message from her, which was probably why she backed off with an alarmed look on her face. I don't think I had physically done anything, but the undead look in my eyes was probably enough to freak anyone out.

"OK, OK. So I asked her what you asked me, whether you should attend the funeral." *Attend the funeral?* Oh right, I had asked her that . . . when? It had seemed like months earlier. "And she said, 'It's up to you, but yes, you can go.'"

I mouthed, "She said I can go," as if they were words handed down to me on a stone tablet. I mulled the words around in my dilapidated mind for a few seconds. *She said I can go.*

"I wrote out the details. It will be on the west bank of the Rewa River just before sunset tonight. Here," she said as she timidly handed me a folded piece of paper as if she were dispensing a dead rat to a hungry snake.

I took the paper and pleaded to Sumi, "But does she want me to go? Does she think I should go? Will I be able to talk with her there?"

"I don't know about all that. I told you what she told me. You can go if you want. You don't have to. But she won't be there."

"She's not going to her father's funeral?"

"No. Just the men go to the cremation."

"Oh. But did she tell you anything else to say to me?"

"No. We didn't have time to talk about *you*. There were a lot of people in her home—family, friends. She could not talk openly with me. You understand."

"Yes, of course. But . . . well, how is she?"

"Her father just died," she said as if she were speaking to an imbecile. Then something, perhaps my bleak expression, softened her. "She seems to be as you might expect at a time like this. I don't know how she really feels." Sumi hesitated for a moment and looked out the window. "I really have to be getting back to my work."

"I understand, but please, one more question." It was not easy getting it out. "Are they like . . . do they . . . do they blame her for her father's passing? Do they blame us?"

Sumi backed away. "I don't know what people are thinking. For now they are just getting used to the idea that he is gone. They are missing him and preparing for the funeral and such." She looked at a clock on the wall. "I must go."

I looked down as I began to speak. "Please tell Rani when you see her that I . . ." but Sumi was already standing by the elevator doors. I watched her as she entered the elevator, staring at me and slowly shaking her head in seeming disbelief.

CHAPTER TWENTY

The Anglia crept up the rumpled road near the riverbank. I turned off the ignition. I was a few miles from where the boating fiasco had taken place a few weeks earlier, and the terrain was almost identical. As then, I had a suffocating feeling that I was plunging forward into something that could soon be over my head. The horrors of that day rose from my gut as I surveyed a few cars and a couple of empty buses in the parking area.

I consciously knew what I was doing was dangerous—going to a funeral where the mourners held me complicit in taking the life of the deceased. I felt like the poster boy for insanity. But I also felt it was my mission to pay my last respects to Mani Gupta, no matter what might happen to me. I also felt compelled because I was starved for even this indirect contact with Rani, when all other doors between us had been locked. Perhaps word of my attendance would get back to her, and she would find some comfort in knowing that I paid my respects to her dad and hadn't let our adversaries intimidate me.

Despite my addled mind, I decided to do a couple of things that I thought would improve my odds of surviving the event. I arrived several minutes late, so the sun was starting to set—the oncoming darkness favored my anonymity. Similarly I thought the clip-on dark lenses over my gold-rimmed glasses would help hide my identity. The all-Indian audience would be already captivated by the ceremony and less likely to identify the tall white guy hiding behind shades. Yeah, right.

I sidled up behind the back row of a standing crowd of about a hundred men, all shorter than me. Everyone was facing the opposite direction, focused somewhat downhill on an extensive, dark pile of logs and sticks near the river's edge. On top of that pile, I could make out a bald, chubby man in a white suit lying on his back. He appeared as if he were taking a nap. There was some gray ash on his forehead. Red hibiscus petals were scattered over his suit. The smell of incense permeated the air.

I watched as Rani's brother Sunil walked counterclockwise around the pyre three times while throwing a yellow substance from a bowl, later verified as ghee (clarified butter), on the pyre. Then more wood was thrown on top of the body, partially covering it. Only the whiteness of Mr. Gupta's suit peeked out between the sticks and logs as daylight evaporated and colors faded.

Some men threw more ghee, and other things I didn't recognize, on the pile of wood. Nobody spoke. Sunil picked up a thick baseball-bat-sized wooden club, walked to a pot filled with embers, and stuck the top in it, lighting his torch like a giant match. He turned and held it out in front of him, showing it directly to the crowd, which reacted with some muttering. Though I assumed Sunil could not make out who I was in the darkness, the fire reflected in both his eyes seemed focused in my direction, and he did not move. After a while he made a speech, the words of which I couldn't decipher, but the emotion was clearly a mixture of pain and anger. It felt as if we were the only two people there. My eyes locked into his rage while my body vibrated from its impact. It was the strangest sensation. I could not look away.

Sunil turned and put a rubbery gray pot on his left shoulder and began to walk around the pyre again as he had done so before. Each time he completed the circle, a man from the crowd stepped forward with a knife and stabbed the pot, and a ribbon of liquid would start flowing from its wound. I winced a little at each plunge. After the third time, Sunil stopped walking and dropped the pot. Finally, he touched the head of the torch to the waiting pyre.

The flame spread quickly, and the pyre was totally engulfed within a couple of minutes, burning so intensely I could feel the blast of heat reach me from more than fifty feet away. The fire was sadly beautiful, and I stood there mesmerized by it for several minutes. I was so captivated, I didn't notice that after a while the other mourners were no longer paying much attention to the fire. Several of them had turned around, were visibly taken aback, and were shooting wide-eyed stares at me. I returned the crazed stares with one of my own. The men looked grotesque, frozen in the dancing orange light. And no doubt, so did I.

Sunil was already leaving from the other side of the crowd, and as he walked from the riverbank toward the parking area, an orderly parade of some other mourners followed him. I stood there like a deer caught in the pyre-light, not knowing whether to make a hasty exit or act nonchalant. I chose the latter as I watched the men pointing at me and talking about something, which I imagined was how it wouldn't be difficult to just throw me on the funeral pyre. After all, nobody would ever be the wiser about who had done it from among the hundred men there. And who would blame the perpetrators, anyway?

Officer, yes, he threw himself on the pyre. We tried to stop him, but he said it was the only way he could atone for his responsibility in Master Gupta's death.

But everyone was also at a funeral and probably felt the moderating tugs of religion and respect for the dead. So one by one, they pried away from staring at me and moved toward Sunil's parade of followers until only I was left to observe the crackling fire, now waning.

Later I would reflect that the only one there who could actually identify me was Sunil. That is, if he had noticed me at all. So perhaps the others had some doubt about my identity. My notoriety did not come with photos. To them I could have been a European acquaintance of the deceased, and their uncertainty about my identity was why they refrained from attacking me. But then I remembered I had been wearing clip-on sunglasses in the darkness, and that probably screamed *guilty* as much as it did *dorky*.

I waited a couple of more minutes after I heard the last vehicle drive away, then used the smoldering pyre-light and crescent moon to guide myself back to my car. I was mildly surprised that none of the tires were slashed. Nor were any of the windows broken. And no mob was waiting for me in the bushes.

Thank you, Krishna.

☙

"I hear you went to the funeral."

My friend Tom was sitting across from me at the Nanking slurping down wonton soup three nights after the cremation. I hadn't been able to talk with anyone at length about the week's events and was ready to burst. My roommate Emmett was off vacationing on the other side of the island.

"True. And I'm lucky to be here to tell the tale."

Which I then told, and Tom's response was, "That's some crazy shit you got going down, Lutwick." Then he added, "How's Rani holding up?"

"I wish I knew. All I get back from her friend Sumi is a bunch of general bullshit." I sighed. "For all I know, she never wants to see me again."

Tom looked toward the ceiling in contemplation. "Hmmm . . . that might not be the worst thing in the world, you know. You'd get out of this looking good," he said, then hesitated a moment. "Well not *that* good, what with her father dying suddenly and people feeling you're responsible and all. But good in that she'd be the one breaking it off, so what else could you do? You'd have to accept it. And you'd be a free man once again. Free to roam, you know, like the deer and the buffalo."

I finished chewing a chunk of sweet-and-sour pork. "Tom, I've thought about that, and though it would be nice to go back to living the somewhat normal life I used to, no, that's not how I want this to end."

"How do you want it to end? With a machete in your back?"

"Like I need to hear that." I sipped my beer and pondered. "Besides, I don't know that I'll ever want it to end."

"So you do love her?"

"Yes."

"But are you *in* love with her?"

"I think so, but it's impossible to know with all the craziness. Sometimes I think, maybe I'm just in love with the idea of her."

"Let me get this straight. You're in love with the idea of a woman who, because of your differences, makes having a normal relationship impossible. You have to watch your step every time you're in public. You have more than half the people in Fiji hating your very being. And when her father dies, they blame you and hate you so much that you can't even be in communication with her, much less be with her. And on top of all that, you don't even know if you're in love with her personally or just all these fun things she represents?"

"Yeah that sounds about right." I stared down at the floor, embarrassed.

Tom stood up, his face getting red. "Jesus H. Christ, Lutwick, can't you see how insane this is? You really could get yourself *and* her killed!"

"Sit down, man, and maybe I can try to explain it—to both of us." He sat, so I continued. "Before I came to Fiji, I didn't have much of a love life—unlike you, of course." I could see he liked that comment. "I've been hiding most of my life from confrontation, from bullies, even from just being with other people in social situations. I come here and I meet a girl who's straight out of my erotic dreams. And there's much more than just her looks. She's smart, she's got integrity, she's brave—she won't let anyone stop her from getting what she wants or doing what she thinks is right. And she seems to like me too. We work together, so we can't help being with each other. We know a romance is absolutely out of the question, but we can't stop ourselves, and pretty soon we're meeting in secret. I don't know about you, but I find the taboo to be a turn-on." I could see from his pursed lips and a slight nod that Tom was intrigued, but not yet buying. "And it's also invigorating to say no to the mob when the mob is not only wrong, it's none of their goddamn business. At the same time, trying to carry on a romance this way is a nuisance at best and dangerous too—you're right—but we don't have the option of turning any of that off. The only option is turning the relationship off, and I refuse to do that, not unless Rani or I decide that it's over. And she's the one most in harm's way. So if she chooses to keep going, then I do too. Meanwhile, how can we truly know how we feel about each other with all the madness spinning around us?

"Exactly, don't you see you're in a catch-22? You can't see how you honestly feel about her in the midst of all this turmoil, but that's all there is." Tom gathered his thoughts, then continued, "It's not going to somehow miraculously disappear. That is unless you marry her and take her back to the States, in which case you will have let the mob decide by forcing your hand to choose marriage. In short, you're fucked, my man."

I pushed my angst aside, shook my head, and said, "Well, at least then I'd have the satisfaction of knowing that they drove us to do the exact opposite of what they wanted."

"But maybe the exact opposite of what you wanted."

This was starting to seem like a chess game, and although I was exasperated, I felt compelled to play it out. "Maybe yes, maybe no, but in their case definitely not what they wanted, so I get a half point, they get none, and I win."

"Yes, but they will have gotten rid of the both of you. Point for the Indians. They go on with their lives and forget about you two, while you're stuck with the consequences. Second point for their side. You lose."

I was getting fed up with this conversation, probably because it was too close to the truth. "Life's not a game, Tom."

He looked up from his beer. "Oh really? Since when?"

❦

After a death, the living must move on. I knew she wouldn't stay away from work forever. Trying to stay positive, I had fantasized our reunion moment for days. She'd come into the office and sneak up behind me. She'd tap my shoulder, and we'd kiss passionately. Everyone else in the office would break into spontaneous applause. Then we'd go upstairs and make wild monkey love on the conference room table. Or under it. Wherever.

Of course, it didn't turn out *quite* that way.

When Rani did return, she had a scowl on a face that for once looked less than perfect. Whatever had happened to her in the eight days since her father's death had taken its toll. Her posture was slumped, her eyes sunken, and her hair frayed. She went straight to her desk, put her handbag down, and went into her boss's office to talk with him. She didn't even look in my direction. A few minutes later, she came out and sat down with some handwritten notes and began typing away.

I went up to her, ready to explode with a dozen conflicting emotions and a thousand questions.

"Oh, hi Will."

OH, HI WILL?!

"Rani, I . . ."

She stopped me short, thrusting her palm toward my face while continuing to look down. "Don't start, Will. Please. We'll talk later." Even her voice sounded different—flat, breaking up.

"What is it? The other people in our office? They all know about us. I don't care about that anymore."

"Well, I do, so we'll talk later . . . at lunch. And I need some time to just be back at work—before we get into it."

Into what? "But I've missed you so much. I'm so sorry about your father. And . . ."

Again, the palm of her hand stopped me from talking further. I sensed the others in the room, some half a dozen people, all had their eyes focused on us. "Well, Rani, if you leave me no choice . . ." I backed away like a rejected puppy.

"At lunch, Will. Then we'll talk." Her voice was emotionless.

We walked towards the conference room. We had been silent the whole way from our office. She looked down the whole time, not giving me even a glimpse of an opening.

Maybe that message about not wanting to see me had meant what I had feared.

She unlocked the conference room door, and we both sat, turning our chairs to face each other.

We looked at each other silently, and I knew things had changed forever.

Tears welled up in her eyes. And in mine too.

I took her hand in mine. She climbed into my lap and put her arms around my neck, and we held each other as the tears rained on the pile carpet below. I rocked her like a child for what felt like an eternity.

Nothing needed to be said.

That night she came back to my flat, and I finally found out what had happened during our crucial week apart. Even more than Rani, her mother was devastated and spent much of her time secluded in her bedroom. Sunil was aloof when around his mother, but kept his simmering anger from boiling over in front of her. Not so for Rani— he openly blamed her for killing their father. They had yelled at each other when the non-family guests had departed, but it never got physically violent. Rani had three other sisters and another brother living in Suva who monitored a physical cease-fire in the war between their siblings. Two other sisters had emigrated to Canada and England but were too poor to come back to Fiji for the mourning period.

"But what about later; do you think Sunil will try again to hurt you?"

"No," Rani answered quickly, but then thought about it and said, "Two reasons. My father told us the night Sunil hit me that the violence had gone far enough, and I think Sunil knew he meant that for forever. So Sunil has to respect his father's wishes, particularly now that he's died. And like I've told you, he's rather afraid of me since I stabbed him in the hand."

"Yeah, I would be."

"Don't worry. I only stab men who do bad things to me." At least she was smiling when she said it.

"Glad to hear that." Then I shifted gears to talk about one of the two eight-hundred-pound gorillas sitting patiently in the room. "So we're still OK, you and me? I mean, you still want to continue being together?"

"I don't know, Will." I shuddered, not expecting that, but she continued, "I just lost my dad. Right now, I can only decide things about today, not tomorrow. Let's put it this way—I'm still OK . . . we're still OK, till one of us says we're not. And so today we're still good. Unless you have decided to end it."

"No. I've missed you terribly. I want us to continue." And then I dropped the other gorilla right in her lap. "Rani, do you think we . . . I mean our relationship . . . do you think it had something to do with your father's death?"

"Yes," she snapped. "We killed him. Are you happy now?" Her dark eyes glowed and shot angry flares my way, reminding me of Sunil's fiery glare at the cremation.

"No," I said hanging my head, "I shouldn't have asked that stupid question."

"Good. And don't bother to get up. I'll manage my way home on my own."

CHAPTER TWENTY-ONE

The flames of anger died down, but she kept her distance. I tried to keep in mind she had been through a horrendous double trauma—her father's death and people blaming her for it. She needed some time to process all that and heal. My well-intentioned but bumbling presence would only keep opening the wound for her.

I'd watch her at work and began to realize how terribly I had handled our relationship. I hadn't protected her. I had been impotent in taking control of the situation. It probably seemed to her that I had reacted to her father's death with morbid curiosity more than comforting reassurance.

Rani always took the brunt of the anger and repercussions our controversy created. Although I told myself I would have wanted to take on most of the burden, I wondered, did I really? Could I have put up with what she had for the sake of our relationship? And if not, how could I have expected her to do so? And to continue especially now that her father had died. This only turned up the heat on her. What kind of man would allow his sweetheart to be treated this way?

I had strung out the romance for my own personal pleasure and inability to make a decision, waiting for a break from the tumult, an intermission that would never come. I had these vague altruistic arguments about making the world safe for forbidden love and not giving in to prejudice—the kind you might argue late at night in your college dorm with other intellectual wannabes. But this was no ivory tower; it was the real world, and it didn't give a damn about high-minded platitudes. Rani was in the trenches in our war, dodging machetes and being wounded, and I was on the sidelines cheerleading through a megaphone. The stark contrasts of that picture in my mind's eye were humbling and emasculating.

Perhaps the right thing to do would be for me to break it off, even though I didn't want to lose her. Maybe it was what she secretly wanted—to end her nightmare. After all, she said no Indians would ever accept our marriage. Maybe she was continuing primarily out of consideration for me and my feelings. Or perhaps her family members thought she had casually embarked on a dangerous liaison that shamed them, a relationship that they felt had brought on her father's death. Then she might feel she could never break it off, in order to show how serious her intent had always been. However, if she became the jilted lover, then she would become a more sympathetic figure to them. Was she hoping I would break it off, freeing her from such a trap?

But regardless of her motivation, how much longer could she put up with the madness before telling me to permanently get out of her life? For the first time, I genuinely thought that I might lose her forever, and it hurt to even think about life without my beloved Rani.

But something was still holding me back. What was I waiting for?

❧

Rani's anger gradually dissipated and we resumed the relationship, but it seemed changed in a way I couldn't quite bring into focus. She seemed distant; her spirit had taken a severe beating and along with it, the virtue of our togetherness. It felt as if I were losing her.

At work one morning, she walked toward my desk. She had the look on her face of someone who had just had the wind knocked out of her. I thought, *oh shit, now what?*

She leaned on my desk to support herself. "Will, I've been told that Sunil and my father's brother, Kumar—they're talking about kidnapping me and forcing me to marry an Indian. It won't happen for a few weeks; they have to line up someone, make arrangements with his family, but . . ."

Something essential snapped inside me. I jumped from my chair, got down on one knee, took her right hand in mine, and looked into those liquid dark eyes. I was hyperventilating. A white aura surrounded her body.

"Rani Vinita Gupta, will you marry me?"

"Are you serious?"

"Never been more serious in my life."

"Are you sure you want to do this?"

"I am absolutely sure, and I'm hoping your answer is yes."

"But why now?"

"Why not now? Listen, Rani, I've been thinking about this for months and all this thinking, it's making me sick and getting me . . . us . . . nowhere. I've been *thinking* when I should have been *doing*. So I just heard what I'd been waiting for, I guess, not that I knew I was waiting for it. For sure, I didn't know they were thinking of kidnapping you, but the thought of losing you to another man, of letting them do one more fucking thing to you . . ."

"Stop it, Will."

Uh-oh, didn't see this coming. "So the answer is no? Maybe you need some time to think . . ."

"No, the answer is yes, I just don't want to have to wait another second to give you my answer."

"Yes?"

"YES, YES, YES!!!"

"Yes to not waiting for me to shut up or yes to my proposal."

"Both."

"Oh, well, that's a relief."

We simultaneously broke into childlike laughter. She leaned down to pull my head toward her and kissed me. We embraced and I heard people clapping. Then that just dissolved into the background.

For in that moment, it was just two hearts melting into one, nothing else but the world spinning round and the Beatles singing "All You Need Is Love."

∿

It had been six months since we first took our working relationship into another dimension. Although there were many remarkable things that happened during our courtship, the most surprising thing to me was something that didn't happen. Rani never once pressured me to propose marriage to her, even though the strain on her was intolerable, and marriage was the conclusion she wanted. Sometime after she said *yes*, I asked her how she could have been so patient. Her response was "I believe everyone needs to do what's right for them, to follow their destiny with as little interference as possible. So you had to decide whether or not to marry me on your own schedule. And because I loved you, I wanted to do what was right for you."

Our engagement would not calm the forces against us. Rani had indicated that marriage would never legitimize our relationship for most of our adversaries. Instead, our plan for matrimony would stoke the fire of their anger and motivate them to try to stop us. Meanwhile, we had a wedding to plan and were in a race against a potential kidnapping and a forced arranged marriage. Which team would cross the finish line first was up for grabs. And we were further handicapped by having to keep it all quiet. The last thing we needed was for the opposition to learn of our plans and literally crash the wedding, perhaps with a show of violence. Yes, that would make it memorable, but not quite in the way we would prefer.

. . . and look honey, here's a picture of your Uncle Kumar swinging in on the chandelier as he lands on the wedding cake. Perfect timing, because the reception was starting to drag. And remember this one? That's Sunil with his machete rushing toward you while I'm breaking a Fiji Bitter bottle over his

head. He was such a cutup that day. Luckily the guests thought it was all part of the entertainment.

Logically then, we should have had a justice of the peace meet just the two of us in a secluded place—perhaps the middle of a mucky mangrove swamp or in a cave in the mountains—say our vows, and be done with it. Yet you don't get married every day, and I was not in the mood to be a minimalist after all the aggravation we'd been through. This was no time to begin doing things sensibly. After all, defying logic had been our hallmark since Day One, and there we were, still together despite everything. Taking stupid risks had obviously worked so well for us. Why change tactics just before crossing the finish line?

I wanted us to have a fun reception and Rani was agreeable with that, but wanted to leave the details to me. I figured I would pick a wedding site by checking out those at premium prices, then work my way down to get something reasonable. So I tried first with the most distinguished hotel in all of Fiji. The Grand Pacific was built by The Union Steamship Company in 1914 to serve passengers on its trans-pacific routes. Its rooms were designed to make the passengers think they had never gone ashore—they were like first-class staterooms, complete with saltwater bathrooms and plumbing fixtures similar to those onboard their ship. The logic of pretending you were not actually at the places you chose to visit escaped me, but then I had never been part of the early-twentieth-century luxury-cruise target market.

Just four months earlier the reigning queen of the British Empire and Prince Phillip had bunked there for a couple of nights. They had been visiting Fiji to celebrate its impending independence from themselves. So I thought the Grand Pacific might be up to my sophisticated standards. Worth a look-see and a laugh when I would hear the price to produce a wedding there. It was only a five-minute walk from where I worked, so I stopped in there during my lunch break the day after the proposal.

A Fijian man in traditional dress pointed me toward a teakwood door marked "Banquets: Bryan Wadsworth." I knocked and was ushered into his office by a thirtyish British guy dressed in a sparkling white naval-like outfit that would have been suitable for the commander of a grand cruise ship. Possibly a further nod to the you're-still-onboard motif upon which the hotel was founded. I immediately felt out of place in my grubby jeans and a goofy Fijian *bula* shirt, a top similar to its garish *Aloha* cousin.

Mr. Wadsworth looked distracted. I wondered if he perceived me as one of those Peace Corps rubes who by both example and intention were destroying the concoction of European superiority in Fiji's final days as a colony. His compatriots and their ancestors had expended so much effort for over a century cultivating the façade of the white man's supremacy in those islands, and then we Peace Corps types showed up and ruined the party in no time at all.

"Are you interested in scheduling a banquet?" I always got a kick out of the British pronunciation of *scheduling*—the soft "sh" sound in the first syllable made the speaker sound inebriated—well, to this Yank, anyway.

"Yes, I am, Bryan. I'm thinking of getting married next weekend and wonder if you have a room available for the reception."

"My goodness! That is rather short notice. How many people."

"Good question. I don't know. Forty . . . forty-five, tops. Just friends. No family in attendance."

"No family? Oh my. But . . . then that's not my concern. Let me see here . . ." he peered into a large black leather book, "Well yes, we can nicely accommodate a crowd that size in our Hibsicus Room."

"How much?"

He quoted a price of about four hundred U.S. dollars. I gulped as I thought about it.

"That's a lot for just a room for one night."

"It does include our standard full buffet dinner for forty-five people, Mr. Lutwick."

"Of course, I know that." Of course, I didn't. "And the music and drinks? Maybe a photographer?"

"Those would be extra."

"Great. We'll bring our own. Deal, Bryan?"

"Deal." We shook on it.

After I signed off on some papers and wrote him a check, he said, "One last thing, Mr. Lutwick, we need the bride's name. You understand . . . for the sign in the lobby."

I hadn't planned on that. "I think we'll just keep that a secret for now. OK, mate?" And then walking further out on the limb, I told him, "Actually, it's a surprise."

∽

I prepared the invitation and Rani printed copies on the mimeograph machine at our office.

> *You are cordially invited to the reception for the world's first underground Hindu-Jewish wedding*
>
> *Pairing Miss Rani Vinita Gupta of Suva, Fiji and Mr. William Roy Lutwick of Richmond, Virginia, United States*
>
> *The Grand Pacific Hotel, Suva*
>
> *Saturday the eighteenth of July in the year nineteen hundred and seventy at half-past seven o'clock in the evening*
>
> *Dinner will be served*

I wanted to add "Attire: Camouflage semiformal with battle helmet recommended. Weapons to be distributed to guests at the discretion of the wedding party," but Rani was not amused. The front of the invitation consisted of a Star of David, the symbol Om, and wedding bells. My rudimentary artwork would have to suffice.

The printed invitation was only for the reception. The wedding ceremony was to be held in that top-secret place—my flat. Like none of our adversaries could ever possibly guess that. But to limit any chance of the word getting out, there would be only four of my closest Peace Corps friends in attendance. We timed it for just before the reception to limit the window of disaster. Lining up a justice of the peace on short notice proved surprisingly easy, and he agreed to wait till the wedding itself to get the bride's name. Although I doubt the *surprise-wedding* excuse was any more convincing for him than it had been for the banquets manager at The Grand Pacific Hotel.

Sadly, none of Rani's friends or family were invited to either the ceremony or the reception. We couldn't chance the word might get out to the potential wedding-busters. We also didn't want to put any of those she cared about on the spot for attending, although almost all of them would have boycotted it anyway. Even Rani's heroic mother would not be able to attend her beloved daughter's wedding taking place just a few miles from her home. It was heartbreaking, but necessary.

In the case of my family and friends back in the States, there just wasn't time for them to be invited and make plans to come eight thousand miles. So the guest list consisted exclusively of my Fiji-based friends, most of them Peace Corps Volunteers, and some of our coworkers.

I put a Peace Corps friend in charge of the music (homemade tapes played on a reel-to-reel player), put another in charge of photography, and bought several cases of Fiji Bitter at the brewery to be delivered to the hotel. We were set to party.

With a few hours of effort, I had set up a wedding reception costing only a few hundred dollars at a hotel literally fit for *the* Queen, on nine days notice in a Third World country. I don't know why people make such a big deal of this wedding-planning thing. It can be such a breeze.

Of course, we did have that one little security issue racing after us like a great white shark. Whether it would pull us under before we could pull off the wedding—that was anyone's guess.

॰૭

We had the wedding fully planned when I realized I had forgotten one minor detail. I had purposefully never consulted with the controversy-averse Peace Corps Administration about my relationship with Rani. Not to mention that little car issue I had been hiding from them.

I didn't want to stay in Fiji any longer than we had to, mainly because of continued concern about potential violence. Given the hostile environment and the trauma surrounding her family and our relationship, staying in Fiji was not a viable option. We wanted to make a fresh start where we wouldn't be the local freak show with a hostile audience. So, I really had to get the Peace Corps on board with the plan—and pronto.

To my surprise, the local office was very accommodating. There I was admitting that not only had I broken their biggest commandment, *Thou shalt not piss off the locals*, I was the first in Fiji to take it to the level of a majority of the citizenry. Yet they didn't give me a hard time about it. They even offered to pull strings to expedite the immigration paperwork for Rani, so we could leave for the States in about one month. It was almost as if they couldn't get rid of us fast enough.

Hmmm . . . ?

CHAPTER TWENTY-TWO

T he day before the wedding, I left work and drove home as I usually did. I pulled into my driveway with outsized anticipation for the next day's events, pleased that nothing had gone wrong yet to interrupt them. I was about to open the back door when I suddenly felt transported to a dizzy, rolling world where a black cloud was closing in, suffocating me. I had no idea what was happening or its cause. I couldn't go inside. I had to get out of there— out of Fiji. I started walking northeast—toward the United States. I felt nauseous and was salivating like bulldog. Sweat was flowing from all over my body. My heart was racing, but my thoughts were the scariest part. *Oh shit. Oh God. I don't think I love this girl. We have nothing in common. This won't work. I'm too young and immature to be married. What the hell was I thinking? It's too late to stop it. We have guests coming. Everyone will hate me and for good reason. This is just like with Billie. I tried to talk myself into loving her until I could no longer deny the truth. I'm not capable of real love.*

This cerebral self-flagellation kept going on until I realized I was lost geographically as well as mentally. I leaned against a coconut palm to catch my breath. After a while, the rest of the world stopped spinning, and I got my earthly bearings. I started back toward home, my mind still racing, so caught up in the vicious cycle of my thoughts and emotions that I walked almost all the way to the ocean, a half-mile past my flat, before realizing what I had done. Finally finding my way there, I collapsed on my bed, immediately falling asleep and into a dream.

I'm walking down the street, and Rani is beside me. We are in a large American city, maybe New York. All the people on the street are Indians. They are staring at us with enraged, piercing eyes. We stop at a bench in front of a large tree and sit down. Rani tells me, "You don't have to marry me. I know you're not in love with me."

"But I do love you, at least I think I do."

"That's not what you were thinking before."

"I just panicked. All the craziness. How do I know if I'm in love?"

Just then four Indian men jump from behind the tree, grab Rani, and one holds a pistol to the side of her head. "What's it going to be, sahib? You or the girl?"

I rush toward them. The gun goes off—a blast of fire, a ball of smoke . . .

I bolted upright in my bed, my ears still ringing from the cerebral gunfire.

∞

"Will, wake up. Time to get your ass married."

Emmett was shaking my shoulder. I rubbed the sleep from my eyes and the drool from my chin. The daylight was blinding. "What time is it?"

"Time for you got to get crackin' and me to get packin'."

"Huh . . . what?"

"Man, have you forgotten? Today you lose your freedom. Tomorrow I get mine." Emmett had had it with the Peace Corps life and was homesick, so he was heading back to the States early. Not wanting to miss the wedding, he moved his flight back to the day after it.

As I tuned into the physical world, the prior day's conscious and unconscious nightmares came fluttering back. I felt dizzy. "Emmett, I don't know if I can go through with this."

"Aw, that's just wedding-day jitters. Happens all the time. Or so I'm told."

"No, really. I don't know if I'm in love."

"Shee-it, man. Have you gone plumb loco? Well, I think you're in love."

"You do? How can you tell?"

"Could it be because you've gone through hell and put your life on the line to be with this little girlie? Could it be because you've made it to this point, despite all those people trying to stop you?" Emmett put his hand on my shoulder. "Lookee here Will, when we first met you at Peace Corps training, me, the other guys in our group—we all thought you were a wimp. No offense."

"None taken."

"Good. So when you started going with Rani, we all thought you'd fold at the first sign of trouble. We'd have all bet against you except nobody wanted to take your side."

"Thanks. That's very reassuring."

"Anyway, this relationship you have with Rani has completely changed how you seem to us. Now we see a man instead of a wimp. Maybe a crazy man on the verge of a nervous breakdown, but still a man. If she can have that effect on you, why would you ever let her go?"

"I hadn't really looked at it that way."

"So if you don't go through with this wedding, you'll undo all that magic. Is that what you want to happen?"

"No. I want to keep the magic. Magic is good." I was still half asleep.

"And if you don't go through with this wedding, you'll have all your Peace Corps friends *and* Rani hating you. With so many people in Fiji already wanting to skin you alive, do you really want more enemies?"

"No, I guess I have enough enemies. More enemies would be bad."

"So what's it going to be?"

"I'm . . . marrying . . . Rani . . . today." The words came out slowly and not just because I was groggy. I knew this was total commitment. There would be no more hesitation, no turning back.

Emmett backed away from me and said, "Unless . . ."

"Unless what?"

"Unless she comes to her senses and dumps you."

"Yes, there's always that possibility." I glanced at my watch. "Oh shit! I've got to get ready. I'm getting my ass married today."

∽

Emmett's pep talk did the trick. Or at least from that point on, all I could think about were wedding necessities and logistics. The awful thoughts of the previous day were forgotten as I moved into obsession mode over whether we would get through the day without a catastrophe from violence. Or perhaps from a more mundane cause, such as Rani coming to her senses.

Rani was still at her house. We were to meet at the appointed hour in our secluded spot a block away. I had not seen her in almost twenty-four hours. *What if she doesn't show up? What if they know about the wedding and are waiting till the last minute to kidnap her? What if she's already been married off to some Indian guy? What if she does come to her senses like Emmett said? What if the beer doesn't show up?*

My mind was consumed by a thousand *what-if*s that could derail our special day.

"Stop pacing and talking to yourself. Calm down, will ya?" said Emmett.

"Was I doing that? Well, there are so many things that could turn this day into a disaster."

"Yeah, I'm going to really miss having you as my roomie. Hey them weenies, they're not going to attack our flat, are they?"

"No, you'll probably get out of Fiji in one piece tomorrow."

"Probably? Well I better, because there's a truckload of honeys, and they're gonna be mighty ticked off if I'm not on that plane when it touches down on Texas soil."

But I was already drifting away, biting my nails, pacing the floor, lost in my world of anxiety and doom.

∽

With Emmett going back to the States, my new roommate, Bob, was already living with us. Bob and I had been good friends when I lived in Lautoka on the western side of Viti Levu. As I had done before him, he managed to get the Peace Corps to transfer him to Suva and away from a job he hated. To pull that off, he had to get himself in trouble over his old job. He tried to get his cooperative to have an overdue board election where the more crooked members might actually be replaced. This benign quest could have gotten him kicked out of the Peace Corps. After all, it did offend a group of local hosts, even though they happened to be a bunch of scoundrels. But instead, he talked his way into a Suva job. Until Emmett would leave, we had Bob sleeping in the Pleasure Dome.

To complete the guest list for the ceremony, Peace Corps friends Bill and Tom arrived at four o'clock to lend moral support and help me get set up for the wedding scheduled to start two hours later.

As they came in the front door, Tom said "Hey, Lutwick, I just saw three creepy guys with knives and a map standing in front of your place. I think they were planning something."

"Oh shit. Where are they?" I bolted for the window and pushed the drape aside, just enough so I could peek outside. I didn't see anyone. "They must have gone into hiding when they saw you guys coming here. Oh God, I knew something like this would happen." I turned around in time to see my friends bursting into laughter.

"Very funny, Tom. That's the last time I make you best man at my wedding."

"Yeah, that'll teach him," said Bob.

"Hey, I tried to talk him out of it," said Bill.

"Sure you did, Bill. Look, I don't have time to amuse you guys anymore. You can go in the Pleasure Dome and amuse yourselves. On second thought, I need you for other stuff. I've got to go pick up Rani. Bob, would you queue up the music on the tape recorder, so it's at the beginning of that Stones song when the ceremony starts? Emmett, would you straighten up the place? We've got a wedding here in a couple of hours, and it looks like a dump. Bill and Tom . . . Actually, why don't you two come with me and . . . oh yeah . . . grab some knives from the kitchen, just in case."

Tom said, "In case of what? Are you planning on carving a turkey while you drive?"

"No turkey, but better safe than sorry. You know about her family's kidnapping plan, right? I just don't want anything to go wrong at the last minute."

"And arming us with kitchen knives is going to prevent that? Get a grip, Lutwick."

"It's better than nothing."

"Better keep the cutlery away from this dude," Emmett said, pointing at me. "Will's more dangerous with a knife right now than a rattlesnake in heat."

～

I rolled the car up to the patch of mangrove swamp where I usually dropped her off. I had wanted to be there first, so she wouldn't have to wait at all and risk detection. But we were running a couple of minutes after the appointed time.

"Shit, she's supposed to be here already. I have a bad feeling about this," I said, slinking down in my seat to avoid detection. I just wanted so badly for the wedding ceremony to be over. "Hey guys, get down in your seat, so no one can see you."

"Oh man, look at me, I'm James Bond," said Bill as Tom passed him the open beer bottle in the backseat.

Tom said, "Hey Lutwick, don't look now, but an Indian is running toward us."

"Oh fucking shit! Get the knives ready!" I gasped, turning to see only Rani pressing the door latch and my friends howling as I had taken the bait yet again.

"Hey Bill, Tom. What's so funny?" she said.

"Never mind those fools," I said with a mixture of anger and relief. "Don't I get a *hello*?"

"The face looks familiar, but I'm not sure we've been introduced." She kissed my cheek.

"Cute. How are things at home? Do you think your family is on to us?"

"Yeah, here comes Sunil with a machete," she said, tranquil as a trade wind.

"Did those guys in the backseat write your lines?" I wasn't going to be the butt of yet another boy-or-girl-cries-wolf joke.

"No. I know how nervous you are. I couldn't resist. You're so cute when you're . . . when you're paranoid. Is that the word?"

"Yeah, that's definitely the word for me today. Now close the door, and let's go get our asses married!"

I floored the pedal and the Anglia took off, splattering gray mud in its wake. All four of us let out a simultaneous whoop as we sped down the road to destiny.

֎

We got back home safely, and I fell back into my default mode of biting my nails and manic pacing. At least we had passed one key threshold in whisking Rani away from her home, with two more to go: the ceremony and the reception. My four Peace Corps friends, and even Rani, seemed relaxed, but I just couldn't escape a gnawing fear that someone would try to stop our wedding or at least go berserk and do some damage. Things were just going too perfectly. I feared it was the calm before the storm.

Rani and I went into my bedroom to powwow.

"How come you're so calm?" I had to ask her.

"Because it's my wedding day? Because nothing has happened yet? Because if they've decided to make a scene, there's nothing I can do about that? I don't know. I prefer to be an optimist."

"Great. That means I have to do enough worrying for the both of us."

Rani shook her head as if she might be having second thoughts about the loony-tunes guy she was marrying. Or maybe that was my derangement talking again.

She went in the bathroom to make herself even more beautiful.

Tom came over to me and put his hands on my shoulders. "Lutwick, would you just relax? You're driving everyone crazy with your lunatic imitation. We got Rani, no problem. In less than an hour you'll be a married man. Hmmm . . . forget what I just said—now *that* is something to be nervous about."

"Seriously Tom, you don't know all the things that could still happen to royally screw this up."

Emmett overheard the conversation and came over to us. "How's about I fire up this here pipe? Maybe that will take the edge off Mr. Worrywart."

I thought about it. "You know, I felt like I wanted to be straight for this, but I'm such a mess, I suppose a toke would help me relax and get through it. Not enough to get stoned though. I still want to be ready for the unexpected."

"Yeah, right," Emmett said.

"Well, we can't do it inside because the Justice of the Peace is going to be here soon, and that weed of yours, Emmett, it's pretty stinky, given it's also weak. And we can't do it out back in the daylight cause the neighbors might see us. So we'll stand inside at the back window, then blow all the smoke outside."

Bob ambled over. "Yeah, that works for me."

I knocked on the bathroom door and told Rani what we were doing. "Should I assume you don't want to join in?"

"Don't be ridiculous. I'm certainly not going to try *ganja* for the first time just before my own wedding. But you go ahead."

"Really, are you OK with me doing a toke? I won't get stoned or anything."

"Will, if it stops you from driving everyone crazy it will be worth it. Just do it."

I took only one toke as the corncob pipe was passed among the five of us. I told the guys I wasn't feeling anything. "Must be my nervousness." But Emmett filled the pipe again, so I decided to take a toke of that one. And then, still waiting for it to hit me, I figured I might as well do one more hit of Emmett's low-grade weed.

Or so I had thought, because suddenly it seemed as if I were watching a movie of me and my friends in slow motion.

"Hey Emmett—what was in that second bowl?" I asked him.

"Oh yeah, forgot to tell you, I met some hippie freak. He was working on one of the cruise ships here last week—he was from Texas, even, and he sold me a bit of his stash. Called it *Acapulco Gold*, I think. Pretty good stuff, huh?"

"Oh man, that's some far-out weed." Bill slurred his words or maybe my brain just slurred them for him.

"Great pot you got there, but I still have a wedding to do. You did this on purpose, Emmett."

"Man, I had to do something to put you out of *our* misery. Not to mention I have to use this stuff up. Can't take it with me when I fly home tomorrow."

The conversation floated on for a few more minutes in that inane way it does when a bunch of immature young men get stoned. Then a sound I perceived as a knock at the front door entered my movie, stage right.

Wonder who that could be? Someone who wants to get high? And then I remembered. *Holy shit! I'm stoned out of my gourd, and I'm supposed to be getting married in a few minutes. Maybe it's the friggin' guy who's supposed to marry us! This is not good I think, for me to be so-o-o-o stoned.*

I looked at my watch: 4:45. I thought, *I really like my watch. It's been with me through thick and thin with Rani. Rani? Uh-oh, she's not gonna like me getting this stoned, because we're getting married today. Oh wow—I'm going to be starring in my own wedding. How cool is that?*

The knock was louder the second time, and it scared me straight, or at least in that general direction. Rani had moved from the bathroom and was changing clothes in my bedroom. I skewed up my persona to appear dignified. After all, I was wearing my dark blue suit and a silk rep tie with diagonal blue, red, and yellow stripes. *That should do it, right?* And then I finally opened the door to let the man who was supposed to marry us into my humble abode.

"Vijay Sharma, Justice of the Peace," he said as he vigorously shook my limp hand. "At your service."

It took me quite a while, or so it seemed, to get my dropped jaw back in its sockets.

"Are we doing this inside or out?" he asked me as he walked in.

Finally I got it together enough to say, "Inside . . . but excuse me, Mr. Sharma, I was expecting a Fiji native Justice of the Peace. His name escapes me at the moment." At that moment, even my name escaped me.

"Oh yes, Mr. Lutwick, that would be my eminent colleague, Talei Vanuaonoilau. He had a family emergency. His wife had a baby earlier than expected, so I'm here in his place. A new baby is always a joyous occasion, don't you think?"

"Oh." That was the best I could come up with as I continued standing there looking at and through the Indian man standing in front of me. The thought occurred to me that this was some sort of setup where my worst fears were coming to fruition. I peered behind him to see if he were being followed.

"Is there some problem, Mr. Lutwick?"

"Nothing personal, Mr. Sharma, but my fiancée is like you. She's . . ."

At that moment, Rani came bounding out of my bedroom. "How do I look," she asked, pirouetting to show us her shimmering mane of hair and skimpy lilac minidress that barely infringed on her thighs. Then seeing our Justice of the Peace, she reflexively covered herself like she was naked and her jaw, as mine had before, dropped. "Why is there an Indian man standing in front of me? Is he here to kidnap me?"

Vijay Sharma looked as bewildered as Rani did, then after a double take said, "Oh you must be that couple I've been hearing about. I understand now why you did not leave the bride's name." Rani moved one foot backward and raised her arms, getting into a fight-or-flight stance.

"Yes," I said. "That would be us. This is Rani Gupta."

"Well, it is very nice to meet you both, and I'm honored to officiate at your wedding."

"You are?" Rani and I spoke, simultaneously incredulous. I was blown away by both what I was hearing and what I'd been smoking. The combination was beyond surreal.

"Yes, it would be an honor," said Vijay Sharma, somewhat perturbed we were giving him the third degree.

I replied, "Because if you're not OK with doing this—we know marrying us could put you in a delicate position—then we can reschedule with the Fijian gentleman." Although it was more than a bit late to reschedule the reception, a concept my impeded brain could not assemble at that particular moment.

"Well, that is your choice, Mr. Lutwick."

"But why would you see marrying us as an honor?"

He paused, then opened his hands. "You see, I officiate at maybe fifty weddings a year. I see couples of all the races in Fiji getting married here in Suva and mixed-race marriages happen from time to time. On several occasions, I have married a European and Fijian couple. Once, I married a Chinese man and a Fijian woman. But never do I see an Indian marrying a non-Indian. And I do not know if it has ever happened before in Fiji, but why should my people be the only ones never to mix with the others? This does not seem right to me. So to be able to say I married a European man . . . an American, to an Indian woman, this would be a great privilege for me."

Rani and I looked at each other with an is-this-guy-for-real look, but our eyes were tearing too. "What do you think," I asked her. I felt this had to be her call.

"Let's do it."

And then our audience of stoned PCVs, whom I had forgotten were even there, erupted in laughing applause.

"Excuse me, Mr. Lutwick, but what is that odor?" Vijay Sharma inquired.

"Uh . . ." I couldn't smell it, but I knew what he was talking about. "Oh that . . . um . . . Rani was just burning some incense, doing some Krishna chants before the ceremony." *Lame*, I thought to myself.

"Ah, yes. Of course." I doubted that he bought it, but I appreciated his pretending he did. I was absolutely adoring this guy.

"Why don't you get set up and let us know when you're ready?" I told him.

"I'm ready. There is nothing to be set up. But could I use your water closet for a minute?"

As soon as the bathroom door shut behind him, I peered out the windows—front, back, and side— just to be safe. I perceived no evidence of Indians standing by to attack our fort.

Tom sidled up behind me and said directly in my ear, "Looking for the Mahatma, Lutwick?"

I jumped backward, almost knocking both of us down, then said, "Yeah, Tom. And thankfully he's not there." Tom never missed a chance to mock me. "Bob, take your position by the tape recorder. Let's get this show on the road."

Rani and I went into my bedroom, and I gave her a small bouquet of hibiscus flowers to hold during the ceremony. We stared at each other. Her look asked me, *Are you sure you want to do this?* I replied in kind, *Sure, didn't have much else going on today.* Then I pulled her into my side, and we giggled.

And in that moment I finally and absolutely knew we were doing the right thing.

A female choir sang out the first two verses of our taped wedding song as we walked in step the length of the living room toward the wood-framed front windows of the flat. We stopped and faced Vijay.

"Gentlemen, we have come together today to witness the marriage of William Roy Lutwick and Rani Vinita Gupta . . ."

He did the rest of his spiel, which I don't remember. I'm sure I didn't remember it even at the time, my mind being a teensy bit distracted. He finished with a couple of *Do you take*s followed by our *I do*s. Rani and I exchanged wedding bands. Vijay didn't throw in "You may kiss the bride." Public displays of smooching were utterly verboten in the Indian community. But we didn't need a script. So I gave my bride a long, penetrating kiss as Vijay shaded his eyes. Then I lifted her up and swung her around to the applause and whistles of our friendly foursome. It had been your basic garden-variety wedding ceremony, and we were ecstatic that was all it had turned out to be.

Despite the tiny audience, the bride and groom walked with ceremonial dignity to the back of the room as Bob turned the tape recorder back on for the rest of our wedding song. It kicked in where Mick Jagger takes over the vocals on "You Can't Always Get What You Want."

Not the most romantic sentiment in the world, but the instrumentals and choir worked and we didn't care. We had pulled off our coup. The world's first underground Hindu-Jewish wedding came out of its lair and opened its eyes to the bright tropical sun.

CHAPTER TWENTY-THREE

The reception started an hour later at the Grand Pacific Hotel. I cannot speak for the guests, but I had the time of my life. Of course after what Rani and I had already gone through that day, that week, that month, and that year, I could have spent the evening staring at a mime playing dead and it would have been the time of my life.

My boss, Sitiveni Naitini, was there with his wife. "I see you didn't take my advice," he said. "I think I better stick to work suggestions," he chortled with a mile-wide grin. His wife was an elegant Fijian woman with orange-tan skin, traditional frizzy big hair, close to six feet tall, dressed in a long blue island dress with white flowers on it. The perfect spouse for the man who would someday rise to be Number Two in the Fijian government hierarchy.

Rishi, my trusted inside adviser on Indian cultural affairs, was dressed in a pink and blue sari. She was there with her husband, Arjun—the only two Indian guests. They came over to congratulate us, but unlike her spouse, Rishi exuded no warmth. Rani and Rishi glared like two gunslingers circling each other, each waiting for the other to flinch—while their men stood aside and made amiable small talk. Nothing visibly negative ensued, but the vibe was palpable. I had thought they would warm to each other as the only two Indian women there during a moment of symbolic progress in their world.

I had told Rani that Rishi had advised against our being matched, albeit for safety concerns. But then so did almost everyone else who weighed in on the subject, besides, of course, those who were the reason for those concerns. So why take a particular disliking to Rishi? But during reflection later, I thought their standoff was more about two spirited women vying for some sort of competitive dominance—the older matriarch, a lioness of her social community, facing down the young upstart. Maybe Rishi didn't yet know that the young upstart was leaving town—I hadn't talked with her since the engagement. Rani would later give me her take: Rishi was jealous because she had a crush on me. Whatever the reason, Arjun also picked up on the toxic vibe, and we hastily separated the two contenders, walking them back to their figurative corners.

A few more than the estimated turnout had shown up, but not so many that the cozy room was dangerously overcrowded or that there wasn't enough food and beer. Although we had an invite list, the word got out that there was going to be a Peace Corps wedding at a great hotel in Suva, and Volunteers from all over the island came flocking in. Some of them were from the newer groups, so I didn't even know them.

∾

It was bizarre to see people we didn't know attending our wedding when so many we did know, didn't attend. Couldn't. Rani particularly lamented that her mom couldn't ". . . be here to see all this. She would have loved it."

All my wedding jitters had been totally for naught. No angry villagers showed up to protest. No sign of any kidnappers or other party poopers. The thought occurred that maybe it wasn't because we had done such a thorough job of keeping the wedding secret. There were so many ways the word could have gotten out in such a small society, so it probably had. Maybe the Indians of Fiji, at least the ones in Suva, had just given up and would leave us alone. Victory! Yet, the thought of *not* being under the microscope felt unnatural after so many months of always being there. But I could learn to live with that.

It was pleasant to be the center of attention, to have everyone congratulate us. Yet it also felt so commonplace. Few of the guests had any idea of the tumultuous journey we had been on to get there. And only Rani and I could know what it had actually been like. To try to explain it to our guests, I would have had to write a book. But unbeknown to me, Tom was about to take a shot at the happy couple's story.

Dinner was served buffet style, and when the guests had filled their plates and returned to their seats, Tom stood and tapped his glass with his fork.

"Ladies and gentlemen, my name is Tom Kinkaid, and I am a Peace Corps Volunteer." Tom paused for a response and got only one clap and a whistle, then continued. "OK. Maybe I should have said, 'My name is Tom Kinkaid, and I am about to take off all my clothes.'" And that got a full round of applause. "Thank you, thank you. I see you have excellent taste. But tonight is not about me. Tonight is about these two people sitting here on my left, Lutwick . . . I mean Will Lutwick and his new wife Rani. Please hold your applause and boos till I'm done.

"Let me start by admitting that when these two people started going together, Will climbed the mountain to visit me, and he asked, 'Oh wise man, what should I do? I want to be with this girl, but I'm told this kind of relationship is not allowed.' And I said to Will, 'Son, you can stop it now and get on with your normal life of being rejected by every other girl in Fiji, or you can take a very big chance and take the road untraveled and expect that it will be dark, disturbing, difficult, dangerous, and maybe even downright deadly. Because this is a road that nobody has ever been on, so why else would someone put it there except to lure you into something really awful? I must advise you to dump this girl before it gets even more serious.'"

Rani led the guests in a chorus of *boos*. Jim held a palm to them, then said, "I know. I agree. Bear with me." He yanked his tie knot, then continued, "So Will paid my exorbitant fee—he's a lousy tipper by the way—and descended the mountain, completely disregarded my expensive expert advice, and took off down that untraveled road along with Rani. And as I had feared, it was a rocky road at first, and then it just kept getting worse and worse. It went through a jungle and then a mangrove swamp, and there were lions and tigers and bears along the way, but Rani and Will, they persevered. When the road went through quicksand, Will fell in, but Rani threw him a life preserver and dragged him out. And though they could have turned back at any moment and taken the easy and traditionally smart way out, they kept going forward into the unknown. When Rani slipped on the road and fell halfway down a cliff, Will pulled her back up, and they pushed on and on, clinging together to fight the dangers that challenged them around every turn, until that untraveled road led them . . . yes, that road finally led them here tonight. Yes . . . Amen . . . thank you. And I asked them why they put themselves through such an ordeal following the untraveled road to the ultimate dead end, also known as marriage, and they told me . . . " Tom paused and pointed at the crowd while declaring, "'BECAUSE IT WAS THERE.' That's it. Makes no sense to me, but who am I to argue with success? So let's all raise our glasses and toast the happy, married couple. Ladies and gentlemen, I give you . . . Will and Rani Lutwick."

❧

When we made it back to my flat that night, it was time to carry Rani over the threshold, but I was too exhausted to do it the traditional way. I told her, "Just jump on my back, and you can ride me in," which she did while kicking me in the sides of my stomach with her heels.

"What are you doing that for?"

"Isn't that the proper way to ride a horse?"

I let her dismount and asked, "Why is this night different from all other nights?"

"Because we're married?"

"Yeah, but that's too obvious."

"OK, Will, I give up."

"Because you don't have to go home tonight."

"Oh my, you're right. I never would have guessed. Although I did pack a bag, didn't I?" she said, pointing to her suitcase that she had brought in that morning.

"OK, it's been a long day. And the second Passover question is why do we eat *matzah* and bitter herbs?"

To which she gave me an *are-you-crazy* look and said, "Passover, is that like pass out?"

"Not exactly," I chuckled. "Oh right, we've never talked about Judaism except for that one time about how Jews are paranoid of being assimilated." Oddly enough, this was true. Rani had spoken some about Hinduism when I asked about its importance to her family. But our differing religions just never came up much, what with all the other more urgent topics of discussion.

Barely a mention till after the wedding? What kind of Jew are you, William?

Oh, hi Mom. The secular kind I guess. Hey, when did they get inter-dimensional calling up there?

I have my connections . . .

Rani's voice brought me back to the physical world. "When we started getting together, I mentioned to some friends that there was a Jewish guy working in my office. I asked them what they knew about your religion, because I didn't know anything about it."

"Oh really? So what did they tell you?"

"They thought Judaism was a type of Islam—that Jews are just like Muslims."

I had to chuckle. "Where, oh where, did they get that idea?"

"It was something like . . . both religions are from the same part of the world, so they must be very similar."

"They do have a point, and I'll pass it on to the guys in charge. Maybe they just solved the crisis in the Middle East. We'll have to talk about that some other time, as it gets complicated. Besides, tonight is my wedding night, and I have some other things I'd like to do to Mrs. Lutwick."

The morning after, I was the first to awaken. I turned to look at her. I relished watching my new wife sleeping, thinking how blessed I was to have this extraordinary young woman beside me.

"And why is this morning different from all other mornings?" I asked when I saw her eyelids open.

"Because I'm here in bed with you?"

"No, because I get to see you before you put on any makeup. You know, it's not too late to call this thing off."

"Wrong on both accounts. I don't use makeup. Well, not much," she giggled. "But the real reason this morning is different is because I just learned you snore all night. Why didn't you tell me this *before* the wedding?"

"I snore? How was I to know? I sleep right through it. Hey, if I'd been your typical arranged husband, you would have barely known what I looked like before the big day, much less anything about my alleged snoring."

"Must be a lot of things I don't know about you that you should have told me."

"Yeah. No more need for me to be on my good behavior."

"That goes for me too. You know, I can be a real bitch."

"This comes as a complete shock to me."

"You haven't seen anything yet."

And then we had a pillow fight to cap off our first morning as a married couple. She let me win.

❧

After saying farewell to Emmett and wishing him a happy return to the States, we packed the Anglia and headed to our honeymoon hideaway, the Korolevu Beach Hotel. Our destination was only fifty-five miles west of Suva, on Viti Levu's southern coast. But it took two-and-a-half hours to get there via the ruts and rocks in the Queens Road, Fiji's most-traveled highway. Being midwinter in July, the temperature was only about seventy in the morning, excellent travel weather when in the tropics and your car's passenger cooling system consists of fresh air. It had rained earlier that morning, so no dirt clouds drifted into the cab when we rolled the windows down to cool off. Rani cut up a fresh papaya and threw the black caviarlike seeds out the window as I drove toward the hotel.

"So now that you've learned about my snoring, what else would you like to know about me?" I said as I took a chunk of the bittersweet orange fruit.

Rani put her slender hand on my neck. "Tell me some good things about your country. What will I like there?"

"Well, it's such a big place and the land varies so much. There are deserts, plains, and forests. And mountains so high there's snow around the tops even in the late summer, when we'll be arriving. Actually, I haven't seen that much of the States myself. When we land in California, we can get a car and take some time to see a lot of it as we drive to the East Coast, where most of my family lives."

"Oh, that sounds like fun." She kissed my cheek, and I patted her knee. "I want to see all the natural places. I'm quite keen on the jungles and beaches here, but I know the land in America will be so different and delightful."

"Yes it will be. We can stop and see Emmett in Texas, and I have other friends we can visit on the way."

"Do you think they'll like me?"

"Of course, they will. What's not to like?"

Rani scrunched her nose. "I don't understand."

"I mean you're so great, they'd be crazy not to like you."

A brief thundershower came down on our journey, and then the sun came out again. "Hey, there's the hotel. Up there on the left."

❧

The Korolevu Beach Hotel was one of Fiji's first two resorts. In order to take advantage of the postwar travel boom, it was built in 1948 around a then-unique concept. Instead of putting all the guest rooms apartment-style in one or two concrete buildings, the rooms were individual Fijian *bures* arranged along paths like a native village, with the lobby and restaurant at the center. The tourists got to tell their friends back home they had stayed in an authentic native abode. However, no *bure* in a real village was outfitted with a queen-sized bed, an overhead fan, and indoor plumbing. It was far cheaper to have the structures built by the natives in a way that had been part of their culture for thousands of years. If a hurricane blew some *bures* away, not to worry. It wouldn't cost much or take long to rebuild them.

Our plan was to enjoy a two-night honeymoon at the hotel. All we wanted was a respite before tackling the basketful of tasks we had to complete in less than a month before leaving Fiji.

We parked the car and walked up to the open-air, wood and bamboo check-in counter. A Fijian man in ceremonial garb stood behind it with a red hibiscus flower stuck behind his ear, its long stigma sticking out like a yellow trumpet. He looked expectably stunned when he first saw us but reverted to friendly-yet-subservient as he had been trained.

"How may I help you, sir?"

"I have a reservation for a *bure* for my wife and me. The name is Will Lutwick." I certainly wasn't going to use Rani's name when I made the reservation and give them any advance notice of our uncommon pairing. No telling what kind of plans that might have set in motion.

Glancing at Rani, he questioned, "So this must be Mrs. Lutwick?"

Rani stepped forward in more ways than one. "That's right. I'm Mrs. Lutwick!"

He looked at me for assurance.

"My wife just told you who she is. Now will you check us in, or should I talk to your manager?"

He mumbled something to himself as he handed me the key. Just as I started pulling away from him, his left eye seemed to blink.

"Did you just wink at me?" I asked him, not sure whether he had or not.

"Oh, no sir. Something in my eye. Enjoy your stay here at the Korolevu Beach Hotel."

And so it went for the rest of our stay. After all, it had taken comparatively sophisticated Suva more than six months for us to feel some dissipation of our sideshow status. Therefore, in Fiji outside the capital, even in tourist-oriented locations, it felt as if we had to start all over as a curious couple of outcasts. People would assume despite our wedding bands that Rani was a whore and I was her trick. The fact was that Indian prostitutes were almost as rare in Fiji as Indian intermarriage, but people still jumped to the more prurient assumption when given a choice.

As in much of rural Fiji, the area around our hotel was occupied by separate Fijian villages and Indian enclaves. The hotel drew its service staff from both groups. So the word got out quickly about the nontraditional couple staying in *Bure* #34. There wasn't much privacy for our honeymoon—the hut's walls were not only thin, they were permeable as far as sound was concerned. After awakening on our first morning, we opened the door to go to breakfast, and a small group of Indian kids scattered like cockroaches, laughing as they ran. Their adult counterparts, many of whom seemed to neither be working nor staying at the hotel, gawked at us as we walked through the garden between our *bure* and the main building. I glared back at them and asked, "What are you looking at?" They shook their heads and looked down, but then they continued staring at Rani as if unable to look away.

We were used to it. We were married. We no longer had to put up with this behavior. *Fuck 'em!*

At night, we walked along the beach under a starlit sky. We continued our discussion about what life might be like when Rani would discover America. The tumbling waves beckoned us to cross the vast ocean. Despite earlier misgivings about life in my country, she was beginning to come around. I talked to her of an open society where she could do anything she wanted. She could live out her dreams. There was so much to see. Rani began to think she just might like life in those United States as the great unknown began to take shape.

Back at the hotel, we stopped at the bar for a nightcap or three, then made our way to our *bure*. There we made passionate noisy love in retaliation of our inquisitors, even though we assumed they were not around to eavesdrop on us at that hour. It didn't matter. We would have the last word whether they heard it or not.

"Only a few more weeks of being the freak show," I told Rani as we ate breakfast the morning of our departure. "Then all this will be over."

"Yes, that will be nice, but I'll still be like a . . . What's the title of that science fiction book you mentioned?"

"*Stranger in a Strange Land*," I told her. "Somewhat true, but eventually you will love it there, and I've told you they are going to love you. Just like my Peace Corps friends do. You're going to take my country by storm."

"I'm not familiar with that expression. Is that a good thing?"

"Yes."

"Then that is what I will do. I will take America by storm."

୬

On the way back to Suva, I asked Rani, "How much does your mom know about the wedding and the honeymoon? I mean, I hope she didn't expect you home anytime soon."

"Home?" Rani seemed startled by the word. "Where is my home now? It's at your flat, I guess." Then she clammed up and dropped her hands.

"Hey, what's the matter?"

"Oh, Will, I don't live with my parents anymore. I've always lived with them. My father is gone forever. This seems so strange. And in a way, I won't be going home ever again. Not to stay, anyway. And in a month . . ." She stopped herself while choking up.

"You're worried about leaving your mother?"

"Yes. I'm worried about how she will be treated after all this . . . and just losing my father, it's all too much for her. And I'm going to miss her terribly."

"I'm so sorry about your mom, but we can't stay. You know that." I massaged her neck and noticed a hard ribbon of tension.

"Yes, but it doesn't make leaving her any easier."

I looked over at my new wife and realized that while she was celebrating our marriage, she was also grieving her losses—probably more the latter. I had wanted to think that our wedding would put an end to her mother's suffering along with Rani's own, but now I saw that wasn't realistic. Kiran Gupta would always be somewhat of a pariah in this society, blamed for not stopping her daughter's *sinful* behavior, considered partly accountable by some for her husband's death. And at forty-nine she was newly a widow. The last of her eight children had just moved out. It was heartbreaking to think of all she was going through.

I patted her hair and said, "Maybe we can bring her to the United States."

"No, that wouldn't work. She'd be so isolated."

"No more isolated than you."

"But she doesn't speak much English. And I'll have you, and I'm young, more Westernized, and I chose this. Her life is over."

I hated not being able to fly in like Superman and save the day. Oh, for life to be like in the comic books.

Rani touched my arm lightly and said, "But there is a something we're working on. My sister Gita lives in Canada, near Calgary with her husband and children. My mom might be able to move there. Then she'd be able to still be part of an Indian community. She wouldn't be able to do that through me in the United States."

"Why not?"

Rani looked at me incredulously. "Do you really think I can just walk into, say, a party of Indians with you? Even without you, as soon as I try to make friends with Indians in the United States, and they find out who I married, that's the end of any friendship. Besides, there are few Indians there anyway."

I had never heard of or seen East Indians living in the States. But at that time there were actually a couple of hundred thousand, mostly in the big cities, but nothing like the late-twentieth-century migration that would later cause their numbers to soar into the millions. "But wasn't that why the United States would be attractive to you? We'll be free—no more looking over our shoulders, feeling self-conscious, worrying about your safety."

"Yes, Will, that is all true. But let me ask you: Suppose you are the only European person in Fiji, the only American here. And you find out this is where you will spend the rest of your life. You have none of the Peace Corps friends that you trained with—in fact there is no training for what you are about to do. You have nothing in common with these people. You try to belong, and some may accept you, but you will always be an odd one, an outsider. You even look different from everyone else. You grew up in an entirely different culture, a society with very different values. That is what it will be like for me when I step off the jet in your country."

I gulped and responded, "Well, it's not exactly that way."

"Why not?"

"Because you'll have me with you."

"Yes."

I waited for her to continue, but there was silence. *Just "yes"? No "we love each other, and I know that everything will work out. I need only you to make me happy and complete"?*

I had hoped getting married would put all our problems behind us. We were supposed to drive off into the sunset and live happily ever after. At least I thought that was the deal. Yet there we were, still on our honeymoon, and the collateral damage was already rearing its ugly head. The last moments of my youthful naïveté were evaporating as I began to understand how truly complicated life can be when two people from different worlds decide to share a committed relationship.

We had broken all the rules and still managed to get what we wanted. And I had been so consumed with winning our war that I had not looked ahead to what would come next. *Mission Accomplished,* I had wanted to proclaim to the world.[5] Whatever I had bought into, a Pottery-Barn-like policy was starting to kick in: *You break it, you own it.*

We drove the rest of the way home silently lost in our individual thoughts.

---

5   Just as those words on a banner hanging above the deck of the aircraft carrier USS *Abraham Lincoln* would reflect another naive, premature celebration some thirty-three years later.

CHAPTER TWENTY-FOUR

A few days later, Bob, Rani, and I had to move from our flat on McGregor Road. Emmett had just departed Fiji, and our lease had run out. The landlord didn't want to renew for just the four months that Bob would be there. But Bob was energetic in searching for the ideal short-term abode. He struck oil by finding a house owned by a young European couple who were looking for house sitters while they went on an extended overseas leave. So we got the fully furnished home for next to nothing. It was ideal for Rani's and my final weeks in Fiji as well as the new crash pad of choice for wayward Peace Corps Volunteers.

The five-year-old house was a green wooden structure with a view overlooking the modest skyline of Suva and the Pacific just beyond. There was even an upright piano for me to bang on—the first piano I had lived with since my mother's death over half my life earlier.

At work, it was satisfying to be wrapping up my projects. My Orange Marketing Scheme had had middling success. But after I had proven the orange trade was economically viable, I had turned the actual business activities over to the growers on Rotuma and their contacts in Suva, taking myself out of the equation. I had kept the faux-organization alive on paper only because it owned my car.

My promotional effort for passion fruit had gone nowhere. It was politely ignored by the local food-processing-industry leaders as the work of a wet-behind-the-ears amateur, which it was. My marketing campaign exploiting the fruit's naughty name to sell marmalade and purees had gone nowhere. Ahead of its time, or so I wanted to think.

I had also been doing research into the export markets for Fijian handicrafts—tapa cloth, war clubs, whale's teeth, and the like. But I had not found much demand. In this case, I was perhaps behind the curve. Gorging on human flesh was no longer gastronomically correct, so the cannibal forks went wanting. War clubs were no longer the weapon of choice for modern military machines. And our tapa cloth wall hangings were upstaged in the overseas markets by the more sedate competition from the neighboring Kingdom of Tonga. I buried my research in the office archives, hoping that, in perhaps a hundred years, someone would discover my writings and proclaim my Nostradamus-like ability to predict future trends in handicrafts marketing.

I had gone to Fiji with the intention of making a difference with my work endeavors. Two years later I was leaving, having made my mark in a totally unexpected way. Life was full of surprises.

The Peace Corps office followed through on their offer to expedite our move to the States by cutting through the red tape surrounding Rani's immigration paperwork. As the spouse of a U.S. citizen, she would be eligible for the title of Permanent Resident Alien, which to me sounded like a tenured professor from some distant planet sent to study earthlings. This status included access to the highly coveted green card and would allow my spouse to legally work and play in America, but not vote or sit on juries. I found it odd that the only color cards for immigration were green. True it was the color of our revered money, but I envisioned something more competitive and colorful. Why not also issue bronze, silver, and gold cards? They could even make a TV game show out of the competitive quest, raising money for Uncle Sam the capitalistic way—by selling commercial space. I thought of sending this idea to the Immigration and Naturalization Service, but with Rani's case pending and knowing how humorless bureaucrats could be, I decided against rocking the boat. Rani and I had already had enough boat-rocking to last a lifetime.

Another situation with a federal bureaucracy I began to work on in my final weeks in Fiji was my plan to shirk the Selective Service Draft. I now sensed that Rani was going to be my ticket to freedom. I didn't marry her to save me from going to Vietnam. It didn't even occur to me till after the wedding what a lifesaver she might become. But I certainly wasn't going to pass up the chance to use her as my only lifeline. The plan for my case was still nebulous as I could do limited research on the statutes and strategies until I actually returned to the States. But I knew the general direction of where I was headed. And of course, the truth could use a little embellishment when the stakes were that high. I drafted a letter for the Fiji Peace Corps Director, Wayne Warden, to sign, which went *something* like this:

To the God-Fearing Members of Local Board #55:

William Lutwick is a Peace Corps Volunteer here in Fiji, and as I understand it, subject to your determination regarding his military conscription. He recently married a local woman who now goes by the name of Rani Lutwick. The newlyweds are being run out of Fiji on a rail (actually on a jet plane, because we're on an island). This is because her people, East Indians, who constitute over half the population, are up in arms when they see our red-blooded American boy with their recently innocent girl. In fact, there have been credible threats on the lives of these two, and so Mr. Lutwick will be leaving his Peace Corps service shortly, some three months before his scheduled departure. And the persecuted pair is going to the USA where they will be out of harm's way.

Rani Lutwick has been thoroughly disowned by her family and is accepted by neither them, nor the community at large here in Fiji where incidentally, cannibalism was still an accepted fact into the twentieth century. Now I'm not saying that she would be eaten if she returned, but I'm also not saying she wouldn't be, and regardless of local dietary customs, this place is not safe for either of them now. It would be even less safe for Mrs. Lutwick without Mr. Lutwick, because she needs her man to fight off the angry descendants of indentured servants.

Additionally, Mrs. Lutwick can barely speak a word of English and has never been off her island. Indian women in Fiji traditionally live their entire lives in the home, venturing out only occasionally to buy some curry powder or worship their non-Judeo-Christian gods. So you can imagine the culture shock Rani Lutwick will have when she lands at LAX in a few weeks. The freeways, the bright lights, television—all those splendid things about America that our troops in Vietnam are dying to protect—will take some getting used to for this little lady. I'm no psychiatric professional, but if I were I would estimate that it would take at least ten years for Rani Lutwick to be able to minimally care for herself in the USA if Mr.Lutwick were somehow not to be there for her 24/7.

So here's the conundrum: If Mr. Lutwick is to serve in the military, and particularly if he be sent overseas, Mrs. Lutwick can neither return to her motherland, nor can she live on her own in the USA, despite its many freedoms and opportunities available to all regardless of race, religion, or creed. If you classify William Lutwick 1-A, you might as well just call out the firing squad or get the chair ready (however you do it in the state of Virginia) because you will be giving Mrs. Lutwick, who has already suffered enormously, a death sentence.

This letter should in no way be construed as indicating we are in cahoots with Mr. Lutwick to help him evade the draft, or that we are the least bit concerned for his life or safety in these machinations. We realize it is his duty to his country and his low draft lottery number to join our fight in Southeast Asia, risking life and limb. Like all young American men, he is expendable. But Rani

Lutwick has braved horrors in her quest to become an American Permanent Resident Alien and if you saw her you would never ever want to put a tear in either one of her big, brown, doe-like eyes.

Besides, Mr. Lutwick is hardly the type to win any medals in our fighting forces. Personally, I don't think he'd even make it through Basic Training. The American military is better off without his sorry rear end.

So please think of this poor girl and her inability to survive without him, as you cast Mr. Lutwick's fate to the winds of war.

Patriotically yours,
Wayne Warden,
Fiji Peace Corps Director

Although Wayne appreciated my eagerness in drafting his letter, he toned it down some in the signed version. But in that way and others, the Peace Corps administration came through when I needed them most.

❧

It was emotionally easy for me to wrap up my affairs in Fiji. I had made some endearing friends that I would see again in the States in a few months and then throughout the rest of my lifetime. I would miss Fiji, but not the hysteria surrounding my relationship with Rani, and I was eager to start anew in the States and see old friends and family. I had a new marriage and a blank slate ahead regarding where in the U.S. we would live and what kind of work I might set my sights on.

A cultural revolution had occurred in my home country over the past two years, and though I had watched it from afar, I was curious to know what it was like up-close. I wanted to be where the action was, and for me it definitely was no longer in Fiji. I found the thought of my American rebirth invigorating.

Not so easy for Rani to say good-bye to her mother, siblings, and the rest of her family amid tragedy. Her clan's fabric had been ripped apart over our relationship. She had to say farewell to all her childhood friends, knowing she might never see them again. She was not only saying good-bye to a life spent entirely on an island two-thirds the size of Connecticut, she was leaving a unique idyllic culture that blended British, Indian, and native Fijian influences into a singular version of a tropical paradise. She would end up packing all the memories of her life into just two suitcases.

Rani had liked her life before she met me. She said later that, had I not come along, she would have been happy to stay in Fiji, conceivably forever. Though it might seem inevitable that someone as outspoken, courageous, and beautiful as she was could never be contained by such a traditional culture, there was a side of Rani that was comforted by that secure structure with its familial bonding, predictable routines, and unpretentious personalities.

The clock ticked down and our final hours in Fiji arrived. Rani rode in a taxi to the local airport fifteen miles from Suva, together with her mother and sisters while I drove the Anglia a final time with Bob, Bill, and Tom. When we arrived at our destination, I turned the Anglia's keys over to Bob for his final three months in the Peace Corps. He was thrilled to have a car, generally a forbidden luxury for the Volunteers. He promised to take care of it and send me the proceeds from its sale before he would depart Fiji three months later.

The Nausori Airport lounge was not much bigger than the size of a large living room, and our bon voyage group constituted most of its inhabitants. In addition to the friends in my car, a few others who lived near the airport joined our farewell party. For us Peace Corps

Volunteers, it was a joyful occasion filled with happy reminiscing and laughter. But next to us, Rani was saying good-bye to her family and some of her friends. And their farewells were filled with tears and grief. It was as if a party and a funeral were sharing the same small room, the surreal result of a scheduling mishap.

Rani introduced me to two of her sisters, Pooja and Anokhi. I politely shook their flaccid hands and looked at their difficult smiles and liquid eyes. All of us were apparently awkward, using politeness and language barriers to keep the banter simple and our emotions in check. How surreal to be meeting my sisters-in-law for the first time so incidentally a month after the wedding they could not attend and at a time when I was taking their sister almost halfway around the planet from them. There was nothing I, of all people, could say to take the sting out of the occasion, much as I struggled to conjure up some magic. How difficult and excruciating this choice must have been for Rani!

After that, I just wanted to finish the farewells and get on the turboprop that would take us to the international airport at Nadi on the other side of Viti Levu. Rani's good-bye was such a sorrowful scene that I thought she might even change her mind at the last minute. And then I too would be caught in an impossible situation. Stranger things had happened in our time together.

But she didn't change her mind. I gave her mother a pained hug and then backed off, as she and Rani embraced in a whirlwind of tears for one final time. Rani pried herself away, and the two of us walked across the tarmac to our awaiting vessel. We walked up the passenger staircase and joined the dozen or so travelers already on board. Settling in, Rani sat next to the window and continued waving painful good-byes to her family and friends who were staring like despondent puppies through the lounge's plate-glass window. I felt almost devastated by the circumstances, so I couldn't even begin to imagine what it must have been like for Rani at that moment.

Eventually the engine started, the propellers rotated like pinwheels, the plane rolled and took off, and the neon-lit rectangle of the sad people in the lounge shrank until it disappeared. The buzzing turboprop lifted itself higher, and the airport became just one more of the lights around Suva twinkling up at us through the dusky sky. That view was quickly replaced by the mountainous interior of our South Pacific island appearing like mounds of spinach layered on a bed of muddy ribbed rocks.

Rani had never flown, and I had wanted to ask her how she was doing with it, but held back owing to the gravitas of the moment. I watched her for some mollifying signal that all was OK with her, though I knew it could not be. Her eyes were red and sunken, and she looked like someone who had been awake for days.

I took her hand and put my arm around her, but there was no response. I withdrew, assuming she preferred solitude. In a few minutes and after an uneventful ride, we were descending toward the western, dryer side of the island and landed at Nadi as the orange in the sky morphed to cobalt blue.

The desolate look on her face had mostly subsided as we walked into Nadi's larger, more conventional terminal and sat across from each other at a table. We had an hour before our next flight. It was scheduled to stop to refuel and take on additional passengers in Honolulu before completing our overnight journey to Los Angeles. My father's brother Harry lived in LA with his wife and two daughters, and he would be meeting us at the airport the next afternoon. After that, we had no particular plans beyond buying a car and pointing it east, probably visiting a couple of friends en route to Virginia. What I did know was that wherever our journey might take us, I would introduce Rani to America and America to Rani, and I would be praying they would like each other. There was no acceptable alternative.

"How was it for you . . . the flying?" I finally asked her, my curiosity getting the best of my desire to give her time and space.

"You know, I didn't even remember that it was my first time till we landed. I was so caught up in how difficult it was saying good-bye to everyone, how much I would miss them. And my poor mother." Rani wrung her hands and shook her head. "Awful as that was, I suppose thinking about my family was a good thing, or I might have been quite nervous. And yes, I liked flying like a bird over Viti Levu and looking down on it. It's a beautiful island." She choked up. "*My beautiful island.*"

"I thought maybe you wouldn't come with me," I confessed, reaching across the table and taking her hand in mine. I could feel bulging eyes from some airport workers and even some travelers staring at us, but that no longer registered as a concern.

"Me too. It wasn't easy to leave, particularly Mum," she said. "But then I realized God wouldn't have brought me this far if he didn't have a good reason for doing so. I don't like to start something and then quit."

"I've noticed," I replied and laughed tensely. She did too.

The sky darkened, and after a while they called our flight number. We boarded the plane and got settled in our seats.

"This is a jet, so it will be a smoother flight than the airplane we were just on," I told her.

"You know, Will, after all we've been through in the past year, you needn't be so concerned about how I'm reacting to flying." She said it lightly while taking my hand.

"You're right. You seem to be able to handle anything. If you walked up to the cockpit and took over for the pilot, I'd feel confident you could fly this plane all the way to Los Angeles. Well, Honolulu anyway."

"Don't give me any ideas. You never know what I might try."

"Right again. I'll have to be careful about that." Then I asked her, "Are you ready for your brave new world in America?"

"Now *that's* something that scares me to death."

"You'll be fine. I just know you will." I told her, trying to reassure both of us.

She looked out the window at the runway. At its edge, a group of perfectly parallel coconut palms was illuminated by floodlights, holding back the jungle. Just then a multicolored parrot flew by and landed on the wing close to our window. The bird pecked at its side, then looked at us. Rani kissed her right hand's fingertips and touched the window.

"Good-bye, Fiji," she said, biting her lip. "You'll always be my home."

I too kissed my fingers and touched them to the window. "Thanks, Fiji, for the experience of a lifetime and your greatest gift, this amazing young woman sitting beside me."

The parrot opened its beak as if replying to us, and us alone, then flew away as the jet engines roared to life.

"*Bula* everyone. Fasten your seatbelts and prepare for takeoff," came a commanding voice over the loudspeaker. "This flight is headed for Honolulu and then Los Angeles. If this is not the correct flight for you, please alert a stewardess immediately to get off this plane."

I looked over at Rani, and we grinned simultaneously. She shook her head a couple of times. I squeezed her hand as we braced for takeoff. She looked at me with those dark panther eyes that had first bewitched me nine months earlier. Looking back at them still put me under her spell.

The jet rolled forward, lifted off, and was swallowed up by an inky black sky.

EPILOGUE

"Oh shit! This is it. They won't transfer my case out here." I flung the draft board notice to the floor and banged my fist on the coffee table. I looked out the window as a street car rattled past our boxy little apartment on Ocean Avenue.

Rani came running out of the bedroom. "That is crazy. We just moved to San Francisco."

"And I told them that we were moving here. They're deliberately making it as difficult as they can. They could have easily let a nearby draft board hear my case."

That had been part of my strategy. A Selective Service board on the Left Coast would probably be more receptive to my unorthodox plea for a military deferment than one in Richmond, Virginia, where I grew up. My new home city's intensely antiwar, pro-minorities political bent would have undoubtedly worked in our favor, whereas the home of my youth was a conservative, recently segregated city. Their insistence on seeing us personally was an obvious sign that the gang at Local Board #55 was skeptical of my intentions and not about to let their weak-kneed counterparts in San Francisco save my butt.

We didn't move to San Francisco to improve my deferment odds any more than I had married Rani for the same reason. The realization that those life changes might be helping my case was a welcome after-thought for both situations. Actually, we had moved to San Francisco pretty much on a whim.

We had landed at LAX from Fiji. Even I was unprepared for the culture shock that would hit after living in a Third-World environment for almost two years. A mostly sleepless five-thousand-mile overnight flight and a four-hour time change accelerated the initial impact. I couldn't imagine how overwhelming it must have been for someone who had been on an island her entire twenty-one years.

I remember the drive to my uncle's house in West Los Angeles from the airport. Riding the vast freeways in his seemingly immense Cadillac felt like being on a roller coaster, one of my worst phobias. I thought I was going to vomit and probably would have, had the trip been more than a few miles. Los Angeles circa 1970 reflected American cultural attributes at their most extreme. Everything seemed immense and complex, luxurious yet decadent to those two refugees from a simpler world.

"What do you think so far?" I asked Rani after we unpacked and sat on deck chairs adjacent the sparkling turquoise swimming pool at my uncle's home.

"Your family is very welcoming, but right now, this is like a strange dream to me. Maybe later I can tell you what I really think," she said, implying that I would not like the thoughts racing through her mind. I didn't press the issue.

The next night, my cousin Naomi took us to the stage version of *Hair*. We had seats in the third row. It was a spectacle the likes of which neither of us had ever seen. Though we enjoyed the music and the pageantry, it portrayed a world very unlike the one I had left two years earlier, but reflective of the one just outside the theater doors on Sunset Boulevard. How could America have changed so much so quickly? When all the actors came on stage nude, Rani's eyes bugged out, and her face was contorted with distress. Penises and vaginas were wiggling in all their glory just a few feet away from her overwrought face.

"Is this what people think of as a theater play in your country?"

"No. Just close your eyes if you don't want to look at it." I took her hand to reassure her, but she yanked it away.

"I want to leave," she told me. And we both knew she wasn't just talking about the theater.

Rani later told me she had thought that must be typical American evening entertainment, because there it was on her first night out in the United States. She wondered what kind of grotesque nightmare she had stumbled into. The rebel in her had struggled for freedom, but this seemed like degradation and madness, and it frightened this usually fearless young woman. She had sacrificed everything—for this?

It would be an extreme understatement to say that was not how I should have introduced Rani to America, but it was too late to undo it. I tried to reassure her that not all America was *La-La Land* and the stage production of *Hair*. I needed to get her out of Los Angeles fast, so the next day I bought a car, a cherry-red Datsun 510. Something small and unassuming that would be like the cars she was used to in Fiji, even if we did have to drive it on the wrong side of the road.

We made our way up the California coast on a two-lane highway, State Route 1, and the initial nightmare receded for both of us. Los Angeles sprawl was replaced by slower-paced coastal towns, yellow-sand beaches, and forested mountains that reminded Rani of those back in Fiji. The tension in her face and apprehension in her speech seemed to dissipate as she began to appreciate her new home country's natural beauty and lose herself in its serene aura.

We were on our way to the Bay Area. We hung out in San Francisco and Berkeley for a week, and Rani learned not all American cities were L.A. clones. It was my first time in that region too. In the late 1960s, San Francisco had been the epicenter of the cultural and political changes that were polarizing the nation, particularly across generations. In 1970, it was still the *happening* place to be—if you were under thirty.

It was almost required that you look different from mainstream America in San Francisco, although only hippie-freak couture—earth-mother dresses, military-style jackets, embroidered Guatemalan shirts, and tie-dyed apparel—seemed acceptable there. Even anti-fashionistas had their uniforms. This was a place where we could blend in as just another bizarre young couple. That characteristic was acutely appealing to us after all those months under the microscope in Fiji.

"Could you be happy here?" I asked her as we sipped Irish coffees at the Cliff House our last night in the Bay Area.

"Yes. It seems like it might be a good fit for us." Rani laughed, relaxed for once. Her attention was drawn to a bevy of barking sea lions, the largest wild animals she had ever seen. They were splashing and clashing for a sunny spot on their rocky little outcrop just a few yards from us. She pointed at them and laughed aloud at their playful antics.

The girl I had fallen in love with had come back.

"Then so be it. San Francisco will be our new home," I said as we clinked our glasses to make it official. Far from everything familial and familiar to both of us, the city by the Bay seemed just what we needed for a fresh start.

We drove east across the country, a first for me too, visiting sights like the Grand Canyon and the Painted Desert. I had been sponsoring and writing a ten-year-old Native-American boy on a New Mexico reservation through Save the Children. We took advantage of our route's proximity to drop in and meet him and his mother at their little trailer home on the high desert. We visited my Fiji roommate Emmett in Austin and another friend, a former Thailand Peace Corps Volunteer, in Chicago. Rani was seeing more of America in her first few weeks than I had in all my years before going to Fiji.

The American racial landscape in 1970 was mostly black and white. This was particularly true outside the big cities, so it was not surprising that Rani was a curiosity on our magical tour of the heartland. Strangers would occasionally let their curiosity get the best of their propriety, particularly in bars, and ask about her ethnicity. If they seemed genuinely curious and benign, we would tell them that she was Indian. The next response was invariably. "Oh, really? What tribe?" When we explained that she wasn't *that* kind of Indian and where she was from, actually as well as ancestrally, they would look at us as if we had escaped from the loony bin. They just couldn't wrap their geographically insulated brains around her people's journey.

My family members in Virginia turned on their Southern hospitality for Rani. And the ones in New York threw a house party in our honor to make up for none of them having been able to attend our family-free wedding. My parents were already dead, and the other family members didn't have to be so personally affected by what we had done from a she's-not-one-of-us standpoint. Everyone, including the newlyweds, was on their best behavior, and Rani was heartened by the warm treatment.

We spent a couple of weeks on the East Coast exploring my roots, but Rani and I had left our hearts in San Francisco. So we loaded up the Datsun with my childhood possessions and headed back to the Bay Area.

❦

Rani was becoming well acquainted with her new homeland by the time the letter from Local Board Number 55 awoke us at the beginning of our California dream. As the initial shock sank in, its immediate complications joined my longer-term concerns. I told her, "They easily could have scheduled this for when we were already in Virginia if they weren't going to transfer the case out here. I kept in touch with them before, during, and after our visit. And since they waited us out then, why couldn't they have scheduled the meeting for a month from now instead of a week? Now we have to shell out a thousand dollars for two short-notice round-trip flights for a meeting that will maybe last an hour. This is just another way for them to harass me."

A thousand dollars was a significant chunk of cash in 1970—it was almost as much as my entire Peace Corps salary for the twenty-one months I had been in Fiji. And both Rani and I were only beginning to look for work in California. I envisioned my draft board members' amusement as they yanked my puppet strings. To win a deferment from these guys, we were going to have to get them to go from hating us to loving us in about sixty minutes. And that was about as likely as turning the same trick with the people who despised us in Fiji.

At least I had done my homework. I had researched and developed what I thought was a well-honed case to win my freedom.

When I had gotten a low draft lottery number while still in Fiji, I had been at a loss as to what I should do once my Peace Corps deferment ran out. It was too late to discover I was a conscientious objector, though my personality had always been pacifistic. Self-mutilation might turn my body into something ineligible for military service, but I was too squeamish to go to such lengths and perhaps immobilize myself for life. There was always the possibility of slipping away into Canada as a tourist and then staying there. But the United States was my home country, and the thought of being a fugitive criminal there was not something I could easily choose.

I wanted a better solution. After the wedding, my male intuition whispered to me that something about the singularity of my marriage could be my ticket to freedom. When I got back to the States, I found what I was searching for. The rarely bestowed Selective Service Classification III-A was only for situations of "extreme psychological, emotional, and cultural hardship." Not hardship for the potential soldier being shipped to the front in Vietnam. Nobody ever cared about him. But hardship for someone else, anyone else, preferably a sympathetic figure. Rani was that obvious someone. She was no abandoned puppy, but she was an exotic child-woman, and that would have to be sympathetic enough.

In the following weeks, I interlaced our forbidden-love story into a case and sent it to my draft board. But I knew they would not just take my word for it, so I went hunting for additional expert testimonial to add to the letter I had already procured from the Fiji Peace Corps Director. While I was in Richmond, I obtained statements from my rabbi and family doctor attesting to Rani's inability to live without my constant attention. We spent about fifteen minutes with each, Rani sitting there silently while I kept urging them to sign the tear-jerking letters I had prepared for them. In each case they signed, probably just to get the raving lunatic and his mysterious wife out of their offices.

Being married, by itself, was not enough to win the hardship deferment. Even having children was usually not enough, and in any event there was no time for us to score a kid or two. This type of deferment had to be given rarely and only for unique cases, lest too many potential soldiers slip away from the military's grasp. My draft board would have to buy that my poor little wife had no options. She couldn't return to Fiji, and she couldn't make it on her own in the United States. The former was true; the latter seemed something of a stretch and harder to prove. The board members would have to feel intense concern for a woman who would seem to their good-ol'-boy sensibilities as if she were from another planet. And that concern would have to overcome their instinctive disdain for a Peace Corps guy who was trying to get out of his military obligations.

Only three years earlier our biracial marriage would have been a felony in the state of Virginia, punishable by up to five years in prison for each of us. How could they possibly empathize with our plight? And this almost certainly was their last chance to get me. Ten days before the hearing, I turned twenty-five. Once I would reach twenty-six, I would legally be free from their clutches for the first time in the seven years since I had coincidentally registered for the draft at approximately the same moment President Kennedy was being assassinated. I didn't just need a miracle; I needed a bunch of them along with some divine special effects—maybe some lightning bolts shooting down from the ceiling and God commanding the board members in his best James Earl Jones voice to either give me the deferment or be condemned to hell. Even a biblical prophet would have been hard-pressed to pull that off.

"Rani, I don't even know if this is worth the trouble. I can't see any way of us winning, and if I get drafted, you're going to need the money we'd spend on the trip."

"Oh wow!" Rani was becoming fluent in American. "I cannot believe that you would give up on this. That doesn't sound like the man I married—the man who would not accept other people judging that we shouldn't be together. The man who stood up for what he wanted and believed in." Her posture drooped, and she looked at the floor. "And besides, I don't care about the money. I'll get a job soon and if I don't . . ." Her voice trailed off.

"And if you don't get a job soon, then what?"

"You can't get drafted! That's all there is to it!" she yelled. "You're not the military type, and I didn't go through all this just to see you come back in a body bag from Vietnam. I lost my father. I can't lose you too!"

"Whoa! That won't happen. We won't let it." The words came out of my mouth, but I knew they weren't convincing either of us. I would have to try harder. "OK, we'll invade Richmond like Ulysses S. Grant and march to the sea like William Tecumseh Sherman."

"What are you talking about? Is this more of that Jewish holiday stuff?

⁂

Invigorated by Rani's refusal to give up, I applied my energy to enhance the arguments of our case. The draft board members would have to buy into our Fijian soap opera—love Rani and me and hate our adversaries. To convince them of the hardship angle, I would have to reinvent Rani as a slight exaggeration of her real self and tweak her personal history a tad.

"OK, Rani, here's your character. You're a poor helpless Indian refugee in a strange land. You speak almost no English. You don't know how to use a knife and fork except maybe to stab your brother. You were run out of your native land, by outraged relatives who spit when they hear your name. They would slice you into little pieces if they could find you, for you have offended their Dark-Ages sensibilities through no fault of your own. Rani good; other Fiji Indians bad. They hate America, but you love America."

Rani started to speak, but I was nowhere near done and held my hand up to silence her. "However, you have found America takes some getting used to. It is difficult to handle without constant attention from Will. Tall buildings, automobiles, TV, hula hoops, plastic lawn ornaments, loud noises—these and other embodiments of American culture terrify you in your emotionally weakened state. It is only through the constant attention of your brave, patriotic husband that you can keep your pretty little head together. He cheers you up by telling you stories of the land he loves with its purple mountain majesties, rockets' red glare, and roaming buffalo. Oh, and for these particular guys, you also yearn for plantations and Civil War history. That is, as long as they're all white. If anyone on the Board is black, drop that last part. Of course you won't actually say these things, because your English is so limited that I will have to translate your sentences. But don't be surprised when I tell them you just said things in Hindi like 'The Civil War was fought over states' rights, not slavery.'"

"What about you? How are you different?" she asked.

"Well there's my conservative, pro-war politics—I really want to do the patriotic thing and join the military, but gosh darn, it's a tough choice—my wife or my country. I figure once you're established here in a decade or so, I can voluntarily join the Marines and fight the Viet Cong. Because at the rate we're going, the war will still be going on then. Oh, and don't forget, you are married to a man who fluently speaks a unique Fijian dialect of Hindi that is your native tongue, and it is known by no one else but the two of us in all of North America. This makes me your essential communication link to everything in this country. And it also forces the draft board members to communicate with you through me."

"And allows you to control my answers," she pointed out. "I don't know that I'm too keen on that."

I wasn't expecting such a response and had little patience for it. "Listen, Rani, we're absolutely on the same side in this battle, and I know the information they need to hear and how they need to hear it. I know how these guys think and what is necessary to get this deferment. Your presence there will be necessary, but more as . . . uh . . . decoration. Your job will be to look utterly foreign to them. And cute, sad, and helpless—particularly helpless. And you can't look helpless if you start talking to them in English, except maybe for *hello, good-bye,* and *where is the bathroom?* Remember it's essential to my qualifying for that deferment that you speak and understand no more than a little English."

"Yes, sahib, whatever *you* say." She showed me her palms and genuflected.

I should have known better than to think Rani would happily accept a window-dressing role in a performance that might affect her life as profoundly as mine. I shrugged it off, figuring she'd eventually come around to my way of thinking.

So we took a break from beginning our new life in San Francisco and flew back to Richmond for a few days. We stayed with my former guardians, Uncle Jacob and Aunt Tillie. It had been just over seven years since they had run the Chicken Little routine on me when I went to a movie with an African-American friend, so I could imagine what they thought when I brought home as my bride, a woman whose skin was as dark as Cecil's. Then again, maybe the rapid social changes of the 1960s might have increased their tolerance. In any case, they were polite hosts, despite Tillie's historical unwillingness to allow my friends in the house.

I left my hair in San Francisco . . . well, most of it, having gotten the tangled bush on top of my head clipped down to more like a manicured lawn before the trip. It was the morning of the draft board hearing. Now the mustache and the muttonchop sideburns would also have to go. I hated to cut them, but the facial hair was associated with peacenik hippies, a look I couldn't afford at the upcoming meeting. I put on a suit for the first time since our wedding. I looked in the mirror, and a straight young man squinted back at me. Circa 1970, *straight* was considered the opposite of *hippie*, not *homo*. I wanted to project both of those images to my draft board—heterosexual and conservative.[6]

Rani, as requested, also dressed the part. This was the first time I had ever seen her in a sari.

---

6   By hindsight, the desire for a heterosexual appearance was a little peculiar. Gays had always been officially banned from the military, yet it did not even occur to me and my draft-averse friends that we might masquerade as homosexuals to get out of military service. It was as if *the love that dare not speak its name* was so quiet that it wasn't even on the *gaydar*. Then again, maybe fear of being labeled gay, particularly around macho military types, was enough to kill it from consideration.

"I never thought I'd live to see the day," I told her as we stood in the bleak living room of my childhood home.

"What? This old rag?" she said pointing to her splendid red sari with gold trim. "And what are you supposed to be? You look like a banker."

"Yeah, that's me. You can bank on it."

"Oh, that's terrible," she said, wincing.

"And that red dot on your forehead. Just the right touch. But shouldn't you be wearing one of those jeweled headdresses?"

"Not bloody likely. Too formal for daytime."

๛

We jumped into my uncle's car and drove downtown. I reminded Rani of the silent role I wanted her to play, but my heavy-handedness was shutting her down. Which was alright with me, because I wanted to mentally run through the innumerable arguments I had rehearsed a dozen times—points I would need to make while pretending to answer the board members' piercing questions. *Just like a candidate at a political debate*, I thought, *except one scrambling to save his ass.* The more I rehearsed, the more nervous I got. I just wanted this seemingly hopeless ordeal to be over.

We parked in a lot a couple of blocks away from our destination. It was a warm day for the first of December, the temperature in the upper sixties. We weren't wearing topcoats, so our costumes stimulated lots of ogling. We must have been quite the sight for that place and time—the bumbling tall white banker with his petite sari-clad Indian girl.

Selective Service Board Number 55 was housed in a gray concrete fortress that was also the location for several other federal government offices. We got into an elevator with a bunch of normal-looking people and watched them staring at us as if we were space aliens. They seemed to push themselves up against the elevator's walls—apparently fearful of our other-world cooties. I was tempted to bark at them, but this was not the time for such antics. We had serious business to attend to. Their glares, however, added to my escalating anxiety.

We got off the elevator and found our way to the draft board's suite. It consisted of an outer office, a meeting room, and a door, behind which, I knew not what—perhaps an empty elevator shaft for flinging victims down when they had finished their hearings. Beads of sweat were already beginning to coalesce on my forehead, giving it the reflective sheen, Rani would tell me later, of a high-gloss wax job on a sports car. I wiped my brow, but the leakage immediately began anew.

I went up to the front desk where a gray-haired woman was perusing a military manual. I introduced myself to her, and she was reasonably polite until she got a gander of whom the cat had dragged in.

". . . and this is my wife Rani Lutwick," I said, directing her vision toward the only other person in the room.

"Oh . . . oh my . . . oh, OK. Sit down over there." She shot up out of her seat, opened the door to the meeting room, and shouted, "William Lutwick and his wife are here for his hearing." And then in a much lower voice, she said, "You guys are not gonna believe this in a million years."

Maybe we should *give Canada a try.*

I looked at Rani to see if she heard what I had. Her rolling eyes voted in the affirmative.

"They're ready for you in there."

We walked into the conference room, and as the secretary was closing the door behind us, she graciously drawled, "Now good luck you two." But I could see her face before the door fully closed. Her fingers were across her mouth suppressing a laugh.

The lady in the red sari and I continued our hard-to-miss entrance and took our seats on the near side of the oak conference table. Across from us sat the five board members, four white men who looked as if they could have been brothers—all with short light-brown hair and bright piercing blue eyes—and one quite obese woman of about fifty with straggly blond hair.

Together they looked at me, scrutinized Rani for a while, looked at one another, then repeated the cycle. I looked for a sign of empathy and found none. I noticed that their chairs all were set a few inches higher than ours. They looked downward on me and would have to lean forward and stretch their necks to look Rani in the eye.

Finally, the man in the middle slid his glasses down his nose and introduced himself as ". . . the Selective Service, Local Fifty-five board director Mr. Samuel Thompson. That's Thompson with a *p*," and then he introduced his fellow board members. And I introduced myself and Rani. All quite chummy. *So far, so good.*

"Now William, does your wife, here, Ruh . . . Rah . . . Rain-eye . . ." He spoke methodically in a syrupy *Vuh-gin-ya* accent, the kind only used by those whose aristocratic families had lived in the state for centuries.

"Rani," I corrected him.

"Yes, Rah-nuh-hee." He stumbled over her four-letter name as if it were *hippopotomonstrosesquippedaliophobia.*[7]

"Does she speak much English? Can we address questions to her directly?"

"She's learning, but she knows only a very small amount of our language and is very shy as is typical of women of her persuasion, so it would be best if you go through me and I will speak with her in her language and rare dialect." And then realizing he was still waiting, I added, ". . . and translate into English what she says." That seemed to placate him.

A quick glance at Rani showed me she was doing an admirable job quietly posing as sad and helpless, even as I knew she wanted to speak for herself.

"Rain-eye. What kind of name is that, anyway?" Samuel Thompson leaned back and rubbed his chin between his thumb and forefinger.

---

7   Definition: fear of long words.

Idiot! Did you even read my case? And if not, can't you tell by simply looking at her dressed like this?

"It's an Indian name, sir."

"Really, which tribe? I've got a little Cherokee in me, or so says my granddaddy."

O Canada!!!

Fortunately we were already used to this uniquely American inability to keep one's Indians straight. "Her ancestors came from India. They are not from America."

"Right, she's from the Fijis. I remember now," he said. Both of us seemed pleased we had finally achieved a successful communication. "So the Fijis, they must be nearby Injuh in the Injun Ocean."

"No sir, they are seven thousand miles away in the Pacific Ocean?"

"Well, who put them so far away from Injuh?"

"I guess God did, sir." I thought that might appeal to his sense of faith-based geography.

"No, no. I mean what's a girl from Injuh doing growing up in the Fijis?" It hadn't worked. He was just getting flustered.

"Her ancestors were brought over by the British almost a hundred years ago to work the sugarcane plantations. They were indentured servants, and then they stayed in Fiji after their contracts were up."

Samuel Thompson turned to the other board members to mull over what I had just said. Then he said to me, "'Indentured servants' . . . so her people were like our slaves, but in the Fijis. Is that right?"

I looked over at Rani and could see daggers shooting from her eyes to Mr. Thompson's. I made a nonchalant restraining gesture to her with my hand then had to say something, lest she burst and blow my carefully constructed language façade.

"Well . . . uh . . . once they were free, after they completed their servitude, they became the prosperous middle class of Fiji."

"Well, good for them," he seemed impressed. "Good for her people. Tell her that I said that."

I turned to Rani and started throwing down random Hindi words such as *I very love to eat green and blue vegetables, but lower the bad price,* while she appeared to be processing my gibberish, but Thompson interrupted, "I meant later. We need to move on."

And move on we did. He wanted to know about our history together in Fiji, so I told him the true story of our courtship, and the violent reactions it had unleashed. He asked me to ask Rani what she thought of America. I counted to twenty in Hindi, directing my impressive command of the rare Fiji-Hindi dialect in her direction. She replied back in Hindi, although I only caught a couple of words, which translated roughly as "that stupid asshole," and then I said, "Rani loves America. Everything about it. Can't get enough of America. Loves the flag, big American cars, supermarkets. Particularly she loves the South. She thinks it was wrong for the North to attack us in the Civil War." I thought I had been particularly astute to sneak that last sentence in, but there was some headshaking on the other side of the table. Maybe they thought I was shamelessly and gratuitously patronizing them, which, of course, I was. Perhaps I had overestimated their appetite for ass-kissing.

"Well I'm glad she sees American history the way it should have been written, although I don't understand why in tarnation she would be so interested in Civil War matters," Thompson said, looking away and not smiling. "And I don't quite understand how she could love everything in America, because you wrote in your request for this hardship deferment . . ." at which point he slid his glasses down his patrician nose and read from my file, "'Rain-eye is afraid of many things in the United States and needs my constant attention to help her adjust to them.' And then you list twenty-seven examples, including 'number nineteen, supermarkets.' It seems to me that most of these things would occur on a daily or weekly basis for her." He put the file down, took off his glasses, and looked at me dead on. "So I ask you, William, how can she still love America if she's terrified most of the time?"

The sweat had been collecting on my forehead and was now starting to drip into my left eye, searing it. I took my handkerchief and wiped the rivulets away, then loosened my tie and opened the neck button on my shirt. "Sure is hot in here, isn't it?" I mumbled to no one in particular, and no one concurred. "OK, to answer your question . . . OK, yes, let's take that example of supermarkets. Rani is intimidated by them because of . . . of . . . the bright lights, yes, and all the choices—like Heinz has fifty-seven varieties . . . yes . . . and she can't read the words on the packages . . . she is intimidated because she doesn't know what she would be buying so she needs me there to interpret. Yes, that's it. But all those choices—that's the freedom to choose—one of America's basic freedoms—to choose a steak, although as a Hindu, she doesn't eat beef . . . but she could even buy rabbit meat in the supermarket if she wanted. And there are fresh fruits from all over the world, and they are arranged in geometric shapes on the counters—you don't see that in Fiji. So she loves all these choices even as they intimidate her, because she knows that one day she will be able to go to the supermarket without my help, and so she looks forward to that day and so do I, but not yet . . . I mean she's not ready yet."

I suddenly realized that I had unconsciously been standing during all that rambling, I suppose to be more on eye level with those who would judge me. But now I was towering over them, looking down, so I excused my faux pas, applied handkerchief to sweaty forehead, and sat back down. They looked at one another, did a little conversing, and then returned to their default positions, staring me down with an is-this-guy-for-real look on their faces.

I don't think I won anybody over with that one. Maybe we should just buy those train tickets to Toronto.

Samuel Thompson gathered his papers and continued, "OK, let's move on from that one." A somber pallor came over his face as he looked me straight in my left eye, the one that was now getting bloodshot. "William, we are at war in Vietnam, and as Vietnam goes, so goes all of Asia, and as Asia goes, so goes the world. If we lose to the Communists in that part of the world, our children and our children's children may end up as citizens of a godless state with none of the freedoms our boys have fought and died for during the past two hundred years. We need every able-bodied man to fight the Commies. You know a hardship deferment can be granted in only the most extreme cases. Marriage alone, even to an American girl, will not qualify one for such treatment. So tell me, William, what makes you think you're entitled to this hardship deferment?

Oh my God! All that paranoid falling-dominoes bullshit? And then he shoots me an open-ended question on the broadest possible subject. I never planned for making a speech. Calm down. Be still my heart!

"William, we're waiting for your response. Did you not hear the question?"

"Oh . . . sorry . . . I heard the question—I heard the question, all right." I was killing time, trying to come up with a speech, then realized my stalling was murdering any glimpse of a chance I still had. I prayed something half-intelligent might jump out of my mouth. *Steady, you can do this.*

"Mr. Thompson, fellow board members, I mean his fellow and lady board members . . ." *No you can't. Just grab Rani and run for it. The door is so close.* "Your question goes to the heart of the matter of this case. Why indeed do I, of all people, feel entitled to get this hardship deferment when so many other young American men, some of whom I went to high school with right here in Richmond, why must they die for our country in Southeast Asia while I get off scot-free?"

Gee, that is unfair—maybe I should enlist? No, I don't agree with this war. OK I think I've got my response. I slapped both my hands down on the table and moved my face toward the board members. I stared at them one-by-one, nodding with affirmation for two seconds before aligning my eyes at last on Thompson's. "Well, here's my answer, lady and gentlemen of the board. I spent two years winning the hearts and minds of the people of the Fiji Islands for America by helping their economy, doing marketing research on handicrafts and passion fruit and oranges. Oh my—that was something. But even more important than that, I set an example in my personal behavior that exemplified America at its finest. I fell in love with this little lady here . . ." I took Rani's hand in mine and looked lovingly at her. She responded by digging her fingernails into my palm and flashing me a bug-eyed, what-the-fuck-are-you-doing look. I dropped her hand, turned back to my inquisitors, and said, ". . . and she with me. And even though over half the people of Fiji were against us, we battled tooth and nail to be together. Because as an American, I think you have the God-given right to marry anyone you want to . . . well, as long as the other person also wants in on it too. And so by example, I showed the people of Fiji what America and Americans are all about, fighting for free-dom of choice, both for couples and individuals, each in his own way. Lady and gentlemen, I have already served my country in the Peace Corps, and although I was not killed, I came home wounded in battle, so to speak. But I was proud to do it for my country. And that's why the United States of America has a friend in Fiji now, and that's why I should be given that deferment."

Whew! I sure knocked that one out of the park!

But when I looked at those who were about to decide my fate, I didn't see cheering or flags waving. No confetti falling from the ceil-ing. I saw incredulous eyes and gaping mouths.

Thompson eventually responded, "William, I honestly don't know what to say after a speech like that, but I will try. First of all you say you won over the Fijis as a friend to the United States, but you also point out that most of that country's people were vehemently opposed to your mixed marriage with Rain-eye. So you are seriously contradicting yourself. Secondly, your Peace Corps service is irrelevant to fulfilling your military obligations. But most surprisingly, you did not at all the address the issue of why your being in the military would be a uniquely extreme and undue hardship on this young lady? Now you did express some ideas earlier on that matter, and we still have your written documents to consider, but I'm afraid your answer just now did not help your . . ."

At that moment someone started screaming and every molecule in the room froze. "OH GOD, IF I HAVE TO GO BACK TO FIJI THEY WILL KILL ME! I'M DOOMED, DEAR GOD, I'M DOOMED!!!"

That's it—by a total knockout—this train-wreck of a case is totally DEMOLISHED*!!!*

Yes, that was Rani screaming in fluent Queen's English. But she wasn't done. "You people cannot know how it is to be hated by your family for loving someone. They blamed me for my father's death. They say I'm a disgrace. I can't go back there. And I have no one here.

No one, except Will. Without him, I am done for. I will surely perish without him."

A couple of tears trickled down her cheek. Then, *oh no*, she had more to say. "I came to this country to make a home and forget all the terrible things that happened to me in Fiji. But I am so unhappy here." *No, Rani, remember you're supposed to love it here.* "Nobody understands me, and I don't understand Americans." *Really, Rani? Language suddenly doesn't seem to be a problem. I wonder, can they can court-martial civilians?*

But then I Iooked at my inquisitors for the first time since Rani's epic outburst, and I saw that there was a sea change in their attitude. Instead of scoffing like me, they were absolutely gripped by Rani's dramatic performance, hanging on her every word. The burly blond woman came around the table and put her arm around Rani to comfort her. One of the men offered her his handkerchief. Another was pouring her a glass of water. The third Thompson look-alike's blue eyes were dead on mine, and he was shaking his head in disgust as if to say, "You cad! How could you ruin this sweet girl's life?"

After the soap opera continued a little longer, things quieted down, and the draft board members assumed their seats again. Samuel Thompson said to Rani and me, "Could you give us a minute?" I started to rise, but it was they who stood up and left the room. When the door closed, I looked over at Rani. Her head was down. I put my hand on her shoulder, but before I could say anything, I heard the door opening again.

"Now, then William and Rani," Samuel Thompson was speaking, and he had pronounced her name correctly for the first time. "I think this board has heard all it needs to make its decision. Our usual procedure is to let people know the results by mail in two to three weeks, but in this case, if you don't mind waiting outside a few minutes, I think we can let you know today."

We left the room and closed the door. I was pretty much in a state of shock—somewhere between utterly dumbfounded and flatlining. I still thought the deferment had probably slipped away, but I sensed something beyond my comprehension was happening, and our odds were certainly improved from the one-in-a-billion chance I would have given us when we first walked into that office less than an hour earlier.

The matronly secretary was no longer suppressing laughter at us. "Please take a seat, Mr. and Mrs. Lutwick." She must have heard the drama though the door, or maybe the board members said something to her. Turning to Rani, she said with motherly concern, "Are you OK there, honey? Do you need a coat? Can I get you some coffee? Maybe a Dr Pepper?"

Rani declined the offers. No refreshment proposal was extended to me. The patterns were becoming obvious. The decision seemed to be coming down to whether they loved her more than they hated me.

I couldn't talk openly with Rani, so I put my arm around her and tried to comfort her, but her body neither resisted nor complied. I patted her hand. She looked up at me, and I silently mouthed, "Thank you, thank you," but she just averted her gaze and looked downward. The shock of the hearing's wild ride was beginning to dissipate for me, only to be replaced by feelings of sadness and rejection. I hated it when she withdrew and gave me the cold-shoulder treatment. I was downright powerless at such times. At that moment I cared even more about winning her heart back than getting that deferment. I decided to just let her be, but I dreaded the thought of a long night with her withdrawn into her shell.

One of the male board members opened the door and called us back in. It felt more like a criminal trial than a hearing, and we were being called back to court. The jury foreman was about to read the verdict to the defendant. And then it hit me: Rani was as much the defendant as I was, and despite all my preparation, she was the one who shined that day. She showed the board members how vital this deferment was to her in the most personal of ways, and that had been the key to our case. My carefully overanalyzed, patronizing bullshit wouldn't have convinced a five-year-old, much less five adults who had probably seen and heard it all before from hundreds of other young men trying desperately to avoid being sucked into the Southeast Asian quagmire.

Samuel Thompson told us to take our seats. I wanted to take Rani's hand, but her continuing distance thwarted that. "Mr. Lutwick, Mrs. Lutwick," *suddenly we're Mr. and Mrs.?* "The Defense Department highly discourages Selective Service Boards from giving out the III-A hardship deferment. We do not take that order lightly. I myself served in Italy during World War II. As I've said today, this war needs every able-bodied young man in America to do his duty and fight for his country. We do not give the III-A out because of marriage or children. We do not even give it out because a family has already lost one son to war. So I have to inform you now . . ."

But at that moment, time froze, my mind took wing, and a tweaked last verse of *Casey at the Bat* filled my head: [8]

> *Oh, somewhere in this favored land the sun is shining bright,*
> *The band is playing somewhere, and somewhere hearts are light,*
> *And somewhere men are laughing, and little children shout;*
> *But there is no joy in Richmond—Lutwick's case has just struck out.*

". . . we're giving you the III-A deferment for a period of one year. You will receive official notification by mail within two weeks."

Did I hear that right? After that lead-in? Oh my God! We did it! I'm free at last!

I didn't want to push my luck by celebrating in front of them, even though I was beyond ecstatic, so I toned down my exuberant glee to a mere smile and some humble thank-yous directed to the board members. But they weren't paying attention to me. Rani had totally let loose—transformed in a half-second from despondent CARE poster child into a manic Dallas Cowboys cheerleader. She was yelling, "Oh God! This is so great! I am so-o-o-o happy!" She pumped her arm and jumped up and down, not an easy thing to do in a sari. "Yeah! I can't believe it! We won! We won!"

---

8   Ernest Lawrence Thayer, "Casey at the Bat," 1888.

Please Rani, don't overdo it. This isn't official yet. They could change their minds. They don't want us to be gloating over this. Think of the guys who went to war and didn't come back.

And then I had another revelation of what the decision was all about, taking it to yet another level. It wasn't even about the deferment. It was about doing whatever it would take to put a smile on the face of the distressed young girl that Rani had become to these people. Sadness in Rani was torture to watch. Happiness in her spread joy to everyone in the room. It had always worked on me—why not others? Maybe it wouldn't work on every person, every time. Maybe it would never happen again. But in the angst-ridden crucible that had been my draft board hearing, there was born something bizarre but transformational. Something magical.

So it didn't even matter to the board members if she gloated. In fact, they wanted her to gloat. Her happiness was their happiness. By now, my presence in the room was an afterthought to all but myself. But I didn't mind. I had witnessed a miracle, and my butt had been saved in the process.

We said good-bye to our new friends and thanked them again. This time Rani was a bit more restrained. Then we left the office, turned a hallway corner, and waited for the elevator. When we were out of eyeshot from our liberators, Rani pulled herself toward me and asked me to give her a big kiss, which I was more than happy to do. Her apparent anger had evaporated. What a relief! We were celebrating together, rather than apart.

The elevator came, and we got in it with a few others. It was impossible to assume the default elevator mode—silent, eyes averting—but we tried to contain our overflowing joy. We must have been quite the sight in our costumes as the elevator descended to the first floor while guffaws, suppressed shrieks, and really bad dance moves escaped sporadically from the outlandish-looking couple.

Once we got back on the street, I had to talk. "I don't know how you did it, Rani, but you did it! You're a genius. You . . . definitely . . . fucking . . . did it!"

"Yes, I did," she said, "I . . . definitely . . . fucking . . . did it!" And then she jumped up in the air, raised her fist, and whooped again.

When she landed back on terra firma, I said, "You know, I totally thought we were dead in the water when you started yelling in fluent English. That was the central point of my case—that you completely needed me to communicate with anyone and everyone in this country. So they knew I had lied to them and if I lied to them about that, then maybe I had lied to them about other things. My credibility was completely shot."

"Yes, yours was," she replied. "But I could see we were losing badly, so it no longer seemed to matter. Our only chance was to make the case about me, not you. I got them to believe me. And more importantly, to believe *in* me."

"I guess that's all true, but I have to ask, why were you being such a bitch to me in the meeting room after your . . . uh . . . explosion?"

"I know. That was mean. But I could see that was what I had to do to . . . how you say . . . to seal the deal?"

"What? Ignoring and being mean to me sealed the deal?"

"Yes, because all I was doing was copying how they were reacting to you. They hated and ignored you, so I hated and ignored you. You had become the villain in this story, and I was the heroine. Just like in an Indian movie. So I had to make them forget we were actually on the same side—that giving me what I wanted was the same as giving you what you wanted. I had to completely distance myself from you. I didn't want them to get confused before they made their decision about the deferment."

"So is all this brilliant analysis just twenty-twenty hindsight for something that happened spontaneously, or did you actually think any of it out, either ahead of time, or maybe while it was happening?

"I don't understand what you mean by 'twenty-twenty hindsight.'"

"I mean, were you deliberately manipulating when the outburst began? Was that just a charade, a performance—the yelling, the tears? Were you really so freaked out over the thought of losing me or were you acting? What actually happened back there that turned those people from snarling attack dogs into whimpering puppies in a matter of seconds?" And then my wheels seriously started spinning. "And could you do this again? This is powerful stuff. Perhaps we could sell you as . . . I don't know . . . some sort of swami or guru. That's it! We'll make millions!'"

Rani watched me with seeming indifference as my imagination ran wild. She looked as if she were about to say something, but pulled back and laughed instead. "Will, I think I'm going to keep the answers to all those questions to myself for a while." And then after pausing, she added, "Probably . . . no actually . . . forever."

As I thought about whether her performance had been by intent or by emotion, Rani started walking toward the parking lot. But I absolutely had to learn what had just taken place. I caught up with her and said, "Come on, Rani, tell me if that was all just manipulation or spontaneous or what. Hey, I'll buy you that sweater you liked so much at the department store yesterday."

"No. My mouth is sealed shut—just like the deal I sealed." She mimed zipping her mouth and walked ahead.

When I caught up with her, I said, "Aw, this isn't fair. How about a dog? You said you wanted a dog. We can get one right after we get back to San Francisco."

She pressed her hands against her ears. "La-la-la-la. I can't hear you. And we live in an apartment that doesn't allow dogs." And she continued toward the car.

This time I stayed in step. "OK then guinea pigs. We'll get those guinea pigs you thought were so adorable."

She still had her hands over her ears. "I'm not listening, and guinea pigs cannot make me confess."

We arrived at the car and got in. As I drove off, I said, "But Rani, I have to know the answers. What will it take to get it out of you?"

"Oh, I don't know. Maybe we could move someplace where we *could* have a dog."

"OK, a house. With a yard. You enjoy gardening. As soon as we have jobs, we'll rent a house."

"Oh, I like that."

"So tell me your secrets. We'll use your power only for good, never for evil. I promise."

"Doesn't matter. Stop asking me."

"What if I gave you the sweater, the dog, the guinea pigs, and the house?"

"Keep going, I'm listening . . ."

∽

We celebrated our victory by taking Tillie and Jacob out for dinner. The next morning, we flew back to San Francisco to *really* begin our married life together.

And as for those secrets behind her power . . .

Rani's lips are still sealed.

Regrettably, there are no photos of "Rani Gupta" (not her real name) in this book. "Rani" cooperated with me while I was writing *Dodging Machetes*, but prefers anonymity.

Will, circa 1956, age ten

Will at Peace Corps Training site, Lami (near Suva)

Will with nutmeg

Cumming Street, Suva: Fiji's center for duty free merchandise

Bill's *bure*

Will inside Bill's *bure*

Bill (center) and friends go native

Peace Corps Volunteer and Fijians at their village just outside Suva

Bob and Will at the
wedding reception
July 1970

Saying good-bye at
Nausori Airport
(Will facing camera)

ACKNOWLEDGMENTS

Although the events in this book happened over 40 years ago, the idea of writing this memoir only bloomed in January 2009 when I began a memoir writing course at the San Francisco Writers' Grotto. I started with no particular project in mind, but when forced to choose, I asked myself, "What was the best book-length story that ever happened during my life?" My courtship with the "Rani Gupta" character was the no-brainer that immediately came to mind.

So I'd first like to acknowledge the real "Rani Gupta" without whom *Dodging Machetes* would obviously be inconceivable. Not just because she happened to be the object of my desires, but because her courage, intelligence, and determination were so unique that only such an exceptional person could have traversed the events in this book and weathered our perfect storm. "Rani" prefers anonymity, but cooperated with me while I was writing this book. "Rani" made the impossible possible—then and now.

My two superb memoir-writing teachers, Julia Scheeres and Judith Barrington are both authors of critically acclaimed, bestselling memoirs, respectively *Jesus Land* and *Lifesaving: A Memoir.* Julia's current book, *A Thousand Lives: The Untold Story of Hope, Deception, and Survival at Jonestown* was one of the *San Francisco Chronicle's* Top 100 books of 2011 and won the Northern California Independent Booksellers Book of the Year Award for Nonfiction.

After taking Julia's class at the San Francisco Writers' Grotto, some of the other students and I formed a writing group. LuLing Osofsky, Karen Valiasek, Bina Patel, Sheila McLaughlin, and Stuart Sheldon—we met bi-weekly, for over a year, and their insightful critiques of its first draft are reflected in the published version of *Dodging Machetes.*

Jordan Rosenfeld, my development editor, validated and tuned my writing voice, customized her edit around my concerns, and taught me how to make my scenes come alive.

Three of my fellow Peace Corps Volunteers from our time together in Fiji—Bill Humphries, Bob Hauser and Jim Jourdan—helped me to get through the ordeals described in this book, then forty years later helped me to clarify my memories about what really happened during that unique period of our lives. They have remained great friends through the years.

My sister Marcia Moosnick helped me to clarify even older memories including many personal ones about her life. George Schapiro, who has been my close friend since junior high school, helped illuminate some of our youthful shenanigans.

John P. Coyne and Marion Haley Beil at Peace Corps Writers have given me and other returned Peace Corps Volunteers a productive path for getting our books published and voices heard. Similarly, I'd like to acknowledge the CreateSpace staff who provide the tools and expertise to get writers from final draft to first release.

Kudos to my beautiful, talented, and brilliant wife, Denise Brouillette, who enabled me to see the personal vision of this project, encouraged me to stick with it when I felt like giving up (which happened often), and tolerated my mood swings during the process. All this support for a book where I fawn over my ex.

And finally I would like to acknowledge you, dear reader. You provide the ultimate reason for this labor of love.

AUTHOR'S NOTE

All of the events written about in *Dodging Machetes* happened over forty years ago. I did not take notes or keep a journal at the time. In my efforts to fill the inevitable memory gaps, I have tried to be true to both the emotions and the details of what actually happened. The dialog was recreated to be an approximation of what was actually said. A few of the less significant scenes have been taken out of chronological order or are compilations.

Most of the characters' names have been changed, and some of their identifying details have been altered to protect their anonymity. Such details are unimportant to the story, the events, or the character compositions.

WILL LUTWICK has degrees from Duke University and the University of Michigan. After completion of his Peace Corps service, he returned to the United States, where he has had a successful career in marketing, financial administration, and business systems design. He lives in San Francisco with his wife, Denise Brouillette.

www.WillLutwick.com

Made in the USA
Lexington, KY
29 May 2012